Charmers and Cranks

BOOKS BY ISHBEL ROSS

Charmers and Cranks
TWELVE FAMOUS AMERICAN WOMEN WHO DEFIED THE CONVENTIONS

An American Family
THE TAFTS 1678-1964

Crusades and Crinolines

Grace Coolidge and Her Era

Silhouette in Diamonds
THE LIFE OF MRS. POTTER PALMER

The General's Wife
THE LIFE OF MRS. ULYSSES S. GRANT

First Lady of the South
THE LIFE OF MRS. JEFFERSON DAVIS

Angel of the Battlefield
THE LIFE OF CLARA BARTON

Rebel Rose
LIFE OF ROSE O'NEAL GREENBOW, CONFEDERATE SPY

Proud Kate
PORTRAIT OF AN AMBITIOUS WOMAN, KATE CHASE

Journey Into Light

Child of Destiny
THE LIFE STORY OF THE FIRST WOMAN DOCTOR

Isle of Escape

Fifty Years a Woman

Ladies of the Press

Highland Twilight

Marriage in Gotham

Promenade Deck

Charmers and Cranks

Twelve Famous American Women
Who Defied the Conventions

ISHBEL ROSS

Harper & Row, Publishers
New York, Evanston, and London

FIRST EDITION

LIBRARY OF CONGRESS CATALOG CARD NUMBER: 65-14657

C-P

Contents

Illustrations

═══════════

Acknowledgments

In writing these sketches of twelve remarkable American women
I have used the resources of various libraries and historical so-
cieties across the country, and have done concentrated work in
the Library of Congress, the New York Public Library, the New
York Society Library, the Mercantile Library, and the New-York
Historical Society, which has many of the papers of Mrs. Frank
Leslie's second husband, Ephraim George Squier. The Squier
papers in the Library of Congress proved to be useful, too, as were
the files of the Leslie publications from the days of the Civil War
down to 1905.

For special material on Mrs. Jack Gardner I am indebted to
Dr. George L. Stout, director of the Isabella Stewart Gardner
Museum, Miss Clara Strauss, Curatorial Assistant, and William

Mason. The Museum in itself, with its rich store of Mrs. Gardner's correspondence with famous men, as well as her paintings and objects of art, makes good hunting ground for the biographer.

Mrs. Sherman Rogers (the former Irma Duncan, who was one of the Isadorables adopted by Miss Duncan and who later helped her to run her ballet schools) was most cooperative in answering questions, and was kind enough to give me permission to quote from the dancer's letters to her, now in the Dance Collection of the New York Public Library. In particular, she allowed me to use two letters written by Gordon Craig to Isadora after the drowning of her two children in the Seine.

Mrs. LeRoy Campbell, curator of the Jumel Mansion, helped me at every point while I was assembling material on Madame Jumel. Dr. Blake McKelvey, author and City Historian, associated with the Rochester Public Library and Rochester Historical Society, gave me many valuable suggestions for my work on the Fox sisters, as did Mrs. Elston F. Holton, Curator of History at the Rochester Museum of Arts and Sciences, and Mrs. Margaret B. Andrews, Assistant Librarian in Charge of Special Collections at the University of Rochester Library. Mrs. Muriel G. Thomas, of the Rockingham Free Public Library at Bellows Falls, Vermont, was one of many librarians who went out of their way to round up special material for me—in this instance, about Mrs. Hetty Green.

I am indebted to Emanie Sachs (Mrs. August Phillips), author of *The Terrible Siren*, the definitive biography of Mrs. Victoria C. Woodhull, for her kind advice and assistance; and to Harry Salter, son-in-law of Mrs. Aimee Semple McPherson, for his courteous aid. My warm thanks go to Pettus V. Hoyle for an enlightening glimpse of Hetty Green.

I.R.

Charmers and Cranks

Madame Jumel

Elizabeth Bowen was nineteen when she came to New York
and settled close to Bowling Green. She was a striking-looking
girl with red-gold hair and a shapely figure. Behind her was a life
of abject squalor in Providence, Rhode Island. But as Madame
Jumel she was destined to have riches and fame, to be a favorite
at the French Court, a belle at Saratoga, and to marry Aaron Burr
in his last years. Although mystery and conflicting legend obscure
much of her history, enough of the truth is known to establish
her as one of the great eccentrics and noted charmers of her era.
Madame Jumel was ambitious, intelligent, ruthless, and, at the
end, demented—a gutter flower that bloomed on the riches and
backing given her by Stephen Jumel. He was a solid citizen, a

wine merchant who loved her until he died, and many believed that she hastened his end.

Their mid-Georgian mansion, built by Roger Morris in 1765, remains one of New York's historic landmarks. George Washington made it his military headquarters for a time, and Thomas Jefferson, Alexander Hamilton and John Adams all dined in what is known today as the Jumel Mansion. In those days nothing impeded the magnificent view of the Palisades, Long Island, and the distant hills of Staten Island, and Madame Jumel chose it as her country home in 1810. After that she and her yellow coach with liveried postilions became one of the city's sights. Her romances, her gowns, her whims, and her beauty were legendary in their time, although she was never able to breach the social barricades in New York. The French Court received her but the Knickerbocker families froze her out, and she bitterly flouted them. Her strong, successful husband backed her through every adventure.

Betsy Bowen was born in Providence in 1775, the daughter of a prostitute and a sailor. Her mother, Phebe Bowen, was a notorious character who was in and out of the courts. When she was sent to jail, as she often was, Betsy was in the custody of the Overseer of the Poor, and from the workhouse she could see the brick mansions of the Browns, the Nightingales, and other established Rhode Island families. The future Madame Jumel scrubbed floors and worked in the scullery until she was turned over to a seafaring family. Samuel Allen owned a schooner and Mrs. Allen found Betsy hard to handle; she had a violent temper and a flow of gutter language that appalled her churchgoing keeper. She was uncontrolled, undisciplined, almost savage in her impulses, but she was bright and acquisitive in picking up knowledge. The Allens taught her to read and write, to pray and study the Bible.

In 1786 her father, John Bowen, was drowned in the harbor of Newport, and after that Phebe drifted about, plying her trade and occasionally selling "yarbs and greens" from a handcart in the streets. Betsy and her half-sister, Polly, trailed after her, barefoot and dirty, and helped her to collect her herbs from streams and in the woods. Phebe married Jonathan Clark, an educated but shiftless man who taught Betsy some history, improved her language, and gave her glimpses of a better world. But Betsy stayed behind in Providence when the Clarks wandered off, moving out of her parents' lives forever. She was then eighteen and haunted the streets of Providence with Polly. Betsy had developed into a magnificent-looking girl of medium height, lithe and delicately molded, whose burnished hair with its Titian glow would always arouse comment. So would her eyes, which were of a deep blue that turned to violet under stress. Her retroussé nose gave a piquant lift to her face. By this time she had picked up some worldly knowledge, both from Clark and other men with whom she had associated, usually sailors from the far seas. She wanted to move to New York, to travel far afield, but for the moment she was trapped, because she had become pregnant.

She took a room in the home of Major and Mrs. Reuben Ballou. Mrs. Freelove Ballou was a midwife, and Betsy's son was born there on October 9, 1794. He was named George Washington Bowen, after the fashion of the day to name babies for great men. However, when he grew up he senselessly maintained that he was George Washington's son, and argued the point unsuccessfully in a legal battle over his mother's fortune. Betsy abandoned him at birth and never had anything to do with him again until shortly before her death, when she sent for him, but he did not respond. During the battle over her will in 1872, Chauncey Shaffer, a lawyer who believed Ballou to be the child's father, said that in Providence "George Washington Bowen was just as well known as 'Betsy Bowen's bastard' as the town pump or Congress Commons."

After the birth of her baby Betsy and Polly lived together on Olney Street and were frequently seen wining and dining at the Golden Ball with French soldiers and sailors who had drifted back to Providence, remembering their days there when they fought the English under the Comte de Rochambeau. One of her friends, Captain William Brown, brought Betsy gifts from the Orient, including a monkey that she sported on her shoulder as she walked the streets. She was becoming almost as notorious as her mother, but she had other ambitions and soon left for New York. Various stories surround her departure from Providence, but the best substantiated is that Captain Brown, who already had a wife and family, was responsible for her settling in New York. In any event she changed her name to Eliza Brown and lived in the home of Captain Carpenter, a friend of Brown's. In the course of her long lifetime she was variously known as Betsy Bowen, Eliza Brown, Madame de la Croix, Madame Jumel, and Madame Burr.

The Manhattan that Eliza saw in 1794 was a cluster of buildings at the tip of the island, with an occasional church spire and, in the distance, fields, swamps, and woodland. She walked up Broadway with its tight-fronted mansions flush on the street, wandered through the shops on Pearl Street, and watched the stages heading for Greenwich, the village that one day would be encompassed by Manhattan. The city was beginning to stretch uptown, but the area that Eliza knew best was Bowling Green, with its spiked fence, its public walk and flower plots close to the water's edge at the Battery. Counting houses, shops, warehouses, and homes stretched all the way up to Bowery Lane. The big mansions were on Whitehall and State streets, and rose and yellow brick houses lined the streets in decorous rows. On Nassau Street rambler roses and honeysuckle climbed over trellises, and picket fences separated the houses. Near the wharves the smell of spices and copra was strong.

Celebrities drove past Eliza every day, including Aaron Burr whose estate was at Richmond Hill, overlooking the Hudson. Soon she was meeting Burr at John Simmons Tavern on Wall Street and was going with him to the theater. His short, lean, restless figure created a stir when he walked into a public place, and his manner was arrogant and demanding. Eliza was already sampling the fleshpots and often spent an evening watching the fireworks at Vauxhall Gardens, or eating ice cream and drinking lemonade in the little green booths under lamplit trees at Contoit's.

Then one day she met Stephen Jumel, and the whole course of

her life changed. He was a much respected wine merchant with an emporium on Stone Street and a house at Whitehall and Pearl streets. The Frenchman was a sage and robust character from the Bordeaux wine country, big and muscular in build, shrewd in business, and gallant with Eliza. When she met him he was forty-five and in process of making a second fortune. As a youth he had left France and gone to Haiti, where he bought a plantation, raised sugar cane, indigo, and coffee, and established a settlement that was known as "The Little Paris of America." Its white-washed houses and trim squares, its flowers, fountains, and small cathedral suggested a provincial French town. But when Tous-saint L'Ouverture, the Haitian Negro liberator, led the rebellion after the French Revolution, Jumel had to flee to the jungle. His plantation was wrecked, his buildings were burned, and many of the Creoles were murdered. He was picked up by a passing ship bound for St. Helena, and eventually an American ship, putting in there, took him to the United States. He went into partnership with Benjamin Desobry, and they specialized in importing the Spanish sherry and Portuguese port then so popular with the well to do. Their kegs and puncheons arrived on two brigs, the *Stephen* and the *Eliza*, and they came from Portugal, Spain, France, England, Ireland, the Canary Islands, and the West Indies. Their Holland gin and their rum from Antigua were popular, and they sold to the inns and hotels, to Vauxhall Gardens and other entertainment centers, as well as to private citizens.

By 1800 Jumel was one of the wealthiest merchants in New York. He was a broad-minded man, respected by his competitors for his far-seeing methods. His humor was Gallic, and he was popular socially as well as in the business world. He gave generously to charities, and his two-story yellow brick mansion with dormer windows was a gathering place for bon vivants, particularly those of French extraction or of Federalist sympathies. The guests who walked in through his Adam doorway knew that there they would have epicurean food and the finest of wines.

Eliza Brown met Jumel by chance but pursued him with purpose. As a bachelor he could afford to flaunt her in public, and as a Frenchman he felt no concealment was necessary in keeping a mistress; but he lived in a strait-laced community, and Eliza was snubbed at every turn. However, she took to the abundant life without any qualms and was seen everywhere with Jumel. She marched into City Hotel with him, smartly gowned, haughty in bearing. They went to the Belvedere Club far up on the East River and dined in the octagonal ballroom, or to Ranelagh near Corlaer's Hook, or to the Indian Queen on the Boston Post Road. The vagrant from Providence presided as his hostess, amid Chinese draperies and rare furniture. By this time she had learned to find her way through the knives and forks, the array of wine glasses, the subtleties of French cuisine.

Jumel believed in living well. One of his friends was Jean Anthelme Brillat-Savarin, who had fled from the guillotine and was delighting New York's gourmets for the time being. Eliza was a clever girl, and she picked up French quickly. Jumel found her intelligent, witty, and full of craft. Her sharp comments on the political scene amused him, for she had listened to Aaron Burr and other men holding public office. They were often seen together at the theater. It was still the era when chop bones and bottles were flung about in the Park Theater, but Eliza listened attentively to the words of Shakespeare and Sheridan. Jumel was intent on educating her; she was equally determined to make herself an accomplished lady in the grand tradition.

Eliza never spoke of Providence and had worked up an involved story about her background for the benefit of Jumel and his friends. Some of it bore a faint relation to the truth, but all through life she was noted for her extravagant and apocryphal tales. Her father, she insisted, was an Englishman of French ancestry named Capet who died in the East Indies while her mother was on the way to join him. According to Eliza's story, her mother, too, died en route and was buried at sea. Eliza then was bottle-fed by a sailor until they landed, when she was turned over to the captain of an American ship heading for Providence. She was legally adopted there, but her life was one of such drudgery that she kept running away, although she was always brought back. Finally she fell in love with an officer named De la Croix and eloped with him to New York, but he deserted her and she then fell in with Captain Brown, who was related to her foster parents and was kind and protective to her. This was Madame Jumel's own account of her beginnings, with occasional variations as the years went on. De la Croix was sometimes plain Peter Croix. She knew Saint-Mémin, the artist, and his miniature of Madame de la Croix, dated 1797, is believed by historians to be Eliza Brown, although it has had other identification. The profile, the retroussé nose, make the resemblance almost indisputable, and give some likelihood to Eliza's tale. It was also believed that she visited France with De la Croix some years before Stephen Jumel went abroad with her in the *Stephen*, a 300-ton vessel that took more than a month to cross the Atlantic.

After visiting his family in the Bordeaux country they went by coach to Paris, which still bore the scars of the Revolution. People talked of little else. Brillat-Savarin took them to the salon of his cousin, Madame Jacques Récamier, and there Eliza met Talleyrand, Benjamin Constant, and Joseph Bonaparte, Napoleon's brother. She studied Madame Récamier's pale oval face and sinuous figure with interest. Eliza flourished in the company of wits and savants. They all made much of Stephen Jumel's handsome companion and even had patience with her broken French. They drove to the Bastille, strolled through the Place de la Concorde, and saw where Marie Antoinette had died. While Jumel met wine merchants and attended to his business affairs, Eliza, with unlimited funds at her command, bought clothes and bibelots with a lavish touch. By the time she returned to America she had taken another step in her worldly education. She had been received in the Faubourg St. Germain, where no one had questioned her status, and she had had a glimpse of French life that the American traveler of that era rarely saw.

On her return she moved into the Jumel mansion, to live openly as the mistress of the wine merchant. But the better families were not ready to accept this situation, and Mrs. Alexander

Hamilton alone was courteous to her. Jumel braved even the City Assembly with Eliza. He was an accomplished dancer, and he had had a French dancing master and a fiddler come to the house to coach her in all the steps. She wore an Empire ice-blue satin gown and was the most beautiful woman in sight as she moved through the minuet, the quadrille, and the opera reel. Alexander Hamilton led the cotillion with his wife, and before the evening had ended Eliza had danced with Hamilton, Rufus King, Dr. David Hosack, and Mayor Richard Varick, who had been military secretary to General Philip J. Schuyler. Eliza was adding to her education as she moved smoothly through the dance. She liked to talk to intelligent men, but women froze at her approach.

When Thomas Jefferson became President in 1801 after tying with Aaron Burr, Jumel gave a dinner party for his fellow merchants to celebrate. But the Knickerbocker families stayed away and, except for Mrs. Desorby, no wives at all showed up. Jumel was furious, and it was then that he bought Eliza her coach and two black horses. Her coachman's blue livery and tall beaver hat made her more visible than ever on the social scene, although she did not break the barriers. Her name was dragged without much logic into the gossip surrounding the famous duel between Alexander Hamilton and Aaron Burr in 1804. There were deeper political points at issue between these two men, and James Parton "utterly disbelieved this wretched gossip" and dismissed it in his biography of Burr. But Samuel H. Wandell, author of *Aaron Burr in Literature*, wrote that "there were those, indeed, who went around insisting that the lady had her share in sending Mr. Hamilton and Colonel Burr to Weehawken." In any event, her name was closely identified with Burr's over a long period of years.

This was also the year in which Eliza tricked Jumel into marrying her. Her discontent with her status had been growing, and she saw by this time that she was never going to make any social headway unless Stephen married her. He had gone to Philadelphia on business when she took to her bed and staged a dying scene. A messenger was sent after him, and when he arrived

Eliza, with a doctor beside her, seemed to be in the last extremity. She was almost beyond speech, but when he asked her what he could do for her, she whispered that she could die in peace if only he would marry her. Jumel was a Roman Catholic and a priest was hastily summoned. Eliza dropped her pretense with tactless rapidity. She was up and about the next day and two days later was driving around town. A second ceremony was performed in a Catholic church on April 9, 1804. She was now officially Madame Jumel, but it did her little good, for the barrier of ice did not melt.

For the next six years Madame Jumel presided in her luxurious mansion, but it was dark and silent at night, and instead of entertaining her fellow citizens and being entertained by them, she and Stephen had to seek diversion in public places. His fellow merchants stood by him, and their wives were civil to Eliza, but his business was hurt to some extent. He bought her way into charity functions by subscription, and he was recognized as a philanthropic target, but Madame Jumel was too astute not to know that she lived under a blinding veil of ostracism. Together they made one last move to impress their inflexible critics. When the Roger Morris mansion was put on the market Eliza saw at once that it would be a good buy for them. She knew it well as Warriners Tavern, and she was aware that Mary Philipse had gone direct from Whitehall to the heights with Roger Morris. Eliza was sure that with the Jumel money its elegance could be restored.

Stephen bought the property on March 9, 1810, paying $10,000 for the house and thirty-six acres. Later he added another thirty-nine acres that cost him $9,000, and he had a wharf from which he could ship his produce downtown. There were quince and other fruit trees on the property, and the view was spectacular. He made it a gift to Eliza, so that she now had a country estate like the Livingstons, the Beekmans, the Murrays, the Clintons, and the Astors. Both Jumels were well aware that a pageant of American history was identified with its graceful rooms, from the days when colonial dames and men in powdered wigs danced the minuet, down through the stark days of military occupation, when it housed George Washington and other generals.

Madame Jumel could find no flaw in the house when they had finished the restoration. It was done with exquisite attention to detail. Samples of the colonial wallpaper in the Court-Martial Room were sent to Paris for duplication. It was rehung on wood blocks—green panels with a border of doves, morning-glories, and urns. Furniture of the pre-Revolutionary Georgian period was arranged alongside American Federal and French Empire pieces. An imposing doorway was installed, with flanking sidelights and an elliptical fanlight with amber glass. Eighteenth-century mahogany furniture was used in the stately dining room where some of America's most famous men had assembled. The two-story mansion faced south, with a gallery under its columned portico. The outer walls, two feet thick, were lined with English brick. It had nineteen rooms, including a lofty octagonal drawing room at the rear, thirty-two by twenty-two feet, with marble mantelpieces. The house was painted white, and boxwood hedges were planted along the winding driveway.

When all was as Eliza wished it to be, a hundred invitations in French were sent out to the first citizens of New York. A footman in satin livery took them around from house to house, and some if not all responded. There was interest in the fine old house that the Jumels had restored. The octagonal drawing room was cleared for dancing. Candlelight beamed down on the guests from chandeliers and sconces. The grounds were strung with lanterns, and the Park Theater orchestra played muted music. A huge trestle table was loaded with dishes prepared by the French chef of City Hotel. Nothing had been left undone, from a barrel of oysters to rose-petal ices. The party lasted until dawn, and the guests enjoyed M. Jumel's superlative wines, from the French expatriates to Mr. and Mrs. Rufus King. But dead silence followed. The Brevoorts, the Morrises, the Jays, the Livingstons still turned the cold shoulder to Madame Jumel as her husband continued to prosper and grow ever richer. He bought real estate and gave funds to help defend New York during the war of 1812 when a British attack was feared. The blockade had affected him less than it had other merchants, although two of his schooners had been seized at Bayonne and sold as contraband.

Jumel now fancied himself as a farmer, having become so rich that he no longer needed to give his business daily attention. He took time to enjoy his meadows and orchards, to enlarge his property, and to run it on businesslike principles. It was wonderfully quiet after the clatter of carriages and drays in downtown New York, but Eliza was restless, and when she returned to Providence for the funeral of Captain Carpenter, she adopted Polly's daughter Mary. Her half-sister had died, the Clarks had vanished altogether, and the scene had changed considerably. She stayed at the Golden Ball, the historic tavern that she had often entered on the arm of a casual acquaintance. A veteran on the staff saw through the powder and paint, the fine feathers and grand airs of Madame Jumel. She was Betsy Bowen, and he quickly spread the news. A crowd gathered under her window. Eliza thought they had come for a speech until she heard the shout of a drunken voice: "We came to pay our respects to Betsy Bowen." She banged the window shut and left Providence as soon as possible.

On her return she was faced with disaster at home. Her husband had just heard from a Providence man the true history of Betsy Bowen, of the son she had borne and the way in which she had lived, of her debauched mother and her equally degraded half-sister Polly. It was all news to Jumel, and he took it hard. There were many grim moments in Eliza's life, but she always fought back. When confronted with her past sins she readily acknowledged the truth of the stories and raged at Stephen. Eliza's eyes blazed with a violet light as she threatened him with a pistol.

"Touch me, Stephen, and I'll kill you," she cried.

"I believe you would, Eliza," he said. "Put it away and let us talk quietly."

Henry Nodine, a carpenter who worked around the house, had heard the quarrel. A great chill prevailed between the Jumels after that, and her husband never again regarded her with the same trust. She kept the pistol at hand beside her bed, but in the end she won him back again. Mary Eliza Jumel now became her aunt's idol. She was a docile, pretty child for whom Madame Jumel took pleasure in buying clothes and presents, and she enrolled her in Miss Whitestone's School for Young Ladies. But the lean years continued for Eliza, so far as the social scene was concerned, and in 1815 Stephen, Mary, and she sailed for Europe in the *Eliza*. Jumel had wound up his business and closed his accounts with Desorby. They were still at sea when Napoleon had his brief return to power after Elba. As their brig anchored at the mouth of the Gironde River after a wild crossing, they learned that the storm had delayed the departure of the ship on which the emperor planned to escape. Now British frigates blocked the harbor, and the only chance for flight lay in an American ship which would not be inspected.

Four men muffled in cloaks boarded the *Eliza* to make plans for Napoleon's escape. One was Joseph Bonaparte, his brother, who had been King of Spain. Eliza had met him at Madame Récamier's salon. He said that Napoleon would arrive at the dock in a simple carriage. An emissary would precede him and signal with a lantern. Jumel's boat was to wait at the dock for the signal. The Jumels agreed at once, and Eliza saw herself landing in New York with the great Napoleon, for the plan was to turn around and travel home. Jumel kept his part of the bargain, but his passenger did not show up. Joseph Bonaparte arrived next day to tell them that Napoleon had decided it was undignified for a monarch to run away. He had boarded the *Bellerophon* and thrown himself on the mercy of the British. Three months later he was on St. Helena. But he sent his carriage to the Jumels out of gratitude, and from then on Eliza drove in state, in an equipage lined with morocco leather and cut velvet. She had the gold key to the emperor's army chest and his traveling clock with the royal N in gold.

In later years Madame Jumel grew expansive on the role she might have played had she saved Napoleon from capture. As things were, she and her husband became part of the Napoleonic legend and were warmly welcomed in Paris by the impoverished nobility. The city had changed drastically. The old mansions were shuttered and the aristocratic families had scattered. New buildings had gone up and some of the medieval streets had been cleared out. The boulevards were wider and some were lined with plane and chestnut trees. They settled at the Hotel de la Breteuil on the Rue de Rivoli, facing the palace gardens. Invitations were showered on Madame Jumel, and she rode around Paris in her magnificent yellow coach-and-eight. She lent it to some of her new-found friends, among them the Duchesse de Berry, the Duchesse de Charot, and the Comtesse Henri Tascher de la Pagerie, a relative of the Empress Josephine. The comtesse had just been widowed. She had many of the empress' jewels, and pieces of furniture that eventually came into Madame Jumel's possession and were installed in her New York mansion, giving it the Napoleonic flavor that it has today. One story is that the comtesse sold these possessions to the Jumels for $25,000; the other that she gave them in lieu of rent, after living with them for years.

Madame Jumel played the game both with the Bonapartists and the Royalists and was riding high when she made one of the great blunders of her career. She hung a victory wreath on one of Napoleon's eagles, and a friend dared her to put it on her carriage. Eliza did, and drove through the streets until she was mobbed and the police threw her into jail. She was labeled a dangerous alien plotting a Bonapartist uprising. Stephen Jumel had to use all his diplomatic connections to have her freed, on the understanding that she would leave the country at once. Eliza returned to New York, but Stephen decided to stay on and to push the suit he had brought over his confiscated vessels. It was months before Mary, who was enrolled at Miss Laurau's School for Young English Ladies outside Paris, heard from her aunt. The child wrote to her urgently on December 8, 1816, asking her to come to the school concert and to bring her gauze frock with her lace Vandyke. The school was dreary, she wrote. The English young ladies wept all the time, and they were all freezing cold. She could see only the tops of the trees in their garden, "which makes it look as if they wanted petticoats."

Five months later Mary received an answer to this letter. Madame Jumel wrote from New York that she had had to leave too hastily to get in touch with her, but her thoughts were always with her. Her health was better, and she was putting Mary's room in order at home and was hanging blue satin curtains trimmed with silver fringe. "Do not forget, my dear Mary," she added, "the sacrifice I made was for your good." Meanwhile Stephen Jumel visited Mary from time to time and praised her when she won first prizes for history and drawing. He went to Italy to study the vineyards and returned often to the Bordeaux region which was peculiarly his own.

Madame Jumel stayed alone in her mansion with her servants and lived erratically. Her neighbors looked at her with more suspicion than ever. Many Americans were traveling, and strange stories drifted back about her operations in Paris. And where was her good husband? Had he left her at last? She tried to lease her mansion to Joseph Bonaparte, who had settled in Bordentown, New Jersey, but he wrote to her coldly that he had no thought of moving. Mary rejoined her in 1817 and they returned to Paris in 1821. The ban on Madame Jumel had been lifted, and for the next five years they lived in state on the Place Vendôme. This was the most brilliant period of Eliza's career. The Jumels entertained on the most lavish scale, and they were close to the core of the French aristocracy. Louis XVIII always noticed Madame Jumel when he drove past her yellow coach, and she finally wrote to him asking for recognition for her husband. It was a bold stroke, but Eliza had large ideas. She was often embarrassed, she wrote, because she had no title and her husband had no cross, in spite of all he had done for his country and his king. He had set up manufactories to help those who had lost everything. He had created a demand in the United States for French merchandise and had helped to feed it. He had left France at the time of the Revolution and had established a home in America, resolved

never again to see his native land until the return of the Bour-
bons. Madame Jumel continued:

> What a joyous day for him when he got the news of the
> return of the Bourbons. Immediately he made haste to sell
> his ships and his stocks and to leave his temporary home,
> which was for him a sort of exile. . . . When I see that I
> have no title and my husband no cross . . . I feel utterly
> discouraged and beg him to go back to his adopted country.
> But knowing your Majesty's extreme kindness, I am anew
> inspired with the hope that you will not ignore a subject so
> worthy as Stephen Jumel.

The king took no action, but Madame Jumel continued to
attend court functions and, when he died, she was present at the
coronation ball for his successor, the Comte d'Artois, who became
Charles X. She was in the train of the Duchesse de Berry and
outshone her peers in a gown of white and gold silk, with a
jeweled comb that had belonged to the Empress Josephine in her
red-gold hair. Eliza had found that it was fashionable to be a good
churchgoer in Paris, too, so she often went to the Madeleine. But
the extravagance of these years and the decline in Jumel's fortunes
after he left America had brought them close to financial ruin.
Madame Jumel and Mary returned home in 1825 with the
understanding that the money that had accumulated in Stephen's
accounts with Desorby should be sent to him immediately. As
she left he confirmed his gift to Eliza of the mansion and the
land around it. At the same time he deeded to her for life his
property in downtown New York.

After she had time to study his business assets in Manhattan,
she asked him to send her power of attorney, and from that point
on Eliza stripped her husband bit by bit of all his holdings. She
knew that he wished to part with his New York property for
cash and to settle permanently in France, but she did not intend
this to happen. The title to his real estate holdings was transferred
to her niece Mary, but the revenue was collected by Madame
Jumel. In the end the mansion alone remained in Mary's name.

Stephen wrote to her with a note of desperation, asking for cash to meet his immediate obligations in France: "Be good enough for the love of God to send it to me at the old firm of Jumel and Desobry with the running account," to which she coldly replied: "I have done everything in my power to procure money for you but it was impossible, money being so scarce, but since we have a house at Mont de Marsan wouldn't it be better to sacrifice that, rather than what we have left here for old age?"

Weary, disillusioned, Jumel went back to his family in Bordeaux. Meanwhile, Eliza functioned with such business brilliance that by 1828, when he returned, the value of the Jumel holdings had increased from one to three million dollars, and Eliza held title to fourteen hundred choice, income-bearing properties. On her return from France her mansion was occupied by Moses Field, to whom it had been rented, so that for the time being she boarded with a Dutch farmer on Long Island. She went in to New York every day to attend to business, and she wrote to Stephen that the land was going up in value and should not be sold off, as he advised. New York was growing fast. Fields, woodland, and swamps were disappearing as the streets ran northward and the city joined the village of Greenwich. Every foot of land was valuable, and Alexander Hamilton, Jr., Madame Jumel's lawyer, helped her in her operations. But she needed little advice, for she was a shrewd businesswoman who seized on every opportunity to advance her fortunes. She enjoyed the role she played. The game was fast and competitive, and she felt jubilant as her profits rose. For the time being she lived economically.

When Stephen arrived she and Mary were back in the family mansion, her Napoleonic treasures were installed, and she was living on the old scale. It did not take him long to learn that Eliza had everything under her control. Jumel had no property left in the State of New York other than a tract of wasteland that had no value. His first winter at home was a lonely one, since Eliza and Mary, who had developed into a beautiful girl, went south to New Orleans for the season. But Jumel, a kindly and uncomplaining man, ran the farm and attended to the vineyard. They had six hundred vines, always a matter of interest to the seasoned wine merchant. He rarely went downtown, for he was in his seventies and his health was failing.

One day he was tossed from a jouncing haycart on King's Bridge Road and was badly hurt. During the night a large bandage on his arm slipped off, and he bled to death. Tales soon circulated that Madame Jumel had helped to dislodge the bandage that the doctor had left firmly in place. Jumel was buried under a plain slab in St. Patrick's churchyard on Prince Street. The date of his death was May 22, 1832, and on the anniversary in 1964, a séance was held at the mansion before a gathering of historians and experts in extrasensory perception. In the previous spring a group of school children visiting the Jumel mansion had told of seeing a lady in a long gown on the balcony who ordered them to shut up and go away. Mrs. LeRoy Campbell, curator of the Jumel Mansion, was downstairs and knew that there was no one on the balcony, but the house had always had the reputation of being haunted. In May she invited Hans Holzer, an author who trails down the legends attached to haunted houses, to hold a séance with a well-known New York spiritualist, Mrs. Ethel Johnson Myers.

The medium sat in front of the Napoleonic bed in which both Stephen and Eliza died and listened to Holzer give his thirty guests a briefing on what was to come. He described a ghost as the "thought form of someone who has died under tragic circumstances, and must keep re-living his experiences." Ghosts, he added matter-of-factly, give up when they are told what they are, and that their problems no longer are important. As he talked, Mrs. Myers, a tall, elderly medium who is also a voice coach, began to groan and twitch. Coaxed by Holzer she answered questions in deep tones, and her audience was encouraged to believe that Stephen Jumel was speaking through her. The séance was held in broad daylight, and every agonized move made by Mrs. Myers was visible as she muttered that Jumel had been buried alive, that Eliza and Aaron Burr had connived at his death, and that Eliza had killed him.

Mrs. Myers was soon in such visible distress that Holzer soothed her: "You have been revenged many times," he said. "She died miserably. Let go of this house."

The medium then assumed Eliza's voice. She seemed to be angry with Holzer. "Go away or I'll call the police," came in mutterings from Mrs. Myers.

Holzer bade the restless spirit go in peace, and within a few minutes Mrs. Myers' eyes opened. She seemed to be shaking off a bad dream, and as she resumed her normal manner she complained of a sharp pain in one of her arms. Holzer explained that ghosts had a way of transmitting pain to their mediums, and Jumel had died from the injury to his arm. In winding up the séance, the author predicted that Jumel's ghost would no longer haunt the mansion, but he was less certain that Eliza would stay quietly beyond the veil.

A year after her husband's death Madame Jumel finally married Aaron Burr, the man on whose name she had traded for so many years. She was fifty-nine and still a beauty. He was seventy-seven and near the end of his life. He had lived hard, and he was bitter, shriveled, bad-tempered, and violent. There was great interest in the marriage of the much vilified Burr and the flamboyant Madame Jumel. Philip Hone, who had been mayor of New York, noted in his diary on July 3, 1833: "The celebrated Col. Burr was married on Monday evening to the equally celebrated Mrs. Jumel, widow of Stephen Jumel. It is benevolent in her to keep the old man in his later days. One good turn deserves another."

In the previous year Mary had married Nelson Chase, a young lawyer who worked in Burr's office. Now the former vice-president, penniless and at the end of his rope, and the grande dame with millions were married in the room to the left of the entrance of the Jumel Mansion that today is known as the Tea Room. They went by coach-and-four to New Haven and Hartford on their wedding trip, and Mrs. Burr transacted a little business along the way. She had stock in a toll bridge at Hartford that she sold for $6,000. Later she accused Burr of making off with this money, but another story suggested that she had waved her hand and said: "Pay it to my husband." In any event, there were ructions from the start, Burr was wildly extravagant, and he still philandered. Madame Jumel pursued him to the Astor House, where he entertained his friends and scattered her money. She had hoped that the name Madame Burr would bring her fresh prestige, but in New York it was an empty honor. When Burr announced that he would like to manage her properties, she chased him with fire tongs and then locked him out of the house. After this he had a mild stroke, and she took him in again and nursed him for the time being. But after five weeks they parted for the last time, and Madame Burr told a neighbor: "I don't see him any more. He got thirteen thousand of my property and spent it all, or gave it away, and had no money to buy a dinner. I had a new carriage and a pair of horses that cost me one thousand dollars. He took them and sold them for five hundred."

Burr was a dying man when their divorce suit was brought to trial. He was represented by Charles O'Conor, and he charged that Eliza had a ferocious temper and that she had been "disobedient and insulting." Burr died in 1836 within a matter of hours after the divorce was granted. Eliza had not wept for Stephen Jumel, but she wept for Aaron Burr. His brilliant and adored daughter, Theodosia Alston, had been lost at sea in 1813. His widow now took a childish delight in flaunting his name, and on one of her trips to Europe she stood up in her carriage, when halted on a country road by a company of soldiers, and declared in her high, clear voice: "Make way for the widow of the Vice-President of the United States." She found that the name Madame Aaron Burr met with response in European circles, whereas the name Stephen Jumel had been forgotten.

Her life entered a new phase, and her eccentricities began to show clearly in the years following Burr's death. She stayed less at her mansion, feeling that it was lonely and remote from the stream of life. For many years she kept a suite at the Astor House, where she entertained George Bancroft, James Fenimore Cooper, N. P. Willis, and other literary figures, as well as the

French expatriates. For one brief period her protégé was Prince Louis Napoleon, a nephew of the emperor, who had been arrested and sent to America by Louis Philippe. In summer Madame Jumel was one of the sights of Saratoga, trailing behind her a dash of Revolutionary history and the echo of her Napoleonic associations. She had taken a house on Circular Street, which she named the Tuileries, and continued to occupy it in summer down to the days of the Civil War. Her yellow coach with its four horses and a postilion in livery were always part of the afternoon parade, and her Paris clothes were of interest to all the women observers.

But her pretensions led to ridicule, too, and in her later years, when she seemed bedizened and a mass of ruffles and bows, a cruel prank was played on her by some of the town wits. Everyone knew that she liked to drive with outriders and to create an effect of royalty. A town simpleton took an old carriage, painted it a bright yellow, dressed himself in livery, and drove four scrawny horses. Another of the wits sat in the back, with a low-necked gown and tiny parasol, imitating Madame Burr's way of bowing and smiling as she drove through the streets. When she emerged from the United States Hotel, where she had afternoon tea each day, she drove off unaware of the wild caricature in her wake. Finally she turned around, puzzled by the laughter of passersby, and saw that a clown in the carriage was mimicking her. After that she rode less frequently in the parade, but when she did she kept up her customary style.

Her son, George Washington Bowen, had become a summer visitor at the spa, and he must have seen his mother many times, but there was never any mutual acknowledgment between them. The Ballous had brought him up. He had been a weaver's apprentice and had worked in a bank, but was now in business for himself and had his own house in Providence. He was handsome, proud, and aloof. When Mary Chase died in 1843, leaving Eliza Jumel Chase, aged seven, and William Chase, aged three, Madame Jumel reopened the family mansion and invited the children and their father to live with her. When Eliza and William reached mature years she took them abroad, and they visited Stephen Jumel's relatives in Bordeaux.

At the time of Stephen's death Eliza had informed his family that he had left no estate whatever. But now she found a husband for her namesake, and young Eliza was married to Paul Guillaume Raymond Péry of Bordeaux before Madame Burr returned to New York. In the previous year both Elizas had attended a court ball at the Tuileries and the presentation of the eagle to the army at the Champs de Mars. On their return to New York after the wedding she asked Eliza and her husband to live with her, for she dreaded the loneliness of her house on the heights. But she kept them all dependent on her financially, and there was much squabbling. Will Chase on one occasion picked up an inkstand and hurled it at the painting done by Arcide Ércole in Rome of Madame Jumel with her great-niece and nephew. He had aimed it at his great-aunt but had missed. She was so angry that she covered his face in the painting with a black patch. Then she turned the Chase family out of the house and lived for the most part the life of an eccentric recluse. Actually, she kept the place peopled with figures from the past in her imaginative reveries, as she reviewed her life and sat in faded finery on a dais in her drawing room. Sometimes she gave Sunday afternoon receptions, and then she would rustle downstairs in stiff silks and take her place majestically among her guests.

Miss Anna Parker, who later became Mrs. John V. L. Pruyn, made diary jottings on Madame Burr after she and a group of girls were received in the house of mystery. The picture she painted was grim:

There she stood on the front doorsteps, which were painted with blue moons on a lavender floor—a more fearful looking old woman one seldom sees—her hair and teeth were false—her skin thick, and possessing no shadow of ever having been clear and handsome—her feet were enormous, and stockings, soiled and coarse, were in wrinkles over her shoes —on one foot she wore a gaiter and on the other a carpet slipper. . . . She wore a small hoop, which in sitting down she could not manage, so that it stood up, displaying her terrible feet. . . .

Miss Parker commented on Madame Jumel's rusty skirt with stamped flounces, her threadbare black velvet talma, the soiled white scarf around her neck, and her cap of black cotton lace with pea-green streamers. But she received the girls as if they were all duchesses and she a queen. The house was desperately in need of dusting. Everything was closed up and musty. A dirty molasses pot and shabby cake basket of grapes suggested the remains of her breakfast. But she drew their attention to her superb paintings and her historical pieces of furniture. They questioned her about Aaron Burr, and when Miss Parker asked if he were handsome she said: "Ah, my child, he was a wretch, a combined model of Mars and Apollo." She told the girls how he drove up to the heights to play whist with her after Stephen Jumel's death. One evening he said: "Madame, I offer you my hand; my heart has long been yours." She thought he was jesting, but next evening he said: "We must be married, Madame; I will bring out the priest and tomorrow you shall be my wife." According to Eliza, she was still reluctant and ran upstairs to avoid him, but Nelson Chase, who had come with him, followed her and begged her to marry Burr. He said that the colonel had promised him the deed to a village he owned on the North River and other funds if only Madame Jumel would marry him. When she went downstairs he was waiting for her and then, as Eliza told it:

> He caught my hand and dragged me to the parlor, saying the priest was old and it was nearly midnight and I must not detain him—and he was so handsome and brave and I allowed him to keep my hand and I stood up there [pointing to the place in the parlor on the left] and like a fool was married to him! The wretch, but he did not stay here long.

By this time Madame Burr was weaving many strange tales. She told the girls, as she did others, that Joseph Bonaparte had come to the United States to marry her, that he drove up to see her every day, that she still kept the table all set and the remains of the last meal served him there. She was eighty-four when Miss Parker saw her, and she dredged up other fabulous tales of her life at the French Court. There is no convincing evidence that Joseph Bonaparte was ever in the mansion at all, but stories persisted of the table with the gold service, the china and glass shrouded in cobwebs, the stale crumbs scattered around.

Madame Burr had two servants at this time, and everything was rickety and run-down. She still kept her horses, but they were no longer glossy and well groomed. She argued with tradesmen over tiny bills and would not spend a penny for repairs. A fence was built around her property to keep people from stealing her grapes and firewood. If Anna Parker found her in a state of abject shabbiness, other visitors from time to time gave a different view of Madame Burr. One recalled her appearing in purple velvet, with her skirt slashed with yellow satin. On this occasion she wore side curls and was playing the role of Vice-Queen of America, a title she used for herself when she was not being Madame Burr, widow of the Vice-President of the United States.

Until her last years she attended the Church of the Intercession and rustled in, usually late, with a great flurry of silks. She was heavily powdered and painted and tried to recapture youth with leghorn hats coyly trimmed with ostrich plumes or streamers. Mrs. Alexander Hamilton, whose son was her lawyer, occasionally called to see her, although, ironically enough, Madame Jumel had married her husband's slayer. Mrs. Lucy Audubon, widow of the naturalist, had long talks with her and listened patiently to her tales of her links with the French aristocracy. The older members of the French colony sometimes visited the widow of a man they had liked—Stephen Jumel. When twin boys were born to a family in the neighborhood she asked that one be named Jumel and the other Burr. They were not, but she brought toys for them from Germany on her last trip abroad, which was in 1853, when she was seventy-eight.

Some time later she was seen riding on horseback around the grounds leading a tatterdemalion army of emigrees who were out of work and in distress. Her mock soldiers were quartered in her barn, and she fed and clothed them in their time of need. Carrying sticks for rifles, they drilled and were reviewed by Madame Burr. A sentry was posted at the gate, and sometimes a volley of fire was heard. This was her French Army, and more than anything else it convinced her neighbors that she had gone mad. She no longer held her Sunday afternoon receptions, but she rode her horse until she was eighty. Music occasionally drifted through the grounds, persuading passersby that a four-piece orchestra was serenading Madame Burr as she dined. In these last years she sent for her son, and when he ignored her, she kept threatening that she would follow him to Providence. She was tormented by rappings and strange noises, and she was sure the house was haunted.

But at the end no one really knew what was going on. For the last three years of her life the doors were bolted, the windows were closed, and only dim rays of candlelight gave any sign that there was life in the mansion. Weeds grew unchecked in the grounds and Eliza, who had strained so hard for friends and recognition, was left alone. But the one remaining maid had orders to powder and rouge her every day during her last illness. And thus she was found propped up in bed on a Sunday morning, July 16, 1865, wearing a lace cap with pink ribbons. She was ninety years old and had slipped away in her sleep. Her funeral service was held at the Church of the Intercession, and she was buried in the Jumel tomb in Trinity Cemetery, on the slope overlooking the Hudson. She had escaped from her hallucinations, the banquet spread for imaginary guests, her Napoleonic army, and the rattling of the ghost that haunted her mansion.

The Pérys moved in after her death, but they soon left because they were persuaded that the house was haunted and that Madame Jumel revisited them between midnight and one o'clock in the morning, making terrible rappings in the Lafayette Room. Her silver and jewels had vanished. Her three carriages were valued at twenty dollars, fifteen dollars, and five dollars, and her last gray horse was sold for thirty dollars. Two years before her death she had drawn up a will, leaving most of her real estate and personal property to religious and charitable organizations. The remainder went to the Pérys and their daughter, Mathilde. The boy who had thrown the ink bottle at the Ércole painting was ignored altogether. A bitter fight for the Jumel fortune followed. Various family offshoots, legitimate and illegitimate, contested it on the ground that she was incompetent when the will was drawn up.

The litigation went on for sixteen years, ending in 1881 when the court sold the property and settled all claims. The mansion remained in the possession of the Chase family, and the French contestants were allowed a sixth part of all that had been Stephen Jumel's. The famous case of Bowen and Chase was tried in 1873, with George Washington Bowen basing his claim on a law then in existence in New York State that an illegitimate son could inherit from his mother if there were no legitimate children. He sought to dispossess the resident heirs but failed. However, the hearings gave the public another fantastic view of a wholly fantastic woman. Madame Jumel remained as mysterious a figure after her death as she was in her long, dramatic lifetime.

Hetty Green

—————————

Hetty Green was born an heiress in 1835, with a New England whaling fortune behind her. She died in 1916, a friend-less eccentric. In the intervening years she established herself as the most legendary miser of the nineteenth century, as well as its leading woman financier. Money was her god, her lifework, her hobby, her obsession. Although she had always had it in abun-dance, it brought her little happiness and left her bereft of human warmth. "My father," she once said, "told me never to give anyone anything, not even a kindness."

It was a hard and bitter philosophy, and Hetty did her best to live up to it. Many pitied her but few loved her; yet she was one of the prized legends of Wall Street, where her moves were closely observed and she was recognized as a powerful figure.

Hetty controlled large investments across the country. She juggled real estate mortgage deals, supervised railroad interests, and made huge loans. Henry Clews called her "one among a million of her sex" and Collis P. Huntington described her as "nothing more than a glorified pawnbroker." She was always good for a loan at standard rates, and a market panic was a bonanza for Hetty. Her fortune swelled prodigiously in the moment of others' misfortune; she caught the backwash of the man going down to ruin and bought falling stocks with an infallible sense of the moment to pounce. She foreclosed mortgages without qualms, and in their hours of desperation some of the leading bankers were at Hetty's mercy. In the panic of 1907 she was one of the biggest lenders, giving $6,000,000 to Texas alone.

"I am not a self-made woman," Hetty insisted. "I was born rich. My father was a millionaire, and so was his father, and all my ancestors have been rich." But she fattened her inherited fortune until it passed the hundred million point. Yet she spent most of her life in wretched flats, moving from place to place to avoid tax collectors. Her clothes were shabby; her children were denied the medical attention that they needed in their youth; she lived on the most meager fare; and there were few banquets in her life. From youth to old age she fought an endless series of court battles, and she was always a picturesque litigant, with her bulging umbrella, her waspish tongue, her irreverent defiance of court procedure.

At the height of her power and success she was easy to identify as she hurried through the financial region. There was only one Hetty Green, the Witch of Wall Street, in a moth-eaten cape and dingy bonnet, her grim mouth slanted downward at the corners, her gray eyes hard as steel. She invariably clutched a black reticule that was thought to hold bonds representing vast sums. The fact was that it usually contained nothing more important than Hetty's lunch, flung in without wrappings.

In her youth she had been the picture of health and vitality. As a girl she was graceful and well-proportioned, with a wealth of brown hair and gray eyes that did not pick up the glint of steel until she had fought many battles with hardheaded men. Her creamy complexion was touched with a carnation bloom from the sea winds that whipped around her in her girlhood days, and even in old age she had a sturdy dignity of carriage and a healthy color in her cheeks. Some New Englanders remembered her in her early twenties with ringlets down the back of her neck and camellias in her hair, an unimaginable picture to her Wall Street peers. In her later years she confided to Dorothy Dix, the newspaper correspondent:

> I was forced into business. I was the only child of two rich families and I was taught from the time I was six years old that I would have to look after my property. But I wasn't raised to be arrogant and haughty like the little lordlings you see now. On the contrary, my people were so afraid that I would be selfish, that I was sent to a Quaker school. There I learned plain things, to be thrifty, and careful, not to waste, to be just, and to read the Bible.

Hetty observed all these injunctions and, in addition, was one of the hardest working women in the world, as well as the thriftiest. All through the Golden Nineties, while her fellow bankers bought yachts and art collections, laid out country estates, traveled and lived luxuriously, Hetty was the miser among the millionaires. An old trading tradition was in her blood, reaching back to the purchase of one black cow in 1624 by Henry Howland at Plymouth, Massachusetts. Like most of the early settlers, the three Howland brothers, John, Henry, and Arthur, cleared land, farmed, and traded with Indians. In the post-Revolutionary days they expanded their operations to rum, iron, and the merchant marine. Isaac Howland, Jr., Hetty's great-grandfather, founded the family whaling fortune and gave New Bedford its name. Her father, Edward Mott Robinson, known as "Black Hawk" Robinson, built up a fortune in the whaling trade, and when he married Isaac's young granddaughter, Abby Slocum Howland, a Quaker heiress in her own right, he cemented it further.

Hetty was born in New Bedford on November 21, 1835, heiress to both the Howland and Robinson fortunes. Her mother was so delicate that Hetty never came to know her well and passed most of her childhood with her grandfather, Gideon Howland, Jr., and his spinster daughter, Sylvia Ann Howland. They all lived in the large mansion owned by Isaac's widow, Mrs. Ruth Butts Howland. Whether in her father's house or at her grandfather's, Hetty was never far from the docks of New Bedford. The port reeked of whale oil, spices, and cheese, and she skipped along within sight always of the Howland flag, flying from many masts. Her family owned thirty whalers. For the most part she ran wild, wearing durable, ugly garments of Quaker gray, with an austere bonnet hiding her luxuriant hair. Tales of adventure and of distant lands were her daily fare as she listened to seamen, whalers, and travelers of many kinds. Her father sometimes took her down into the hold of a ship, which was rough training for so young a child, and Hetty's language in later years was occasionally spiced with echoes of these days.

"Black Hawk" Robinson, a tall and handsome Quaker whose family had moved from Philadelphia to Providence, was known as "Napoleon" along the docks. He was a strong and arrogant man who had become a partner in the Howland interests when he married Abby. Gideon Howland had a major interest in the family whaling fortune, and Hetty's mother and Aunt Sylvia each had shares. Little Hetty was the legal heir to all four, and from her earliest years the residents of the world's great whaling port showed interest in the hoydenish child who trotted after her father. They all recognized the fact that she was a potential heiress.

In summer the family moved to their Round Hills farm at Buzzard's Bay. From her bedroom Hetty could see the white tower of Dumpling Light and in the far distance the Elizabeth Islands. By the time she was six she could read, ride, and drive. Her father made her read the stock market reports to him as soon as she recognized numerals, and he carefully explained his business transactions to the absorbed child. She was expected to keep a strict accounting of personal and household expenses. Figures had meaning for Hetty from that time on, since she always associated them with the family fortune. Statistics were her nursery rhymes and, ultimately, music in her ears. Years later she remarked: "I came to know what stocks and bonds were, how the market fluctuated, and the meaning of bulls and bears. When I went to Boston to school, I knew more about these things than many a man that makes a living out of them."

At the age of seven she was sent to Miss Eliza Wing's boarding school at Sandwich, near New Bedford. Three years there did little to tame her spirit, and her letters at all times were conspicuously ill-spelled and almost illiterate. Although Hetty could add like lightning she never learned to put sentences together with grace or clarity. But she was drilled in the usual maidenly accomplishments. She learned to sing and play when Gideon Howland installed a piano in the house, although he feared the wrath of Sylvia, Abby, and Ruth over this extravagance. Hetty's grandfather died when she was thirteen and she missed him, for he had been one of the few mellowing influences of her childhood. But it was her domineering, hard-grained father who had the most profound influence on her. He would have done nothing further about her education had not the women in the household insisted when she was fifteen that she be sent to a finishing school in Boston. The Rev. Charles Russell Lowell and his wife, Anna Cabot Lowell, who ran the school, did their best with her, but she was willful, quick-tempered, and prone to quarrel. During this period she read the Bible three times from beginning to end and quoted freely from it in her later years. Occasionally she used a text to excoriate a trembling victim on Wall Street. The Lowells were well aware of her family history, the millions behind her, the seafaring tradition, but they were not prepared for her rough language and rebellious spirit.

Hetty was little changed when she returned to New Bedford. Again she became her father's shadow along the docks, but she presented the conventional front at her coming-out party. She wore white lawn, with a crown of camellias on her glossy hair and filigreed gold earrings dangling at either side of her strong, handsome face. Beaux gathered around her, for she was good to look at, sharp and knowing in her conversation, and in the background loomed the family fortune. If she lacked the softer graces none of them noticed it as they swung her around the ballroom floor. But Hetty, by instinct or her father's warnings, assumed that all her suitors were fortune hunters, a well-grounded belief that she harbored until she found a man of wealth in his own right who wished to marry her.

The story was much the same in New York, where her father sent her for a winter with an order on his New York bankers for $1,200. Mrs. Lawrence Grinnell, a distant relative, was her chaperone, and when Hetty refused to buy anything for herself, she outfitted her with a charming ball gown, and all that went with it, to wear at a party she was giving in her honor. Hetty accepted them as gifts but showed up for her New York debut in her New Bedford clothes. She returned home with the boxes untouched. During her brief stay she had invested the money given her by her father for clothes, and had made a handsome profit.

On her return home she was restless and discontented. Her mother, who had left "Black Hawk" and had gone to live with Sylvia Ann, died in 1860. She failed to make a will, but Hetty fell heir to some real estate she had owned. When her father quarreled with Sylvia, he sold out his interest in the Isaac Howland firm and moved to New York, where he joined the firm of William T. Coleman & Company, merchants who handled clipper ships. Hetty visited him occasionally, although she could scarcely bring herself to relax her vigil over her Aunt Sylvia, who was threatening to leave her $2,000,000 to charity. Desperate scenes were staged between young Hetty and her aged aunt. When Sylvia announced that she was going to enlarge her house, her niece stormed and wept. She insisted on Sylvia's having a carriage because this was cheaper than livery hire. Hetty nagged, scolded, and harassed her aunt until Sylvia Ann became ill and went with a nurse to their Round Hills farm to recuperate. She predicted then that Hetty would lose her reason over making and hoarding money. It was clear to those who knew her during her adolescent years that she was obsessed on the subject.

She was in New York with her father when the Prince of Wales, traveling as Baron Renfrew, stirred up the city with the great ball given for him in the Academy of Music. Hetty was on the guest list, and in her old age she often told of having danced twice with the prince, and of being amused by his confusion when a jester introduced her as the Princess of Whales. Hetty wore Swiss muslin with a pink sash on this occasion. Her slippers were pink, and the gold filigree earrings she had worn at her coming-out party swung as she danced. There was nothing to distinguish her from the pick of New York society, present that night, but she had little to say to men of her own age, preferring to talk finance with their elders.

With the outbreak of the Civil War the world that she had known changed radically. Not only did the young men of New Bedford go off to fight, but whalers were sent south to block the sea approach to Charleston. Of forty-six sunk by the Confederate Navy, twenty-five came from the New England port. The whaling trade was already suffering from the use of kerosene in place of whale oil. As the Union forces gathered strength for their final assault in 1864, Hetty joined her father in New York, at an apartment on West Twenty-sixth Street, which they furnished with possessions from their New Bedford house. But she would not leave her New England home until she was assured that Sylvia's money had been willed to her, except for 5 per cent that her aunt insisted must go to charity. Hetty had no sooner settled in New York than she learned to her consternation that her aunt had made a new will the minute her back was turned.

For the moment, however, Hetty was diverted by a rich and worldly trader whom her father had insisted she meet. Edward Henry Green was a tall, impressive-looking man who had traveled the world over. Originally from Bellows Falls, Vermont, he had made a fortune in the Philippines, trading in tea, silks, tobacco, and hemp. In the course of his work he had learned to speak a number of languages, including Chinese. His ancestors had come from England in 1635 and had settled in Cambridge, Massachusetts. He was descended from a mayor of Boston, a judge, and a congressman. "Black Hawk" thought him an ideal suitor for Hetty, but he had come home bearing so many gifts for friends that she regarded him with some suspicion as a spendthrift. She was critical of the number of suits he had, and it was not until she received a check meant for his tailor, instead of the valentine he had intended to send her, that she viewed him with approval. Whether Green had made the mistake by accident or guile, Hetty was persuaded that he had paid only a modest sum for the suit in question.

Her father died on June 14, 1865, while Americans still talked with horror of Lincoln's assassination. He left her a million in cash and real estate and another four and a half millions to be held in trust. Sylvia Ann died two weeks later, and her niece learned with disappointment and rage that she had left more than half her fortune to relatives, friends, servants, and charities. Hetty received a life income amounting to $70,000 a year from the remaining million, but her cupidity was so overpowering that this did not satisfy her. Shortly afterward she produced a document that she insisted was her aunt's last will and testament. Its second page, which was legally disputed as a forgery, made her sole heir to Sylvia Ann's fortune. It also led her into one of the most fantastic will contest cases in the history of American jurisprudence. This long-drawn-out contest created a public image of Hetty fighting with tigerish ferocity for what she maintained were her rights.

On October 2, 1865, she filed a bill of complaint asking that the executors and trustees of her aunt's estate surrender it all to her. Hetty charged that Sylvia had had too much laudanum before the will was executed and did not know what she was doing. The defendants, in turn, insisted that Hetty had had access to Sylvia's trunk after her death and could have slipped in anything she wished. A small army of relatives and retainers closed ranks to fight Hetty for their inheritance. The hearings were interminable, with millions of words of testimony going into the records of the Circuit Court for the District of Massachusetts. With so much at stake the battery of counsel on both sides was impressive. Handwriting experts were called in to discuss a blot, or acid stain, on the document. Both Louis Agassiz and Oliver Wendell Holmes appeared for Hetty, and a succession of New England types took the witness stand to uphold their rights. The signature of President John Quincy Adams was displayed to prove a point for Hetty, and the public soon took up the pastime of tracing signatures. Sylvia Ann Howland's name rang throughout New England, and Hetty Robinson became a public personality, known far beyond the borders of her native state. But her spirit wilted as the handwriting experts gave their testimony, and it was whispered that she wished to withdraw the suit. Nothing was proved against her and the case was ultimately dropped. Hetty admitted having written an appendage to the will stating: "I give this will to my niece to show, if necessary, to have it appear against any other will found after my death." She insisted, however, that she did this at her aunt's instigation, and that Sylvia signed it in duplicate in her presence.

Edward Green was one of her witnesses and soon afterward they were married. She was almost thirty-three at the time, and he was forty-six. Characteristically, Hetty had him sign a contract beforehand by which she would not be liable for his debts but he would be responsible for her support. She looked attractive in basque and bustle on her wedding day, July 11, 1867. The ceremony was held at the home of her mother's cousin, Henry Grinnell, on Bond Street in New York. His brother, Moses Hicks Grinnell, a friend of Washington Irving's and a merchant of clipper ship fame, was present, and the echo of whaling days was strong. She looked hard at the ten-dollar gold piece her husband gave to the clergyman, but she felt confident that since he had a million dollars in his own right he was not marrying her for her fortune.

They sailed almost at once for England, with Hetty's kinsfolk saying that she was fleeing from prosecution for forgery. Actually she had been in a highly nervous state since her father's death and was almost afraid to leave the house. She believed that he had been poisoned by a band of conspirators and that her own life was in danger. For weeks before her marriage she slept in a storeroom under a bed piled high with rugs and furniture. She existed mostly on raw eggs and crackers. Her eccentricity by this time was apparent to all around her.

Although exhausted when she went abroad, Green's genial ways brought some warmth and reassurance into her life. He had traveled so much that he settled in London with a strong sense of familiarity, haunting the clubs and finding old friends from his days in the tropics. Hetty quickly learned that he had little sympathy for the spare Quaker tradition, since he was a gourmet and liked the best in food and wines. She frowned at him when she found him sipping rum and smoking Manila cigars, but he was so good-natured and kind in all his ways that even Hetty could get along with him. Besides, he paid all their living expenses, leaving her free to study the operations of Threadneedle Street. In her later years she often talked of her triumphs in London—of being presented to Queen Victoria, a point that was never proved; of staying at the castles of noblemen; of attending great balls and meeting the statesmen of the period.

The Greens lived in luxury at the Langham Hotel, and inevitably Hetty was soon involved in large business deals. Her husband was a director of three London banks and some of his operations involved the house of Baring Brothers. United States Government bonds were in circulation in London banking circles, and Hetty invested heavily in gold bonds, making more than a million and a quarter dollars within a year. In a single day she added $200,000 to her fortune. After testing her husband's business judgment she found it good, but she had her own particular touch of genius when it came to making money. Green had dawdled so much in clubs in the East that he could scarcely keep up with Hetty's lightning financial moves.

During this period she came closest to leading a normal life, although she was regarded by Londoners as the bizarre American woman with all the millions. Her son, Edward Howland Robinson Green, was born at their hotel on August 22, 1868, and she predicted that she would make him the richest man in the world. Her daughter, Hetty Sylvia Ann Howland Green, who was always known as Sylvia, was born on January 7, 1871, and for the time being Hetty was content to play the role of mother. She went regularly to Hyde Park with the children, and she figured in a street accident when a man fell off his cart while having a fit and was badly injured. Hetty gave him first aid; in such ways she was quick-thinking and practical. A marchioness who had watched the shabby woman function with great efficiency came out and offered to give her work. When she learned that she was speaking to Hetty Green she was greatly embarrassed, and afterward kept sending her tickets for bazaars and other entertainments. Hetty was as insistent on her shabbiness as John D. Rockefeller was about the distribution of his dimes. To save on her laundry while in London she had only the bottom flounces of her petticoats laundered.

Strange tales drifted around the City about Mrs. Green's financial operations as she and her husband became well known in Victorian London. When Hetty paraded through the plush and gilt lobby of the Langham, where Mark Twain and Andrew Carnegie also stayed on their visits to London, her unfashionable clothes were passed off as the habiliments of an eccentric. But eventually Hetty grew tired of London and its fashionable life, and in 1875 the Greens returned to the United States. The old charges against her had lapsed, and she had not been indicted as her relatives had predicted, but the fires still burned in her memory. She scoffed when a New York *World* reporter asked her on her return if she had buried herself in London to escape prosecution. "Why do you suppose I'd have named my daughter Sylvia Ann Howland if I had forged my aunt's name?" she snapped. "I'd have had a living picture of forgery before me all these years."

After a compromise agreement the lawyers were paid off and the residue of the greatly depleted estate went to those named in the will, and to various charities chosen by Sylvia. Hetty's annuity was carefully invested in United States gold bonds and brought her added riches; she happened to be one of those who profited by the Gold Corner created by Jay Gould and Jim Fisk.

Soon after their arrival the Greens went to Bellows Falls to live with Mrs. Henry Atkinson Green, Edward's mother. There was great local interest in the fact that the famous Hetty Green intended to settle there, but her neighbors were in for a shock when she arrived, rumpled and obviously in need of a thorough scrubbing. Ned Green was remembered as a jovial youth who had gone to distant lands and made a fortune. His mother was astounded to find how parsimonious Hetty was when they joined her in her square brick mansion and the children went to the local school. Sylvia was myopic and wore thick glasses. At first she appeared in a ruffled dress that her father had bought for her in London, but as time went on she wore ill-fitting made-over garments that dragged around her ankles.

When Ned was fourteen he dislocated his knee in jumping on a sled, and after that he limped. Hetty adored her son, but the thing he needed most at this point she denied him—good medical attention. When his leg did not heal she used hot sand and tobacco leaves for poultices, but he did not seem to improve. Later in New York she donned her shabbiest clothes and took him to a doctor, who sent him to Bellevue as a charity patient. It was soon discovered there that the patient's mother was Mrs. Edward Green. The doctor to whom she had gone in the first place proposed his customary fee, but Hetty never returned to his office.

She was often accused of having made her son a cripple by failing to have adequate medical attention for him at the time of his accident, but though her efforts were tardy and misguided, actually she took him to many doctors, and lived for a time in Baltimore so that he might have treatments there. Big as he was, she literally carried him off and on street cars, and she worried about him constantly. When he had a second fall while watching a parade with his father in New York, Green took him to the Union Club and summoned an outstanding surgeon. He was told that if the boy had had proper attention earlier his leg might have been saved. As things were, it was amputated in 1887, five years after the original injury, and thereafter Ned had a cork leg. The fee for the operation was $5,000, and rather than risk a scene with Hetty, Green sold the last of his securities and paid the bill himself.

By this time the Greens were living apart. Edward had made some investments contrary to his wife's advice and had lost heavily. She saved him several times but tired of this as the sums grew larger. When she had lost all faith in him as a sound operator on the stock market, she dropped him as she would a bad investment. The crisis had come in 1885 when John J. Cisco & Son went bankrupt. The firm's vaults were stuffed with Hetty's securities, and she was accused of precipitating the failure of the house when she decided suddenly to transfer her deposits to the Chemical National Bank. "Black Hawk" had always banked with Cisco, and she had been with the house for twenty years. When she tried to pull out, the bank officials informed her that her husband owed them $702,159.04 for transactions of his own, and that they would hold her deposit of $556,581.23 to make good this obligation. She stormed down from Bellows Falls and confronted Lewis May, to whom Cisco's had been assigned. Witnesses looking through glass were startled to see Mrs. Green rampaging up and down, waving her arms and shouting. The argument went on for five hours, and she returned to the siege day after day. Finally, at the end of two weeks, she gave May a check for $422,143.22 and a receipt for half of her claim against the assets he held. It took several clerks to help Hetty pile her boxes into a wagon as she moved over to the Chemical National Bank with securities that had a market value that day of $25,000,000.

This story spread and helped to make Hetty the most famous woman financier of her day. After the Cisco failure she moved with her children from Vermont to New York, breaking away from her husband, who had committed the unpardonable sin of losing money—his own and also hers. He sold his barouche and horses, took rooms in the Cumberland Hotel, and spent much of his time at the Union League Club. His wife was no longer known as Mrs. Edward Green. She was now Mrs. Hetty Green and in time the traders on Wall Street scarcely remembered that she had a husband. On more than one occasion she remarked: "My husband is of no use to me at all. I wish I did not have him." But she did not rule him out of her life entirely; a friendly feeling persisted, and sometimes she deliberately strolled past his club and beckoned him to come out and join her. They would then discuss the children and their investments, but they could never reach an understanding about themselves.

Hetty continued to haunt clinics in rag-bag attire, seeking medical aid for herself or for her children. In 1898, she was publicly denounced for practicing this deception by the chairman of a medical committee investigating abuses of charity patients. She was equally hostile to doctors and lawyers. Her life was so checkered with litigation that she often required the services of the legal profession. Sometimes she cast them off without paying their bills, and she always said she kept a pistol handy, not for thieves but for lawyers. Her feuds were so notorious that she was a dreaded figure in any court. In 1892 she buffooned her way through long hearings before Referee Henry H. Anderson in New York when Henry A. Barling, the sole surviving trustee of her father's estate, applied for a discharge from his trust. Hetty protested his accounting and testified that she had received only $334,000 of the fortune left her by her father. She gave the dignified Joseph H. Choate, who had once been her father's legal adviser, a particularly uncomfortable time in court, once poking him with her umbrella and on another occasion threatening "to paste him in the face" with the heel of her shoe. Again when he was summing up in his most rhetorical manner she drew a yellowed old pillowslip from under her cape and wept crocodile tears into it over the sufferings of the executor who, he said, was constantly under the lash of her tongue. The courtroom audience roared, and Choate wilted under this assault. More than once

Hetty knelt before a window in court, stared up at the sky, folded her hands in the attitude of prayer, and called on heaven to support her.

Her strange attire caused public comment in the courtroom, as elsewhere. She usually stalked in carrying an umbrella, with a crazy little bonnet tied to her head with frayed strings. Her favorite seal cape, visibly moth-eaten, covered various tears and patches. She saw virtue in wearing a cheap black dress until it literally turned green, and prided herself on the fact that she had worn one bonnet for ten years and hoped to make it do for another decade. But she became more sensitive about her appearance in the last days of her life and wistfully asked a friend who directed a large Fifth Avenue store if she really looked as ragged as the papers implied. At the moment she happened to be wearing a torn veil, and he gently suggested that if she would come to his store he would treat her to a new one. She did, and walked off with the veil. Before leaving she also picked up an eight-dollar skirt for fifty cents, a matter arranged by her friend. This was the sort of thing that made Hetty Green a happy woman for a fleeting moment.

She was a tiresome but much valued figure at the Chemical National Bank, close to City Hall, where she occupied a long, narrow office and never opened the door leading into her sanctum. Visitors spoke to her through a brass grating. She liked to sit cross-legged on the cold stone floor and shuffle her bonds, mortgages, stocks, and deeds from one box to another. Occasionally she would seize a bundle in clawlike fingers and stuff it into hidden pockets in her voluminous skirt and petticoats. Although she was known first as the Queen of Wall Street, and ultimately as the Witch of Wall Street, some of the great financiers had never seen her. Nevertheless they felt her influence in a variety of ways all the year round. She particularly favored railroad stocks or mortgage bonds, and when she saw a good thing going at a low price because no one wanted it, she bought heavily and tucked it away for future benefits. Time and again this paid off, for Hetty had the Midas touch and rarely lost money. From coast to coast she held mortgages on business buildings, city mansions, factories, theaters, hotels, ranches, and country estates. Churches and cemeteries loomed large in her operations, and at one time she held mortgages on twenty-eight churches of different denominations. A man with whom she was negotiating a large loan said to her on one occasion: "I'm almost afraid to borrow so much and give securities to a single individual. Suppose you were to die?"

"Never mind," Hetty responded. "I'll throw in a couple of cemeteries as a margin on the securities."

He concluded the transaction, as men usually did with inflexible Hetty. Sometimes she toured her properties. Her chief interests were in California, Texas, Chicago, and New York, but she also had lots in Denver, St. Louis, and Cincinnati. Between 1885 and 1890 she picked up more than $17,000,000 worth of real estate. Since she bought heavily in the Loop, she had many encounters with Potter Palmer in Chicago. He and his famous wife took note of Hetty Green when she visited their city, and he sent her flowers, a gesture that few ever thought of in connection with the Witch of Wall Street. She stayed at the Palmer House and peered into the barber shop to have a look at the silver dollars that paved the floor, but she noted that they seemed to be far apart. Over the years she made many trips to Chicago and rode in a private car after her son Ned became an official of the Louisville and Nashville Railroad.

Her bargaining rules were primitive. She bought when everyone wanted to sell, and sold when everyone wanted to buy. She set her own price, and when it was offered she sold. It was a point of pride with her that she never bought anything just to hold on to it; her business was always in flux, but before she decided on an investment she rounded up all kinds of information before parting with her cash. She bought by instinct but never blind, and she followed the same principles, from her greatest to her most minor purchases. Some of her biggest profits came from her city holdings. "There is no great secret in fortune making," said Hetty, who found it so easy. "I believe in getting in at the bottom and out at the top. All you have to do is buy cheap and sell dear, act with thrift and shrewdness and be persistent." When asked to suggest a good investment she invariably replied: "The other world."

She foresaw the panic of 1905 and made careful preparation, calling in her money and closing up as many real estate deals for cash as she could. She always preferred first mortgages to buying real estate outright. In any event, when the market crashed, she was ready with all her assets. She had cash; her colleagues were dependent on their securities. In her own words: "They did come to me in droves. Those to whom I loaned my money got it at six per cent. I might just as easily have secured forty per cent." Hetty professed to be scrupulous about her rate of interest, although the impression prevailed that she was a usurer, who squeezed the last possible penny from her victims.

She was an intimidating figure to the powerful men who sought her aid. In time of panic they came in a stream—bankers, brokers, corporation heads—to the shabby woman who stared at them with cold gray eyes, remembering the yachts, the art collections, the elaborate 1890's parties in the background. She had no sympathy for any of them, but when the bargain was good Hetty would look at them grimly and assent with a wry jest. She knew how they regarded her, and on one occasion she remarked: "My life is written for me down in Wall Street by people who, I assume, do not care to know one iota of the real Hetty Green. I am in earnest; therefore they picture me as heartless. I go my own way. I take no partner, risk nobody else's fortune, therefore I am Madame Ishmael, set against every man."

It was her custom to keep from twenty to thirty million dollars in cash for short-term loans. This made her bankers nervous at times; so did her custom of traveling in the public stage with treasure beyond belief. When she walked in one day with $200,000 in negotiable bonds that she proposed to leave with the rest of her deposits, a banker suggested that she use a carriage instead of the stage.

"A carriage, indeed," said Hetty. "Perhaps you can afford to ride in a carriage—I cannot."

She was slow to surrender to the automobile, saying she would rather ride on an ass than in a motorcar. "Jesus did not ride in automobiles; an ass was good enough for Him," said Hetty.

The Witch of Wall Street had strong likes and dislikes among the financiers, and her feud with Collis P. Huntington was notorious. She always blamed him for the ruin of the Cisco banking house. When he was developing the Southern Pacific Railroad she used every means she could to put obstacles in his way, and when he took over the bankrupt Houston & Texas Central Railroad and attempted to reorganize it, she refused to turn in her million dollars' worth of bonds. He reasoned with her and threatened her, but she threw the road into receivership and collected her bonds in full. Her favorite millionaire was Russell Sage, and she was always pleased to be compared with him. Both loved money for its own sake, but he put his to better use.

One visitor who was always welcomed by Hetty was Chauncey M. Depew, who represented the Vanderbilt railroad interests. They had much business to do together at times, and better than most he knew how to handle the irascible wizard. He would sometimes find her sitting on the floor in the bank with a smudged face and dirty hands, after she had been juggling her money and securities. Hetty seemed to get the miser's satisfaction from the physical touch of her wealth. It took considerable storage space to house her treasures; she had packing cases, boxes, and a variety of nineteenth-century portmanteaus stuffed with bonds, as well as a wagon to convey them from place to place. Sometimes she hung a frowsy dress in the bank vault and changed her clothes on the premises. Her safety deposit box keys for various cities were strung around her waist, and she rigged up a revolver at the foot of her bed with an arrangement of strings when she was staying in a strange hotel. Hetty prided herself on having nerve. She did, on the market, but in her personal life she was a bundle of irrational fears. There were few places where she felt safe or at ease as her fortune mounted. Her personal life was lived on a wretched plane, and in time she came to believe that Sylvia Howland and her father had both been murdered.

Her delusions became more pronounced with the years. She believed herself to be the victim of a conspiracy and her black reticule to be a focus of malignant observation. Her fear of assassination gave added point to her furtive way of life. She was sure she had found ground glass in her food in a boarding house in Brooklyn, and when burglars broke into a house where she lodged at Hempstead, Long Island, she decided that they were murderers who had come to kill her. When a block of wood fell from a house that was in course of construction she insisted that this was a deliberate attempt to kill her.

Her eating habits were as curious as everything else about her. While her fellow bankers lunched at their clubs or at Delmonico's, she dug into her reticule for scraps of food, or heated water for gruel on a radiator in a building adjoining her bank. Now and again she darted into a cheap lunch place nearby to see what she could get for a quarter, and she chewed onions constantly, believing them to be good for her health. On her trips to other cities she had her favorite spots for lunch, but it was against her principles to leave a tip, even when her business drew her into one of the better restaurants. In Boston she favored Pie Alley where she could have coffee and doughnuts with the truckmen for a nickel, pie for two cents, or beans for three. In Bellows Falls or Hoboken she bought a quarter of a pound of butter at a time, a single apple, a few graham crackers, and she thought that the entire nation was cursed by its extravagant women and its unreliable men. Hetty fancied herself as the friend of the workers, and liked to tell reporters that not a day passed without her doing something for them. In later years she became quite fond of giving interviews, boasting with wry humor of the tricks she had pulled in the business world. Hetty accepted the fact that she was a public character and even seemed to enjoy the role at times, so much so that she was pictured as being a "laughing, joking, gay old lady."

But for the most part, her life was lived with extreme secrecy. By taking dingy lodgings close to New York she found that she could get to her bank easily, outwit the tax collectors, and also exist on the most frugal level. She moved from one cheap boarding house or hotel to another, hating to part with a cent, even for the bare necessities of life. Her enemies called her a nomadic tax dodger by night and a usurious moneylender by day. When the chase grew hot she quickly moved to another place, so that her children grew up knowing Hoboken, Hempstead, Far Rockaway, Morristown, Harlem, Brooklyn, and other stopping places. Hetty had been known to sleep in a Bowery hotel, and she boarded for five dollars a week at Far Rockaway in the off-season, wearing fishermen's boots as she ploughed through the sand to the railroad station. Landladies hesitated to take in the strange, shabby woman who arrived with few possessions and a bargaining air.

Her most pretentious setting in those days was two small apartments in Hoboken, a city she favored because she could take the ferry to lower Manhattan and be the first at her desk in the morning. She was also invariably the last to leave. Her parlor was tiny and was hung with chromos. It held a table, a couch, three chairs, and a worn rug. A bunch of red roses made of feathers and a crayon of herself before her marriage were the sole decorations. Hetty, like Andrew Carnegie, dined most often on rice, although occasionally she was known to invest in a beefsteak. A soiled card under the electric push button at her door read C. Dewey, for Hetty used many aliases as she moved from place to place. This stood for Cutie Dewey, the name she had given her Skye terrier at the time of the Spanish-American War.

Little as she loved mankind, Hetty was fond of animals, and Dewey was her companion for years. She fed him better than she did herself. Her rent in Hoboken was fourteen dollars a month, including light and heat. Sylvia shared her mother's bedroom; Ned slept on a cot in the kitchen, where they also dined. All the tenants shared one bathtub on the fourth floor. Hetty used her parlor as an office, and sometimes brokers and agents who had failed to see her in the daytime followed her to Hoboken to talk business. She was making $5,000 a day while she lived under these conditions, and was ironically described by one observer as being an "artist among misers."

Hetty was sturdy and could work long hours without sleep. She never tired of juggling figures, and those who did business with her watched with fascination while she made lightning calculations. Her one extravagance was to give her son Ned a hundred dollars' worth of firecrackers every Fourth of July. As he grew older her advice to him was: "Never speculate on Wall Street; never maintain an office; eat slowly; don't stay up all night; don't drink ice water, and keep out of draughts." When he left college she asked him to promise that he would not marry for twenty years. Ned stood in awe of his mother. No one knew better than he how strong-minded she was. "She wouldn't let me dictate if I wanted to," he said when he got away from her and out into the working world.

Ned helped her as an errand boy at her bank until she sent him to Boston in 1889 to get some experience in a broker's office. Next she ordered him to Chicago to look after her property there, but she tested him first by giving him a package which she told him contained $250,000 in bonds. He hid it under his mattress on the train and went to considerable lengths to protect his mother's property. When it was opened at his destination it contained nothing but fire insurance policies. However, Ned had won his spurs. She had been preaching thrift to him from his earliest years. When he left Fordham she drew him into her business orbit, although he was tempted to turn to the profession so satanic in his mother's eyes—the law.

His presence in Chicago was noted with interest, for he was recognized by the press as heir to one of America's greatest fortunes. He was a big hulking youth with his father's geniality, and he talked quite affably about his prospects.

But Ned showed strange tastes for the son of Hetty Green. He hung around the stage door and indulged in worldly pleasures. He carried cigarettes in his cane and was recognized as a sport. The meager spending money allowed him by his mother was cause for merriment with Ned, and he wrote to her from Texas in small-boy fashion on August 22, 1893: "I am twenty-five years old today. I think you might send me money so I could go to the Fair at Chicago in about two weeks before the Fall rush begins. It would only cost about $200. I can get passes to Chicago and return. Let me know as soon as you can so I can get ready. I want to see the Fair *so* bad. Please let me go."

The Columbian Exposition of 1893 had stimulated a boom in real estate, and in the next few years Hetty made many trips west to keep the pot boiling. After Ned settled in Chicago she made her rounds beside her enormous son, who treated her with respect and concealed amusement. He was six feet four and weighed three hundred pounds. He moved awkwardly because of his artificial leg. In time he became a yachtsman, a patron of sports and the arts, a collector of coins, stamps, and erotica, and a grower of orchids. He was also an excellent businessman. Hetty drilled him herself and boasted that he was the youngest railroad president in the United States when he took charge of the Texas and Midland Railroad at the age of twenty-four. She had sent him south to foreclose a mortgage on the railroad, and he handled the matter so well that she telegraphed him: "The road is yours. See what you can do with it." He soon made it a going concern and established a home for himself in Terrell, Texas.

In Chicago he had come to know a red-haired beauty named Mabel E. Harlow, whom he continued to befriend, and whom he married after his mother's death. She joined him in Texas, where he strutted about with a hat brim as wide as his shoulders. He consorted with cowboys and organized a Tarpon Club and a baseball team, with players wearing bright red uniforms. He bought one of the first automobiles to be seen in Dallas and kept a private railroad car that was known as the Lone Star. He set up bachelor quarters and squandered money in a way that his mother would never have approved. But she was devoted to Ned and was proud when he made a token run for the governorship of Texas on the Republican ticket. However, Hetty really wanted him to return to New York and work under her direction. She wrote to him on March 20, 1902: "In the compliment your great and adopted state has tendered to you I know you will *not forget* your *mother* who *needs* and *demands* your assistance."

For years Ned had slept on a kitchen cot in a walk-up apartment, and he was tired of such needless economies. His rebellion was thorough, and Hetty could do nothing to stop it. Her son went right ahead until he owned a stable of horses, a yacht, and all the luxuries known to his fellow millionaires. He told a Texas editor that when he left his mother he felt like a Trappist monk who all of a sudden had been released from every vow he had ever made. But Hetty defended him fiercely when Huntington threatened to have him jailed in the course of their railroad feuding. Her revolver was at hand on this occasion, and she threatened him:

"Up to now, Huntington, you have dealt with Hetty Green, the business woman. Now you are fighting Hetty Green, the mother. Harm one hair of Ned's head and I'll put a bullet through your heart!"

Huntington left his silk hat behind him in his haste as he sped from Mrs. Green's presence. The railroad litigation in Texas continued for years, and although Hetty got little out of it, she liked to think that she was harrying her enemy. She felt no grief when his end came. "That old devil Huntington is dead," she exclaimed. "Serves him right."

Ned rescued himself from his mother's clutches, but Sylvia was aided by Miss Annie Leary, a papal countess who tried to convert Hetty and to persuade her to endow some Catholic charity. She was a philanthropist in her own right, and she entertained on a lavish scale at her country estate and at her Fifth Avenue home. Dissimilar as the two women were, they got on well together, and Miss Leary had considerable influence over Hetty. "If I can do any church any good I am happy," said the Witch of Wall Street, after acknowledging that she held a score of mortgages on Catholic churches at 2 per cent interest, placed through Miss Leary. But she treated the churchmen much as she did the wolves of Wall Street.

When a Presbyterian church in Chicago on which she held a $27,000 mortgage burned down, the minister wrote to her that if she did not cancel it she would not go to heaven. Hetty wrote back that he had "better climb right up on his corner stone and pray for my soul because I am going to foreclose within sixty days." And she did.

Miss Leary was concerned about providing a suitable social background for Sylvia when the time came for her to come out in society. Like Ned, Sylvia had had a shabby and wretched childhood. She had been moved from school to school and finally entered the Sacred Heart Academy in Manhattanville, when Ned went to St. John's, which later became Fordham. Sylvia had watched her mother hunt for a postage stamp in a pile of autumn leaves and for a dime in a heap of dust. She had seen the family laundry done in a bucket by her mother at Bellows Falls and had watched it being lowered from the window, with Hetty following it downstairs to spread it on the lawn to dry. She had nursed her father there during his last days. For weeks he lay dying in a bedroom from which he could see the hills of Vermont and the river that he had always loved.

Hetty was kind to her husband at the end. When he became ill at the Cumberland Hotel she insisted on moving in to nurse him. Then she took him to Hoboken where she and Sylvia looked after him in an apartment above their own. Finally, when there was no doubt that he was dying, she moved him back to his own home in Vermont. During this period she traveled back and forth to New York several times a week, taking a train out of Bellows Falls at three in the morning, working all day on Wall Street, and catching an eleven o'clock coach back to Vermont. She was in New York when word reached her that her husband had had a relapse. Ned was sent for and arrived quite ill himself. Hetty nursed both husband and son. When Green died on March 19, 1902, she made a special effort to dress appropriately for his funeral. For years after that she wore heavy widow's veiling that made her a more fearsome sight than ever in downtown New York. One of her odd theories was that she was comfortable only in rags and tatters because she was marked before her birth. "While my mother was carrying me she was frightened half to death by a ragged, tattered tramp," Hetty explained. "I have to wear old clothes. I suffer, really, when I'm dressed up."

When Ned came north on another occasion for his sister's coming-out party he was struck all over again by the senselessness of his mother's parsimony. He knew that he could never influence her in any way, and he marveled as he watched her at Sylvia's party. Every day he was learning more about her operations, and he could not fail to be impressed. She looked young for her years, although her thin mouth was becoming grim and her hair was slowly turning gray. But with him she could be kindly and even comic when in the mood. It gave her great anguish to make a splash for her daughter, and she could scarcely wait to get back to Hoboken and into her old clothes. She had chosen Morristown, New Jersey, for the event. Some of her fellow millionaires had estates there and, prompted by Miss Leary, she and Sylvia stayed for several weeks before the debut at the leading boarding house in town, even though it cost forty-four dollars a week for room and board. She had no thought of Sylvia's following her example in any respect and briskly observed: "My daughter hasn't been reared to be a business woman. She knows a good deal about business, and she'll be able to take care of what she may have, but I wouldn't want her to follow in my footsteps."

Miss Leary did her best to have Sylvia meet eligible men, both at Newport and in her own Fifth Avenue house. However, Hetty crossed up one budding romance after another. She sized up the Spanish Duke de la Terre at a tea given in the Waldorf-Astoria and promptly decided that he was a fortune hunter. She warned her daughter against the Earl of Yarmouth, convinced that he was after the Green fortune. Hetty was critical of the foreign alliances that some of the daughters of her fellow millionaires were making at this time. "There are thousands of honest young workingmen in the United States good enough to be anybody's husband," she announced. "The girls who go to Europe to get their husbands deserve what they get and more. If my son married a foreign woman because the marriage would bring him a title I would disown him."

Sylvia was thirty-eight when Matthew Astor Wilks became her suitor, and Miss Leary was determined that there should be no slip-up in this case. She persuaded Hetty to stay at the Plaza and thereby provide some background for her daughter. Always the generous friend, she lent her gold plate to the Greens for a ten-course dinner at which wine was served. Wall Street men chortled over Hetty's extravagance, but her stay for a month at the Plaza Hotel was brightened by the fact that she was allowed a fifteen-dollar-a-day suite for ten dollars. With this social mission accomplished and the stage set, she moved to a boarding house at 673 Madison Avenue but was soon back in Hoboken. She was there when Sylvia's engagement to Wilks was announced early in 1909 from his home in Galt, Ontario. He was the great-grandson of John Jacob Astor, and his branch of the family had settled in Canada, where he had property.

True to form, Hetty refused her consent but was talked out of this resistance by Miss Leary and the prospective bridegroom. She could not question the fact that he came from a family whose members knew how to make and how to keep money. Since he had at least a million of his own, he was obviously not marrying Sylvia for her fortune. Nevertheless, Hetty did not swing over to his side until he had signed an agreement before the wedding, relinquishing all claim to his wife's property. Wilks was an amiable bachelor nearly a quarter of a century her senior. Hetty, who never grew fond of him, called him a "gouty old man."

Hetty was resplendent at her daughter's wedding in St. Peter's Church, Morristown, New Jersey, on February 23, 1909. For once in her life she had gone to considerable pains over her appearance and had even taken twenty beauty treatments costing $300 from Madame Claire le Claire, a top practitioner in this field. Miss Leary's dressmaker had made her a striped silk dress, over which she wore a long black silk cloak scalloped with lace medallions, and finished at the neck with a lace ruff. Observers decided that she was more becomingly dressed than the bride, who wore a blue cloth gown, a hat with stiff ostrich feathers, and a white feather boa. They were married by the Rev. Dr. Philemon F. Sturges.

There were no ushers or bridesmaids, but Howland Pell gave the bride away, with a score of guests looking on. Sylvia was much taller than her bridegroom, who because of his gout walked stiffly. They had tried to keep the wedding private, but the news had leaked out and reporters converged on the family group coming out of the church. There was more interest in Hetty than in the bride, and she was full of good cheer, even to the extent of helping the photographers with their pictures. She whacked an umbrella out of the way that a guest had interposed between the bride and the cameramen.

"Let them alone," said Hetty imperiously. "They are all right. If they want to get a picture let it be a good one."

She posed willingly with the bride and groom and arranged for more pictures to be taken at the Morristown Inn, where champagne flowed and fine fare was served and billed to Hetty Green, the nation's pet miser. Hetty further delighted the press by writing her own account of the wedding. Obviously she liked what was going on, and she wished to see it well recorded. In spite of her scorn for snobs, she laid much stress on her daughter's descent from two old colonial families, the Robinsons of Rhode Island and the Howlands of Massachusetts. "The wedding breakfast was bright and gay," said the New York *Tribune* of February 24, 1909. A French chef was in command, and everything was done in the best manner, with Miss Leary's inimitable touch in the background. Hetty had just run over from her dive in Hoboken to see her daughter married, but Ned had not come up from Texas. Hetty carefully explained to the press why she shunned show of any kind. Hundreds of begging letters had reached her after there had been publicity on her stay at the Plaza Hotel.

"I am not a hard woman," she said, "but because I do not have a secretary to announce every kind act I perform I am called close and mean and stingy. I am a Quaker, and I am trying to live up to the tenets of that faith. That is why I dress plainly and live quietly. No other kind of life would please me."

But the richest woman in the world now showed interest in the social columns for the first time in her life. She had never before cared about anything that did not involve finance, but after Sylvia's wedding she subscribed to a clipping service and gave special instructions that all social items involving the Green family should be sent to her. Her daughter began her married life in the house that Wilks owned on Madison Avenue, and she adhered to the formal standards set by him. The shabby bohemianism of life with Hetty lay behind her, and she turned her attention to philanthropy. Her mother had drawn up her will the year before Sylvia's marriage, making no provision for charity. Both of her children were given to understand that her fortune would be divided between them.

Occasional flickers of affection now gilded Hetty's portrait in the press. After years of appearing in the papers as a litigant and a miser, she took a whimsical delight in giving interviews on public questions. She talked fast and sometimes indiscreetly. There were times when she seemed to be almost incoherent. Her thoughts flowed fast; her words were blunt. She jested in a wry way and knew what was expected of her. Often she was aphoristic and trite, but sometimes she talked good sense. She told girls in search of careers in the business world that they needed concentration of purpose, good memory, and adaptability. Once sure of their ground they should stick to their purpose without fear. "A woman need not lose her femininity because she has a good business head on her shoulders," said Hetty. "Some of the most charming and feminine women I know have well-balanced brains which would easily fit them to cope with the business world should the necessity arise."

Hetty sometimes indulged in a maudlin form of self-pity that made her listeners squirm. When she called herself a poor lone woman it was quickly noted that no member of her sex in the country was playing the man's game more successfully than Mrs. Green. But she scorned the suffrage movement and insisted that woman's place was in the home, adding with a final flip at members of the bar:

> I am willing to leave politics to the man, although I wish women had more rights in business and elsewhere than they now have. I could have succeeded much easier in my career had I been a man. I find men will take advantage of women in business that they would not attempt with men. I found this so in the courts, where I have been fighting men all my life.

When Ada Patterson, writing for the Hearst papers, brought a slum child to visit Mrs. Green, she told Hetty that it would be interesting for the richest woman in the world to tell the poorest child in the world what she should do to get rich. Hetty sat behind a table in the bank, her gray eyes boring into the child's frightened blue ones, and rattled off her favorite bromide: "Save your money and when you get a little ahead, don't put all your eggs in one basket." But she did not start a savings account for the child, or do anything more than pose with her for a picture. However, Hetty was known to be kind to children, as she was to dogs.

There were times when Hetty seemed to seek human warmth and recognition. Pettus V. Hoyle, an editor who came to New York and settled close to Washington Square shortly before Hetty's death, found this to be true when he had an encounter with the legendary Witch of Wall Street. He was walking to his office one day when he noticed her standing at the curb on Fifth Avenue, rain drizzling down on her. She was smiling and seemed to be trying to catch his attention. Then she asked him if he knew where Countess Leary lived. He explained that he had just come to New York and did not know, but the aging lady promptly gave him the address on Fifth Avenue.

"I can find that," he assured her and escorted her under his umbrella to the old-fashioned brick house where Miss Leary lived.

Hetty seemed pleased and thanked him warmly.

Next time he passed that way a policeman said: "I saw you speak to that old lady. Did she ask you where Countess Leary lived? Do you know who she is? That's Hetty Green, the richest woman in the world."

It developed that Hetty tried this ruse on many passersby. Was it her wry way of drawing attention to herself, or of seeing if she was recognized as Hetty Green and what the reaction might be?

In her later years, under Miss Leary's influence, Hetty appeared from time to time at social functions quite elaborately dressed. She wore a diamond pendant and a white satin gown with a black lace tunic when invited to have tea with Cardinal Farley at her friend's house. A white chiffon scarf was draped around her throat, and observers noticed that the chain dangling from her lorgnette was strung with jewels. No one believed that she had ever bought diamonds for herself, but it was known that jewels had sometimes figured in her business transactions and had been put up as collateral. But not even the papal countess could persuade her to do much about her everyday wardrobe, and in one of her last interviews Hetty said, with a touch of bitterness: "They say I am cranky or insane because I dress plainly and do not spend a fortune on my gowns."

Since much of the time she was evading tax collectors, she never welcomed an inquiry as to where she was living, and no one was able to assess the number of sordid places in which she had slept. But her health began to fail in 1910. She was lonely after Sylvia's wedding and the death of her terrier Dewey. She wrote pleading letters to Ned, urging him to join her in New York. "I am so tired," she complained, and again: "I want you to come back soon." But Ned did not wish to leave Texas. He was busy with his many interests, his loves and his hobbies. However, his mother persisted, and he returned to New York, but not to a Hoboken flat or any other of Hetty's haunts. He put up at the Waldorf, and it became public knowledge that Mrs. Green was failing and needed her son's help.

Outraged by this assumption, Hetty began to stir around again. Ned was surprised to find her full of ginger, gesticulating extravagantly as she talked, a lifetime habit, and her eyes gleaming like steel. During the next six years he did a great deal of work for her, and after she died he said that his mother had many quiet charities, unknown to anyone. He cited a list of thirty families that she helped to support. Most of them were relatives. Soon after his return to New York in 1910 Hetty was rushed to Holy Cross Episcopal Church in Jersey City to be baptized by the Rev. Augustine Elmendorf, a nephew of Edward Green's. She had decided that she was dying, and since she wished to be buried with her husband she knew that first she must be baptized. It developed, however, that she was suffering only from a severe attack of indigestion, and she was soon back on Wall Street. But she had a troublesome hernia, and in 1911 she was close to death from pneumonia. In the next five years she worked as hard as ever and added considerably to her fortune.

When Ned left the Waldorf and took a house at 5 West Ninetieth Street, his mother refused to leave her Hoboken flat and occupy the adjoining No. 7 that he had taken for her. She did not altogether approve of his ménage, which included Miss Harlow, but they held many business conferences there. Hetty had no wish to establish a New York residence, for the collectors had now closed in on her, and her lawyers had told her that her books needed close attention. She hired a statistician named Wilbur K. Potter, who shared a desk with Ned and long after her death became an invaluable aid to Hetty's children in the disentanglement of the vast interests they inherited. She was now seen riding occasionally in her son's automobile. But when it became apparent that her New York *pied-à-terre* with Ned, however tenuous, made her an easy prey for the tax collectors, she turned elusive again, and made furtive trips to Hoboken. She could not be found on her eightieth birthday for the customary press interview.

In April, 1916, Hetty had a stroke while she was visiting Miss Leary. She had been wrangling with the cook over costs. Her left side was paralyzed and for the next three months she was in a wheel chair. At last she had to live with Ned, under a New York roof, a course she had long resisted. Her nurses did not wear their uniforms, lest she worry about the expense of having them on twenty-four-hour duty, and she was told that they were seamstresses. Her first stroke was followed by another when she was out motoring. But Hetty continued to attend to her business affairs until ten days before her death. She was clear-headed, dogmatic, and interested in the reports laid before her, but she knew that she was dying. "I am not worrying," she said. "I do not know what the next world is like. But I do know that a kindly light is leading me and that I shall be happy after I leave here."

After her second stroke she called Ned and Sylvia to her bedside and talked to them of the great fortune she was leaving. Their faces had become shadowy to the tired woman who had fought so many battles. Hetty died on July 3, 1916, in her son's house. She was eighty-one, and she had multiplied her inheritance as no other woman in history had done. She was buried at Bellows Falls beside her husband. White carnations covered her coffin, and the choir sang "There is a blessed home" and "I heard a sound of voices." Except for four small bequests amounting to $25,000, she left her great fortune to her son and daughter and nothing to charity. But it was bequeathed in trust for ten years so that Ned was fifty-eight and Sylvia fifty-five before they had more than the income. The Green fortune had never been applied to large ends, and Hetty was scornful of the way in which Mrs. Russell Sage had used her husband's money. When Sage died in 1906 Hetty was displaced briefly as the richest woman in the world, but her millions mounted in the last nine years of her life so that she held her own with the benevolent Mrs. Sage.

Few had kind words for Hetty Green after her death, and the newspapers on both sides of the Atlantic drew attention to her arid life, her eccentric ways, her miserly preoccupation, her quarrelsome nature, and, in the last analysis, her failure to help mankind in any way with her great fortune. A few commented on her sturdy Americanism and the New York *Sun* noted that "she contributed to the development of the country, a service not to be held in contempt." But she had lived unto herself alone, and she reaped the harvest of her willful isolation. At the end there were signs that she was groping for some human warmth, but the habit of a lifetime stood in the way.

Within a month of his mother's death Ned proposed marriage to his faithful companion of many years' standing—Mabel Harlow. However lavish he had been before Hetty's death he now squandered her millions with zest and catholicity. The world was changing fast and he kept up with each scientific development, particularly in aeronautics. He had his own airstrip, an amateur radio station, a fleet of ornate cars and a lake steamship that he had converted into a yacht, the largest and most awkward in the world. In his nurseries he grew everything from pear trees to orchids and American Beauty roses. Ned maintained a large staff and had a number of young protegées, some of whom he sent to college. With his mother gone he indulged to the full his passion for gems and curios of all kinds, assembling a ten-million-dollar jewel collection and caressing his diamonds as Hetty had fondled dollar bills.

Ned had quarters in the Waldorf-Astoria Hotel in New York, a magnificent estate at Round Hills, and another in Miami. When bored with these he escaped to Terrell, Texas. His huge frame, his Pickwickian face and flashy attire made him a distinctive figure wherever he appeared, but by 1930 he spent most of his time in a wheel chair, for his health was failing. He died at Lake Placid in 1936 and was buried at Bellows Falls.

Sylvia moved at once to dispossess Mabel, who had decided to claim Ned's fortune. His will had been hard to find but it had turned up eventually under some cakes of soap in an old tin kitchen cabinet. His sister was the beneficiary but Mabel was assured $1,500 a month, tax free, under the terms of a pre-marital trust fund set up for her by Ned. The will contest ran a tedious course and involved hundreds of witnesses, with four states battling for tax rights, before Sylvia came out the victor. Meanwhile, the more lurid aspects of Ned's life were spread on the record.

By this time Sylvia had been a widow for a decade. Wilks had died in 1926, less than a month before she and Ned had come into full inheritance of the $60,000,000 that their mother had left to each of them. Wilks had bequeathed her another $1,500,000, and when Ned's share also fell to Sylvia she was recognized as the possessor of a fortune close to $150,000,000. She would not let banks invest her money but kept millions in checking accounts, disregarding the interest that might have been hers. She had a home on Fifth Avenue packed with ornate Victorian pieces, and much choice silver and linen. Her estates in Greenwich and Stamford were inherited from her husband, but she had chosen her place at Shippan Point for herself. All were run down and neglected. She rarely stayed overnight in any of her country houses, preferring to pack her own picnic lunches in New York and drive in her Lincoln to spend the day in verdant surroundings. Few of the pipes were connected in her Greenwich house and she used an old-fashioned stove to save on fuel bills. She made most of her own clothes and on the Fourth of July dressed her collie Prince in diminutive garments. He was as much of a pet as Dewey had been to her mother.

In spite of her aloofness and her odd, shy ways Sylvia was always recognized as a dignified and philanthropic figure. Her likes and dislikes were strong, and openly expressed. She approved of Dwight D. Eisenhower and Robert Moses, but disliked Franklin D. Roosevelt and Bishop William T. Manning. At the end she shared her mother's fear of conspirators, and was a tired and frightened old woman when she died of cancer in 1951 at the age of eighty. But she turned out to be the true philanthropist of the family, scattering her mother's riches in all directions, and throwing much light on her own personality in her bequests to charities, churches, old ladies' homes, civic officials, firemen and a collection of friends and relatives who were surprised to find themselves the beneficiaries of the most tightly hoarded fortune in American history. Many had never met her, and some could not account for the tenuous links that had drawn them to her attention. A cleaning woman she had never seen was remembered and Robert Moses received $10,000 for beautifying the landscape with his parkways.

Sylvia had given careful thought to the disposition of her great fortune and, in addition to individual bequests, she had set up twenty-eight trust funds of $500,000 each. She had planned to leave the bulk of her estate to Princeton, but her dislike for Woodrow Wilson caused her to switch her bequests to Fordham, Harvard, Yale, Columbia and the Massachusetts Institute of Technology. Such preparatory schools as Groton, St. Paul's and Kent benefited from her riches.

Thus, through her daughter, Hetty Green's money, in the final reckoning, was used for humane purposes.

Mrs. Frank Leslie

Mrs. Frank Leslie brought dash and glamour to the cause of women's rights in the nineteenth century, and when she died in 1914 she left nearly two million dollars to Mrs. Carrie Chapman Catt for suffrage work. She had not taken a vital stand while the battle was being fought, but had run a publishing empire, written a number of books, and entertained many of the more famous figures of her day. She was known for her style, ambition, intelligence, and romantic interests. Mrs. Leslie had four husbands, and her friends were usually men of fame or stature. Her salon was likened to Madame Roland's, and her linguistic skill and business enterprise were much discussed in the Elegant Eighties. But behind the velvet curtain of worldliness lay a history that plagued her in the years of her success and fame. She preferred to forget the storms of her early years and to blank out long stretches that had painful associations. At the time of her death, one newspaper said that she was sixty-three years old, another eighty-one. In actual fact, she was seventy-eight.

She was born in New Orleans of Huguenot ancestry on June 5, 1836, and her maiden name was Miriam Florence Follin. Her Creole forebears were descended from the Baron de Bazus, the name she used in the last years of her life. After the death of her third husband, she legally adopted his name, Frank Leslie, and was so known in publishing circles as she directed a flow of illustrated newspapers and magazines into countless American homes. She was impressive at the height of her power, but at the end Ellery Sedgwick, about to move into an editorial position on one of the Leslie publications, recalled her as a "shriveled old lady, bedizened like a Dresden china shepherdess archly carrying Bopeep's staff with a shining silver hook, smirking and talking as if she had been Queen of Sheba." He thought that her partners fawned on her and that she smiled with a "flutter of her enameled cheek."

A world of living had intervened between that day and the pre-Civil War era when Miriam Follin was a radiant beauty. Her life from first to last had been high in drama, and her settings had changed over the years from New Orleans to New York and Saratoga, to Peru and Spain, to France and England. She attended Lincoln's first inauguration and reported Queen Victoria's jubilee. As a journalist she was usually found where historic events were taking place, and in her own field she had a perceptive eye, an easy gift of expression, and considerable knowledge of the political scene. Yet a veil of mystery hung around Mrs. Leslie as long as she lived. She was best known in Saratoga, where the Leslies had their summer home, and in New York, where she sat behind a white oak desk writing with a long black quill, or moved in jeweled splendor at her Thursday night receptions.

Miriam Follin's earliest memories were of the Vieux Carré in New Orleans. Her father, Charles Follin, was a handsome, worldly man who dealt in cotton, tobacco, and hides. He spoke five languages and made a scholar of his daughter Miriam, introducing her to Latin, German, Italian, French, and Spanish. She had two half-brothers, Ormond Weyman Follin and Augustus Noel Follin. In 1846 she attended a girls' seminary in Cincinnati, where she saw something of frontier life in the beautiful city spread over the hillsides above the deep flow of the Ohio River. As her father's business dwindled, he decided to settle with his family in New York, and Miriam's next home was at 55 Bond Street, where her parents ran a boarding house. But Follin soon drifted away, and as he traveled he wrote urgently to his daughter, pointing out the importance of studying languages. Her brothers were equally determined that she should be a scholar, and she was constantly under pressure to read nothing but history or foreign languages.

There was little need to drive her, for she was intellectually inclined from early girlhood. She had her first taste of newsprint when she was fourteen and wrote a brief memoir on the life of General José Antonio Páez, first President of Venezuela, which appeared in the New York *Herald* of July 29, 1850. Three years later the Follins were living close to the Church of St. Mark's-inthe-Bouwerie at Tompkins Square, and Miriam had become romantically involved with David Charles Peacock, a clerk in a jewelry store. When her mother Susan had him arrested on a charge of seduction, a marriage and subsequent annulment were pushed through. The incident was chalked off as if it had never taken place, but Mrs. Leslie was confronted with it in court years later. Peacock opened a jewelry business on Maiden Lane and married a rich widow, but he became insane in the 1870's. During her friendship with him Miriam acquired a love of diamonds that was to be characteristic of her in later years. Her jewels were showy and famous.

She was drawn into the theatrical world after her half-brother, Noel Follin, tied his fortunes to the notorious Lola Montez, abandoning his wife and children to tour with her. They were returning from Australia when he jumped or fell overboard and was drowned. Emotional over this event, Lola insisted that she had killed him, and she sold some of her jewels to help his wife and family. But Mrs. Follin would accept nothing from her. However, Lola took Miriam under her wing, and the young beauty toured with her as Minnie Montez, her sister. It was worldly tutelage for Miriam, and she never tired of listening to Lola's tales of Dumas, Liszt, and the King of Bavaria. She had her debut in Albany, and a dramatic crossing they made of the Hudson through ice floes was sketched in *Frank Leslie's Illustrated Newspaper*, part of the empire that Miriam would one day control. Soon she was playing the lead in such productions as "Plot and Passion," but they finally parted when Lola went on a lecture tour and Miriam became infatuated with William M. Churchwell, a congressman from Tennessee.

The next man to engage her interest affected her life profoundly, for he became her second husband. Ephraim George A. Squier was an archaeologist of reputation, a writer, traveler, and scholar who had received honors at home and abroad. He had an honorary degree from Princeton, and in the long run he contributed a great deal to the education of Mrs. Frank Leslie. He was a small, bearded man fifteen years older than Minnie, as she was now known. They were married in Grace Church, Providence, by the Rt. Rev. Thomas M. Clark, Bishop of Rhode Island. Henry B. Anthony, who edited the Providence *Journal* and had been governor of Rhode Island, gave a reception for them.

Back in New York they lived on St. Mark's Place, and Minnie shared in her husband's scholarly pursuits. She translated *Demi-Monde*, a satire by Alexandre Dumas, and later adapted it for the stage. At this time her looks were considered striking. She was of medium height, with a graceful figure. Her gray eyes were deep-set and thoughtful, and her hair gleamed with highlights. She had a prominent nose and a strongly bowed mouth. When Squier took her abroad they toured London, Paris, Rome, Brussels, and the towns of Germany and Switzerland. He showed her the best in art, and improved her knowledge of letters. But already she was an accomplished young woman, able to speak the languages of most countries she visited. Her knowledge of Spanish was particularly useful to her husband who on their return edited a newspaper designed for Cuba and the South American countries. During this period Minnie was indoctrinated in printing practices, a skill that she would use to good advantage in later years. But another strong influence passed out of her life when her father died in Mobile in 1859. All of her ambition and her interest in literary matters had come from him, and right up to the time of his death his letters had emphasized the importance of work and study.

The Squiers were in Cuba early in 1860, as war clouds were thickening in the United States. Minnie was at work on a translation of Arthur Morelet's *Travels in Central America*. As an expert in journalistic matters, Squier was soon drawn into Frank Leslie's orbit. Late in 1861, with the Civil War raging, he was appointed editor of *Frank Leslie's Illustrated Newspaper*. The owner had separated from his wife and had rented rooms in the Squier house on Tenth Street. Mrs. Follin joined this ménage, too, and looked after the major household details for her daughter. Leslie, a vigorous, bearded man with tremendous energy, was the son of a glove manufacturer in Ipswich, England. His real name was Henry Carter, but he used the name Frank Leslie for his work on the *Illustrated London News*, and later it became his legal name when he settled down to journalism in the United States. His special field was graphic art and printing, and he understood promotion, for he had worked for P. T. Barnum when the showman was handling Jenny Lind. His paper and *Harper's Weekly* assumed great importance during the Civil War, competing fiercely in a new form of wartime journalism.

Squier wrote to Leslie on March 11, 1861: "Minnie and I went to assist at the coronation of 'Old Abe.' We went through the whole performance with great éclat—particularly Minnie, who 'took down' all the other girls present." Mrs. Squier was indeed a sensation at the inaugural ball. Her coppery hair was meshed in a glittering snood entwined with ivy. Her flounced crinoline was the widest in sight, and she looked commanding, with her strong features and regal bearing. Her cherry satin overskirt was caught up with clusters of roses, and she wore diamonds and opals. Frank Leslie's paper noted on March 23, 1861, that "this lady's personal attractions, youth and graceful manner, made her the acknowledged belle of the ball, while her sprightly and intellectual conversation and her knowledge of various languages placed all who came within her sphere perfectly at their ease. Her dress was also a triumph of taste and elegance."

A year later Mrs. Squier was back in the White House at a presidential party held on February 5, 1862. This time she wore pink silk with swansdown and talked to the Comte de Paris in French, and to Jessie Frémont, whose husband, John Charles Frémont, was under heavy fire at the time. Four months later Squier, who had gone to the scene at Fair Oaks on a journalistic mission after the battle, wrote to his parents, Mr. and Mrs. Joel Squier: "It was a terrible affair. The ground in some places was covered with the dead as thick as they could lie. . . . We have found 2700 dead rebels on the field. It has cost us dear."

At this time Minnie lost a baby, and she welcomed the diversion when she was called in to substitute for the ailing editor of *Frank Leslie's Lady's Magazine.* From then on the position was hers, and she brought a fresh and enterprising touch to fashion news. Leslie's driving ambition impressed both of the Squiers. The trio rode around town together, and when Squier was at the battlefields Mrs. Squier and Frank Leslie continued this custom. Minnie was quick to inform herself on the problems of publishing, printing, and engraving. The Squiers, with their important lodger, moved uptown in course of time and had houses first on Thirty-eighth and then on Thirty-ninth streets.

But Squier's eyesight was failing, and he was glad to go to Peru as a government commissioner, charged with settling silver claims. Minnie went with him for a brief time, but the altitude made her ill and she returned before the end of 1863, intent on effecting a business partnership of Squier, Leslie, and herself. She wrote to her husband on April 12, 1864:

My own darling . . . a month is a very, very long time for even a patient little woman like me to wait for a letter. Mr. Leslie has not succeeded in making the partnership arrangement, which I think with you would have been very advantageous in many senses. His publications were never on so firm a basis . . . but the wear and tear of business is telling upon his appearance and spirits so that you will find him much changed in everything, save his friendship to us all. Why, he has not since my return been home half a dozen times more than ten minutes before dinner time!

Minnie confessed that she felt unsure of their future and was not content to float idly on the stream. She hoped that he would seize on any good opening in Central America or Peru, and she would join him wherever he might go—"but let us not settle down with our luxurious tastes and habits without at least an effort to render ourselves independent of the world." She wrote that he was self-sacrificing to be dealing in mummies and rattle-traps when he might have been writing in "one of the most tasteful of libraries, sleeping in one of the most luxurious of chambers, lunching at Delmonico's and sharing the companionship of one of the nicest little wives in the world." And then she added: "Darling, with you absent, there is a world of light and sunshine taken from our little circle."

This was the sixth year of their marriage, and their friends observed that Mrs. Squier and Frank Leslie had now become inseparable. They drove around town together, dined at Delmonico's, and worked in close alliance at the office. The beautiful Minnie had become an essential part of the Leslie empire, and she had many original ideas to contribute to the publisher. She had just as much of the power complex as he. Leslie was restless, bringing out dozens of publications, and experimenting constantly with type and display. Illustrations were his consuming interest, and he had an unerring eye for the farcical, the grotesque, or the newsworthy item.

In 1865 he and both of the Squiers posed with President Lincoln at the White House, and a presentation plaque was dis-

played to mark the birth of *Frank Leslie's Chimney Corner*.
Horace Greeley looked on in his owlish fashion. Leslie, whose
motto was "Excelsior," had not lost the Barnum touch. The new
publication was aimed at the family, with serials, fiction, adventure stories, and verse. It proved to be a success, like the other
Leslie publications. Mrs. Squier was viewed with great interest as
she whirled into her office on Pearl Street and flashed her black
quill to get things moving for the day. This publication was to be
her particular responsibility. She wrote for it herself, beginning
with sketches on Peru. Her "Ladies Conversazione" became the
opposite number to Jenny June's writings in *Demorest's*, a rival
publication. The chimney corners across the country reacted
well, and coupons and premiums added to the excitement.

There was never any question of Mrs. Squier's capacity in this
field. She had wit and intelligence, as well as a thorough working knowledge of the plant. In the office she was businesslike and
informed. Away from the office she circulated in the most popular spots, taking stock of the fashions, visiting Saratoga and other
resorts, appearing at the race tracks, rustling into the theater in
ravishing gowns, and building up a wide acquaintance among
men of letters.

The ubiquitous trio went abroad in 1867. Frank Leslie, Samuel
F. B. Morse, and Thomas W. Evans were the three commis-
sioners appointed to judge the fine arts exhibits at the Paris Universal Exposition. By some mischance Squier was arrested for an
old indebtedness when they landed in Liverpool. He was clapped
into Lancaster Castle Jail as an "absconding debtor," but he
quickly turned this to his own advantage, with Leslie prompting
him to write his experiences. This was too good an opening for
the ever-vigilant publisher to miss.

"Don't bother about me in the least," Squier wrote to "Dearest
Minnie" from jail on March 8, 1867. "It is better than shipboard
and quite as good as Lima. Besides, the article! Have a good time,
and in that way best please your E.G.S." Leslie stopped in a
luxury shop and sent him a box of sausages, steaks, chops, and
bloaters, which he cheerfully shared with the other prisoners. He
wrote "Two Weeks in a British Bastille" after Leslie had bailed

him out. In the meantime Minnie and Leslie had been doing London thoroughly. They went to the theater, attended art exhibitions, and signed up writers and artists for their magazines. Mrs. Mary Ann Jubber, Leslie's sister, was impressed with the influence Mrs. Squier had over him.

But the full splendor of the era seemed to be concentrated in Paris, where rulers from the Orient and celebrities from all parts of the world had gathered for the Exposition. The French populace seethed politically but shouted "Vive l'Empereur" as Napoleon reviewed the troops at Longchamps. Leslie and the Squiers were invited to all the state functions, and Minnie danced with Bismarck at the state ball given at the Tuileries in honor of the Czar. Her readers in America had a detailed view of the Empress Eugénie wearing a $20,000 purple satin gown at the opening of the Exposition. Her own gowns were newly bought from Worth, and Leslie had added emeralds. At a Fourth of July gathering at the Grand Hotel she was toasted as one of "Columbia's Fair . . . the most beautiful woman in Paris." Napoleon III received the commissioners and gave them medals for serving on the jury. Squier complained of the way in which Leslie worked and drove others. He wrote to his parents: "Coming to Europe is anything but pleasure when Mr. Leslie is about. He works here five times as much as at home. . . . Minnie seems to be in a bad way and I am much concerned about her. I want to get her off to some quiet place."

But she had no time to rest or recuperate, and she relished the excitement. They moved on to Italy, skimming the surface at every point, studying effects and picking up ideas for their publications. Even in a gondola Leslie's mind whirled with plans for his next production, and Minnie encouraged him, while the more leisurely Squier stayed a little aloof. Things were much the same when they arrived home, and Squier wrote again to his parents: "Mr. Leslie's business has grown to be monstrous, and he works all the harder in consequence. While I draw in from effort, he extends his! All for the benefit of these children, each one of which would be perfectly happy to have him die."

When Leslie was abroad his three sons, Henry, Alfred, and

Scipio, had set up a rival publishing firm with the title, Frank Leslie, Jr. He ruled them out of his own empire at this point, but both his estranged wife and his sons were giving trouble. He wanted a divorce, but Mrs. Leslie would not agree, and there was much family bitterness. However, both Leslie and Mrs. Squier were present for Alfred's wedding in Saratoga. They now went regularly to this popular resort, where politicians, social figures, celebrities, and high-powered gamblers made a strange combination of interest and color. One of Leslie's rivals, William J. Demorest, had his summer home there and his wife, Madame Demorest, at the time was one of the ruling figures in the fashion picture. But there was no community of interest between the Leslies and the Demorests.

In 1871 Minnie's translation of Arthur Morelet's *Travels in Central America* came out, done in collaboration with her husband. This was regarded as a good piece of work. The fact was recognized by this time that she had brains as well as beauty. The Squiers now lived with some pretension and more and more the trio became the duo. Wherever a big party or ball was held Mrs. Squier might be found, elaborately dressed, with a cluster of men around her. Mrs. Follin had died of cancer in 1868, and the chaperonage she had supplied was missing. It was clear to many at this time that the Squier marriage was falling apart, but the principals still kept up a pretense of harmony at a clambake held in the summer of 1871 at Round Island, near Greenwich, in Connecticut. There were 150 guests, including Senator Anthony, to fete the author and diplomat, who was celebrating his fiftieth birthday, however unhappily.

Leslie had just introduced his *Once a Week: Frank Leslie's Lady's Journal*, with Minnie in full charge. It was aimed at the younger generation and was much discussed. Again he moved toward getting a divorce, but Mrs. Leslie brought a counter suit, naming Mrs. Squier and accusing her husband of "visiting Europe, keeping a yacht, horses and carriages, and mistresses," while she needed money. Squier leaped in with an announcement that the charges were false, and his wife sanctimoniously added:

"I am in accord with my husband; and our relations are perfectly harmonious." Squier was still working hard for Leslie, whose weeklies and monthlies poured out in a torrent, with a combined circulation of half a million copies a week. But he was finally ousted from the Leslie interests when Mrs. Leslie was quietly granted a divorce in 1872 on grounds of desertion, with a settlement of $28,000. Then Squier's hand was forced, and evidence was supplied under New York law that gave his wife grounds for divorce in 1873. He was intensely bitter and considered that he had been put in a compromising situation by Minnie and Frank Leslie. After the decree was granted he wrote to his lawyer that the whole proceeding was "rotten to the core." He added: "My mouth is sealed, not in anger, but out of regard for her reputation and the fortune that I hope is in store for her. . . . I will not permit my apparent disgrace to be flung in my face in New York City."

A few months later Squier was adjudged insane and was committed to an asylum. The entire incident had depressed him deeply. He had been drinking heavily, and finally he broke down without warning. "Eclipse of genius," the New York *Herald* headlined its story when this well-known scholar lost his reason.

Mrs. Squier and Frank Leslie were married at St. Thomas's Church that same year, settling first at the Gilsey House on Broadway and Twenty-ninth Street, and then at a fashionable boarding house on Fifth Avenue. Minnie now went to the office only three times a week, but as each new publication came into being, she had a hand in its origin, and she and her husband talked constantly of professional matters. Mrs. Leslie's guiding star was ambition, and she had found a kindred soul in the restless editor. They were involved in most of the important social and political gatherings of the period, and brilliant and controversial men circled around them. Mrs. Leslie moved with the tide and was always a handsome presence at the opera, the theater, or the race track. She shopped at A. T. Stewart's and Tiffany's and dined frequently at Delmonico's or the St. Nicholas Hotel. As a working wife she followed the fashion of boarding instead of running her own ménage. Women not only read her fashion news to see what they should wear, but they studied Mrs. Leslie in public, sure that her clothes, however elaborate, would be the last word in style. Simplicity had not yet been identified with chic, and she was reported to be wearing $70,000 worth of diamonds at Samuel J. Tilden's installation at Albany in 1875. The governor was riding the crest of the wave after his successful fight against the Tweed Ring.

By this time Leslie had built his summer home, Interlaken, at Saratoga. It was on Lake Lonely and was a show place, with arbors, gardens, and Alpine effects. The cottage stood snugly under a hill, almost hidden from the highway. Porcelain vases foamed with flowering plants, and vines clambered over the rustic summer houses on the property. Tortuous paths led through its five hundred acres. Turf covered a flower-decked esplanade at the edge of the water, and the Leslie steam yacht lay at a miniature dock almost at the cottage door. A grandstand made a vantage point from which to watch the regattas, and Leslie gave a thousand-dollar Tiffany cup to the winner of the International Amateur Regatta Race of 1874, the year of his marriage to Minnie. He had an office in the tower where he worked incessantly, but his guests enjoyed his croquet grounds and the other diversions on his property. Few famous visitors came to America without making a trip to the Leslie country estate. It was not the most elaborate of its kind, but it was certainly the most original, and Mrs. Frank Leslie in herself was one of its major attractions. When Dom Pedro II, Emperor of Brazil, visited the Leslies in 1876, Minnie spoke French and Spanish to him, and Italian to the Empress. They had come to attend the Centennial Exposition, where the Leslies were prominent, with one of the best advertised attractions of the Fair—the Frank Leslie Pavilion. Afterward they published *A Historical Register of the Centennial Exposition*, a costly venture on which they lost heavily.

The nation as a whole had a chance to observe Mrs. Leslie when she and her husband with a party crossed the continent early in the summer of 1877. Her impressions later enlivened the

Leslie magazines and were also assembled in book form. They rode in the $35,000 Palace Pullman Car that had been exhibited at the Fair and was advertised as a marvel of luxury and comfort. It was named "Frank Leslie," and the fiesta touch was present from coast to coast. They set off with hampers of champagne, and Potter Palmer sent pyramids of flowers to Mrs. Leslie as they left Chicago. Minnie was observant of the passing scene, watching the rolling prairie giving way to low bluffs, then to a quiet lake dotted with wild ducks, and finally to herds of grazing cattle and shaggy horses as they approached Council Bluffs. The people of Omaha seemed to be in an apathetic state. Streets were dirty and ill-paved; clocks lacked hands and shops were deserted, for hard times had stripped the people of money. Men went around in alligator boots and overcoats made from blankets and wagon rugs. Their hair and beards were unkempt. The women wore handkerchiefs on their heads and clearly had no link with Mrs. Leslie's fashion news.

She found Cheyenne, which had been billed as "Hell on Wheels," a fresh and enlivening example of a true frontier town. Transparencies hung as signs on many of the shops, and the streets were crowded with miners, teamsters, drovers, and scouts. They looked ferocious but were "lamb-like in demeanor toward strangers." Mrs. Leslie watched an emigrant train of several wagons starting for the Black Hills. She visited the saloons, theaters, and gambling dives, watching roulette, keeno, and *rouge et noir* being played. When she appeared at McDaniel's Theatre and the Opera House the natives were just as much interested in viewing Mrs. Leslie as she was in them. Wherever they went they ran across copies of their own publications, and there was no lack of self-conscious ballyhoo on this trip.

At Colorado and Manitou Springs she sought out well-known authors. Here Helen Hunt and Grace Greenwood lived. She found Grace, whom she had met from time to time in the Press Gallery in Washington, living in a Tyrolean house with branching antlers over her door.

Mrs. Leslie made it all graphic for her readers, from the Garden of the Gods to her visit to Brigham Young in Salt Lake City. Nothing on the trip interested her more than this glimpse of polygamy, her talks with some of the wives, and her interview with the leader himself. She studied the ladies in Beehive House and the Lion House, as well as the schoolhouse, the theater, and the Cooperative Union Building. It all made her think of the "closely guarded seraglios of a Turkish Prince."

But Mrs. Leslie was not satisfied to have the customary per-functory look at Brigham Young. By this time he was bored with visitors from the East, writers or otherwise, who came to stare at him as if he were some sort of monster. However, he quickly detected in Mrs. Leslie a spark that caused him to give her his full attention, instead of whisking her through like the others. She settled herself beside him on the "sacred sofa" and found him both formidable and attractive.

"Do you suppose, Mr. President, that I came all the way to Salt Lake City to hear that it was a fine day?" she demanded.

"I am sure you need not, my dear," said this cavalier of seventy-six, "for it must be fine weather wherever you are."

The rest of the party were frozen out as he and Mrs. Leslie embarked on a confidential conversation. She longed to ask him about the recreant Ann Eliza, who had deserted his harem and exposed some of its secrets, but she refrained. Amelia, the current favorite, was "an excellent wife and a lovely woman."

"What religion can make a woman happy in seeing the husband whom she loves devoted to another wife, and one with equal claims with herself?" Mrs. Leslie asked. "Any woman, I should think, would spend all her strength, use every effort of mind, body and soul, to attract and retain his love, admiration and attention. Isn't it so, Mr. President?"

He answered meditatively: "You look like just the woman to do that sort of thing, but fortunately, perhaps, there are not many of that kind among us; as a rule, our women are content in trying to make their husbands happy and their homes pleasant. . . . For my own part I always endeavor to show perfect imparti-ality, and allow no one division of my family to claim time or thought too exclusively."

"Then do Mormon husbands feel no preference?"

"Well, perhaps; human nature is frail, but our religion teaches us to control and conceal those preferences as much as possible, and we do."

Brigham Young confided to Mrs. Leslie that Utah in two or three generations would have the finest specimens of men to be found anywhere in the country, for they would have sprung from marriages of "pure affinity, and a state of society impossible except under polygamy. Our young men are pure, our women are virtuous, and our children are born free from inherited disease."

The climax of the Leslies' trip came when they reached the Palace Hotel in San Francisco and took stock of its regal inner court and tiers of balconies, its singing birds and flowering plants. Mrs. Leslie quickly picked up facts about its rooms for twelve hundred guests, its four hundred and thirty-seven bathtubs, and its two-and-a-half miles of corridors. But the sidewalks of the city were still made of wood, and many of the little shops were open to the street like booths. Men tossed dice for drinks, and Mrs. Leslie thought it an "extravagant place in dress, equipage and general tone of living."

She sampled the restaurants and compared them with those in Naples, Paris, London, and New York. She was pleased to see that women could visit them freely without criticism. "The Prunes, Prisms, and Propriety system did not altogether rule in San Fransisco," she wrote. But their street attire was more showy than she approved, and the afternoon promenade on Kearney and Montgomery streets reminded her of a fashionable "opening." She did not neglect the seamy side of San Francisco life, visiting the Barbary Coast, the county jail, an opium den, and a brothel, all in the interests of journalism. She sat in the private gallery for ladies of the Brokers Board and watched a scene of such excitement that she wrote she would "have given worlds to be six feet high, deepen her voice to a baritone, and be in the midst of it all." Mrs. Leslie was not tall, and her husband was quoted as saying that he wished he could add three inches to her height.

The mayor of San Francisco entertained them, and they drove

up the steep streets to view the mansions being built on Nob Hill. Charles Crocker's house was then in course of construction. Much of what she saw seemed crude and unfinished to Mrs. Leslie, but she found Baldwin's Theatre a gem, fitted up in crimson satin and gold. She dined with the Leland Stanfords "who have the most magnificent house on this continent with one drawing-room furnished in Pompeian style, and a superb picture gallery." Mrs. Leslie was impressed with Mrs. Stanford, who appeared in crimson velvet with rare old lace and a parure of diamonds and opals.

Her party visited the Yosemite, the Big Trees, and Santa Rosa. Minnie's first view of the Sequoias was disappointing, and she found Los Angeles a "quaint, mild-tempered, uneventful little city, with its legends and lingering flavor of Spanish and monastic dominion." But she noted that within ten years it had become a "live" American city. One of the most interesting events of her trip was her visit to Eulalia Perrez, of Los Angeles, the oldest woman in the world. In fact she claimed to be 140 years old, and she looked it, with eyes as red as fire and an uncanny look about her. She was a short, shrunken figure with a black merino hood on her head. She asked Mrs. Leslie if she were married, and then she wanted to know to which of the men present.

"Well, I should not think you need have married a man with white hair," the old crone said, peering at Frank Leslie.

Mrs. Leslie could talk with her in Spanish, and Eulalia told her that she had been married twice and had had many lovers. She had grandchildren eighty years old, and she had never in her life been more than eight miles from Loretto, her birthplace.

The Leslies on their return trip visited Virginia City, and stopped at Detroit to see Senator Zachariah Chandler, arriving back in New York full of enthusiasm for the land in which they lived. In the book she wrote subsequently, Mrs. Leslie echoed Horace Greeley: "Go West, my friends, Go West. Within the Golden Gates lies all that you desire. Go West." Although their tour had been vivid promotion for the Leslie empire, they came back to disaster. The financial panic of 1877 was on, and Leslie was deep in debt. He had overextended his properties, started too many publications, made bad investments, and had also been living on a princely scale since marrying Minnie. The circulation of his magazines had dropped, and in 1878 he was forced to assign his property. Much litigation followed, and he fought ferociously, managing to reduce his indebtedness to $100,000. In the meantime an ugly scandal had added to his troubles.

Shortly after their return, the comments that Mrs. Leslie had made in her writings on Virginia City came home to roost. The natives were outraged, and Rollin M. Daggett, editor of the *Territorial Enterprise*, had gone to great lengths to check up on her early history. On July 14, 1878, he splashed the story on the front page with an arresting headline: "Our Female Slanderer. Mrs. Frank Leslie's Book Scandalizing the Families of Virginia City. The History of the Author. A Life Drama of Crime and Licentiousness. Startling Developments."

A twenty-four page pamphlet accompanied the paper, with testimony from old court records dug up in New York. It reviewed Minnie's life through the days of Peacock, Lola Montez, her marriage to Squier, and all the details of the divorce. Frank Leslie tried to buy up every copy. It told him much that he had never known about Minnie. In time it became famous as the Peacock Judgment Roll, and it was to plague Mrs. Leslie for years. She blamed Squier, who had partially recovered, for contributing to this vengeful attack. In the middle of this scandal, and all his business difficulties, Leslie had developed throat cancer. He was fifty-eight years old and even in the last two weeks of his life he worked feverishly over his chaotic business interests, with Minnie at his side to help him. She read to him and he saw a few visitors, but she was busy at her office when word reached her from his nurse that the end was near. She hurried to their house on Fifth Avenue, and in his last hours he told her that he wished her to take his place, to carry on his business, to use his name. She later described what she said was the deathbed scene:

"Go to my office," he chokingly told her. "Sit in my place, and do my work until my debtors are paid. I do not ask you to cherish my memory, my darling, for I know you will do that: I ask you to vindicate it."

On a lecture tour a decade later she varied this version slightly and said: "I put my arms over the dying man's shoulders and looking into his face, asked him to speak to me. He opened his eyes, smiled faintly, then said to me these words: 'You are beautiful and I love you.' His head dropped back. He was dead."

Leslie died on January 10, 1880, two weeks after he had made his will bequeathing to his wife all his property, trade-mark, and his interest in the publications. The funeral services were held at the Church of the Divine Paternity, with his employees present, and he was buried at Woodlawn. When he died Minnie said that she would never again wear anything but black. She now became a whirlwind of professional competence. Her good friend Joaquin Miller, the Western poet, pictured her as rising from her husband's coffin and going straight to his office to direct and control every detail of the publishing house "like a Napoleon."

It was not an easy task. She faced seventeen law suits, while she ran the magazines and cleared her status for the Leslie trademark. In addition, her husband's family contested the will. His sons charged that it was fraudulent and was drawn up under undue influence. During the will contest the Peacock Judgment Roll was hashed over, and the public learned things about Mrs. Leslie that had never been suspected. Her creditors crowded her on all sides, and Mrs. Eliza Jane Smith, a Brooklyn woman, was so touched by her plight that she offered her $50,000 to tide her over her immediate difficulties. Mrs. Leslie gave her jewels as security, and the loan was quickly returned, for within a year of her husband's death she had paid off his debts and was mistress of the Leslie properties. Her journalistic enterprise when James A. Garfield was shot was the talk of publishing circles, and circulation soared. She sent two artists to Washington to make sketches when the news reached her. Then she assembled her entire staff on a Sunday morning and added fresh material to Tuesday's regular issue of *Frank Leslie's Illustrated Newspaper*. This was followed up with an extra edition three days later, and the next regular edition had a complete roundup of all that had taken place. This was fast journalism. In the space of a week she had brought out three illustrated papers and given sensational coverage to one of the great stories of the period.

Her competitors looked twice at Mrs. Leslie after that. It had long been whispered that some of Leslie's brightest ideas had come from her, able though he was in his own right. At any rate, she had been carefully schooled and understood the problems of publishing. Circulation jumped from 30,000 to 200,000, and she kept up this pitch for the three months that Garfield lingered on. When he died in September, 1881, at Elberon, New Jersey, she literally stopped the presses to get out a fresh edition, including sketches of the deathbed scene. This was done under high pressure; she had met the most professional standards. In addition, the courts had given her the right to call herself Frank Leslie.

Minnie worked with intensity and scoffed at people who chose "to take care of themselves." She wrote: "Make your mark and achieve success or, if need be, die in the attempt. . . . I am impressed with the inevitableness, the inexorableness of labor of some kind in every life at all worth living." She found plenty of excitement and stimulation in her own work and in the solo part she played. For a time she abandoned her sybaritic way of living, cut her own expenses, and lived simply while she was pulling the magazines out of their slump. She was at her desk by nine every morning, wearing simple black dresses with tiny black grosgrain aprons, edged with white ruffles. Her black kid shoes were tipped with silver, and her glossy hair was neatly arranged to enhance her businesslike look when at work. But as she waved a feather fan on hot days she seemed the epitome of femininity and leisure until a decision had to be made. Then she functioned with an unerringly hard drive. Mrs. Leslie was never troubled by indecision. She knew what she wanted and got it. This was reassuring to the vague artists and troubled writers who could never make up their own minds about anything. Some of her sketch artists were of major importance, but they listened attentively to her ideas. She was a skilled proofreader and had considerable knowledge of men, politics, and languages, all of which made her strong in her field and not easy to fool. Mrs. Leslie encouraged American talent at a time when English writers were getting a heavy play in American publications.

When visitors arrived she toured the plant with them, and amazed some with her precise knowledge of all the intricate printing processes. She had sixteen presses, and pictures could be drawn and engraved in the space of eight hours. Her thirty engravers and fourteen artists were a source of pride to her. She used women writers for interviews but preferred men for office work and as artists. In one respect she diverged completely from her husband's policies. He had had a mania for adding to his publications. She cut the number sharply until by 1885 only two weeklies and four monthlies were left of the scores of papers that he had started. New methods were introduced; things were speeded up and the overlapping that had developed was minimized. Her own salary was $100,000 a year, no small wage for a woman editor in the 1880's. *Frank Leslie's Popular Monthly* was now the major link in her chain.

Her own contributions to the magazines mirrored Mrs. Leslie's personal tastes. She stayed close to the news and encouraged discussion of current problems. Readers looked for her own account of fashionable and social doings in New York, for Mrs. Leslie went everywhere. In chic black she appeared in boxes at the opera, attended openings, dinners, and receptions, and held a salon of her own to which people flocked. This picture had not changed; in fact it was accentuated after her husband's death. At the close of a hard day's work she joined in the five o'clock parade of carriages in Central Park, and by eight she was ready for the functions of the evening. All the Metropolitan stars knew her well, and visiting actors, lecturers, or writers found it wise to swim in her circle if they sought publicity. She took note of the passing fads, from spiritualism to Banting's method of reducing. Although she showed interest in the suffrage workers and contributed to their cause, she never campaigned in this field or made much stir about it. In fact, she was more consoling to the woman in the home. "A world governed by women would become a mere agglomeration of individualists instead of a composite whole," she wrote. "Let us drive, let us hold the reins, but for heaven's sake have a good stalwart man on the box beside us, to speak a word of warning as we flog the horses down hill, and to grasp the rein when they run away with us." This was not her own case, but it would serve for lesser souls.

After her husband's death she continued to live mostly in hotels, finding this easier for entertaining than a house. Pictures and the trophies and bric-a-brac of her traveled life surrounded her in her suite at the Gerlach Hotel on West Twenty-seventh Street. She saved everything from an Exposition badge to a tiger skin. There was much comment on her jewels, and particularly her diamonds, but in the final accounting they were not found to be of great value. They were showy, in the tradition of the period, with sunbursts and stars, but her favorite piece of jewelry was a wide gold bracelet, with her name in diamonds. She liked to endow each piece with a history, and her Venetian necklace was supposed to have belonged to one of Catherine de Medici's maids of honor, and to have had poison inside a little dove encrusted in diamonds. Her earrings were said to be the largest pair of matched diamonds in the country.

In 1883 she toured the South with the announced intention of meeting representative Southerners. The people of New Orleans studied her with great interest as she paid a return visit to the city of her birth. She wrote of the old French market and of the changes caused by the Civil War. She studied orange culture in Florida and visited Mrs. Jefferson Davis at Beauvoir, her home in Mississippi. Varina Davis was used to traveling journalists, but she had much to discuss with Mrs. Leslie.

Minnie's salon in New York was at its best just before she was momentarily thrown off stride by *Town Topics*, which on March 27, 1886, revived the scandal of her past life in a piece called "From Puddle to Palace." But she quickly brushed this aside and went on to further conquests. She went abroad every year to study fashions, to see her artists and writers, to pick up news and comment, thus becoming a well-known figure in London, Paris, Rome, Madrid, and at the spas. She particularly enjoyed San Sebastian and wrote of her visit to the summer home of the Queen of Spain. Mrs. Leslie was popular abroad; in fact, she now had more acclaim in London and Paris than at home. She interviewed Lady Brassey, who had sailed around the world in the *Sunbeam,* and was entertained by Lady Wilde whose son, Oscar, had toured the United States in 1882. He had arrived in New York with letters of introduction to Mrs. Leslie, and she had done what she could for him by advertising him in her publications.

She flourished in Victorian England until she was involved in a scandal. While she was driving in Hyde Park with Prince George Eristoff de Gourie, who claimed to be a Russian prince, the Marquis de Leuville, an earlier suitor, slashed his whip at the prince in a fit of jealousy as their two carriages met in the park. Her engagement to the Marquis de Leuville had been announced in 1884, when she was forty-eight. He was an affected character with long flowing hair, high heels, and a monocle. But no more was heard of him or of the engagement until the encounter in Hyde Park. Mrs. Leslie defended the prince, but in the long run both men turned out to be impostors. She was highly susceptible to titles, and some strange adventurers rubbed shoulders with men of genius in her salon. Ella Wheeler Wilcox, who was one of Mrs. Leslie's protégées, thought her an easy mark for impecunious admirers, but she also believed that she was quick to appreciate talent of any kind, and to give aid when it was needed. She seemed to be free from petty jealousies, and was always ready to praise beauty in another woman. But behind this amiable front the poet detected such "adamantine streaks in her nature that it was a veritable shock. . . . I have seen her almost angelic in tenderness, and I have seen her as cruel as the iceberg. Surely a strange woman."

The first money Ella Wilcox ever received for her work was ten dollars sent to her by *Leslie's* for three poems. Later Mrs. Leslie became interested in her as a poet and invited her to her soirées; but she would then ignore her. Mrs. Wilcox remembered a particularly painful evening when her hostess insisted that she recite her poem "The Birth of the Opal." She was about to have a baby and did not wish to appear, but Mrs. Leslie decked her with her own opals, a stone that she loved. She disliked the poem and Ella's way of delivering it, showing her disapproval quite openly. But she kept on inviting the young poet to her parties, as she did anyone of rising or established reputation. Mrs. Wilcox gave an unflattering view of her in her memoirs. She commented on the "infantile feet under the Junoesque form" and thought her too slender at the waist, too full in the bust. Her waist could be spanned by a necklace.

"She looked older and less radiant than I had imagined, and her pronounced Roman nose, while it indicated her Napoleonic business prowess, militated against her beauty," Ella wrote. "But her skin, of exquisite texture, was like the finest marble. . . . Her eyes were large and blue, and her mouth too small for beauty . . . but she seemed alive with sentiment and romance, the dominating qualities in her nature, second only perhaps to ambition for power and prestige."

Mrs. Leslie did everything possible to keep herself fit and youthful in appearance. The fashionable women of the period had taken up dumbbells and pulleys, and she adopted this fad enthusiastically, beginning her day at seven with a cold plunge, a brisk rubdown, and calisthenics. She boasted in her old age that she had never had a backache, a headache, a toothache, or any kind of sickness in her life, which she attributed to her healthful regime. She never had a fire in her rooms and wore gauze underwear all the year round, instead of the flannels that her contemporaries favored in winter. After breakfasting on toast and beefsteak she drove to her office, encased in the rigid stays of her generation. As she aged she remained coquettish, a curious blend with her keen professionalism. All through the 1880's she balanced her business and private lives with skill, but she seemed to be most truly herself in her office. She was an honorary member of the Woman's International Press Association, and she found time for a succession of books, including *Rents in Our Robes,* a glossy view of her own life.

But by 1889 her responsibilities weighed heavily on her. She wanted to spend more time abroad, and finally she sold her weeklies to the Judge Publishing Company, keeping only *Frank Leslie's Popular Monthly.* After this her office was in the Judge building on Fifth Avenue, where she worked in the midst of ornate Victorian pieces, with a bust of Frank Leslie on the mantelpiece and a large eagle overhead. With more time on her hands she turned to the lecture platform and toured the country, training for this experience with typical thoroughness. She was a fresh note on the lyceum circuit, where charm had not been the inevitable quality of the emancipated sisterhood. Her gowns were thoughtfully chosen with regional tastes in mind, but observers considered the general effect overpowering. The Boston *Post* called her a "most gorgeous example of what she doubtless believed to be the true taste for all court occasions." But on the trains she wore plain black broadcloth tailored to her hourglass figure.

In her lectures Mrs. Leslie traced the growth of social life and manners. She discussed her health routine, her beauty secrets, her jewels, her past adventures, and the opportunities for women in business. In Detroit she said:

> In all my married life, I never dined with my husband without receiving from his hands the delicate favor of his choicest toilet. No matter whether or not we dined alone, he always wore his dress suit; I my low-cut dress, revealing neck and shoulders. . . . I was always conscious of the deep and abiding interest he took in his courtliness of dress, and all for my sake.

But lively Mrs. Leslie ran into plenty of cross fire as she traveled. Some thought her a humbug, an egotist, a pretentious woman, and when she expressed the view at the time of the Haymarket riots that the anarchists should be hanged, the Chicago *Daily Inter-Ocean* of October 15, 1890, headlined the story:

"Shoot Them Like Dogs." After that the more radical elements described her as an "empty-headed doll, an animated fashion-plate." Mrs. Leslie was many things, but she was never an empty-headed doll. However, she sometimes looked the part, with an Empress Eugénie fringe brushing her eyebrows, bright pink stockings showing beneath her skirts, and a glitter of jewels festooning her bodice. When things got dull and she felt that her audience had little interest in the manners of the French court, she would recite one of Joaquin Miller's poems.

She continued to write syndicated letters as she traveled, and they had wide distribution. Like most accomplished journalists, she could write under any circumstances and had been doing so most of her life. Although her approach to public affairs was professional, she catered to her audience and often whipped off essays on love, marriage, and fashion. Her own view of what she called the *Best Man* was revealing. He should be fine-looking but not necessarily handsome; brave as a lion, ambitious, enterprising, and of untiring industry. He should be reticent to the world, and generously confiding to those he felt it wise to trust. He should be patient, uncomplaining under suffering, and tender as a woman toward the sufferings of others—in short, "a good man, yet not a saint; a cheerful, convivial host and companion, yet unquestioned monarch of his own appetites; loving and faithful and gentle, and yet a tower of strength and defense."

Was this her view of Frank Leslie? Her public seemed to think so. But at fifty-five she had not tired of romance, and she married William G. Kingsbury Wilde, Oscar's brother, whom she had met on one of her trips to England. The ceremony took place at the Church of the Strangers in New York on October 4, 1891. Minnie was all in soft gray, from her picture hat with ostrich tips to the hem of her gray satin gown. The wedding supper was at Delmonico's, where she had been a familiar figure for many years. Their wedding trip was to Niagara Falls. But disillusionment set in at once. Mrs. Leslie had expected that Willie would fit into the journalistic pattern, but he slept most of the day while she went to the office to work. The tall, bulky young man, with features as heavy as those of his brother, was lazy, alcoholic, and untidy. He had charmed her with his brilliant conversation on newspaper work, his law training, his family, and his days at Trinity College, Dublin. But after their marriage it was clear to Mrs. Leslie that he had no intention of helping her. By nightfall he was usually drunk and abusive, throwing bottles around at random.

Willie was fiercely critical of the American scene, and although he liked to sit and drink in the fashionable clubs, he expected his wife to pay his bills. The Lotos Club threw him out. Minnie quickly reverted to calling herself Mrs. Frank Leslie after a brief period of being known as Mrs. Florence M. Wilde. Willie was thirty-nine years old at the time of their marriage. Her two preceding husbands had been much her senior.

They went to San Francisco for the first annual convention of the International League of Press Clubs early in 1892, and here Mrs. Leslie shone and was in her element. Her "Reminiscences of a Woman's Work in Journalism" was a salute to her own life history. It was all fodder for her syndicate writings, but it was also the end of her marriage to Willie Wilde. They went abroad later that year, and she came back without him. She put through a quiet divorce in 1893 in Goshen, Orange County, and soon learned that Willie had married again. She never regretted dropping this troublesome husband from her list, and her next book, *Are Men Gay Deceivers*, expressed her mood of the moment. She had come to the conclusion that American men made the best husbands, and she kept encouraging girls to step out with independence. Commenting on Henry James's *Daisy Miller*, she wrote:

> There is, I suppose, no girl in the world so perfectly capable of taking care of herself and doing it well as the American girl. . . . The failings of our American girls are simply . . . the somewhat troublesome excess of unemployed strength. . . . I have never forgiven Mr. James for some traits in his portraiture, and yet there is a great deal of truth in the innocent audacity, the fearless criticism and the simple care-

lessness of public opinion that stamp his heroine, and one cannot but feel a certain tenderness for the poor child.

Having tried the lecture platform she turned next to the theater, adapting her translation of Dumas' *Demi-Monde* and producing it as *The Froth of Society*. It opened at the Union Square Theatre on an April night in 1893 and went under with the most devastating criticism. This hurt her more than many of the other defeats of her life, and she left again for Europe, after leasing her interest in the Leslie publications to a syndicate. On her return things were in chaos. There had been a big slump in the magazine field. Her *Popular Monthly*, like many other publications, had dropped out of sight. The Arkell Publishing Company went bankrupt as the Spanish-American War was being fought. Once more Mrs. Leslie went to work, reorganizing and incorporating as a stock company, and holding half the stock herself as president. The format changed, and the magazine was smaller, smarter, and cost only ten cents a copy. Such contributors as William Dean Howells, Bret Harte, and Frank Stockton helped to push the circulation to 200,000 copies a month. But when Mrs. Leslie turned her back, as she did with frequent trips abroad, things went wrong again, and finally she was squeezed out as editor. Ellery Sedgwick moved in at this time to edit the *Monthly*, which eventually became the *American Magazine*.

Mrs. Leslie retired in October, 1900, and a year later she had a stroke. She was soon able to travel again, but life narrowed for her after that. She maintained a ghostly echo of her Thursday evenings, but celebrities no longer clustered around her, and at Saratoga she was a memory rather than a living presence. Her heavy maquillage, her tired eyes, her dusty jewels gave her a slightly tawdry air. She was full of strange whims, like insisting that her maid walk the dog while wearing a kimono. When she sold the last of her holdings in 1903, the name Frank Leslie, which had been a household word for half a century, was lost forever, and she assumed her ancestral name, the Baroness de Bazus. She had been both Miriam and Minnie over the years; now she was Florence de Bazus, with a crest, *Tout ou Rien*, inspired by *Demi-Monde*. She moved from the Gerlach to Sherry's, then to the Hotel Chelsea, and finally to the Sherman Square Hotel. She had half a million dollars after the sale of the last of her stock, and she multiplied this by shrewd investments in the years that followed.

In her seventies she was on the verge of a fifth marriage when her suitor—this time seventy-year-old Don Teodoro Martel y Fernández de Córdoba—died in Paris in 1907. He had been gentleman-in-waiting to the King of Spain. She continued to go to Europe and set off for the last time in 1914 after having had a severe heart attack. A nurse accompanied her, and those who had known her in the 1880's could scarcely believe that this was Mrs. Leslie. The outbreak of the First World War caught her in Europe, and on her return she died at the Sherman Square Hotel on September 18, 1914. She was seventy-eight years of age. Funeral services were held for her at Calvary Baptist Church, and she was buried in Woodlawn Cemetery, close to Frank Leslie and Ephraim Squier, the two husbands who had counted most in her life. She left a few bequests to relatives and all the rest of her estate to Carrie Chapman Catt to further the cause of woman suffrage. But a long will contest thinned down the bequest from nearly $2,000,000 to $977,000. The *Woman's Citizen* was established in 1917 with Mrs. Leslie's money, and it remained the official organ of the National American Woman Suffrage Association until the vote was won in 1920. Ten years later the National League of Women Voters named Mrs. Leslie, along with Elizabeth Cady Stanton, Susan B. Anthony, Mary Garrett Hay, Dr. Elizabeth Blackwell, and others, as one of the greats in the suffrage fight. She had challenged society in a number of ways, but by the force of her pen and the strength of her personality she had impressed herself deeply on her era.

Margaret and Kate Fox

When Margaret and Kate Fox of Rochester became famous in the late 1840's for their mysterious rappings, they helped to establish spiritualism as a serious cult in the United States, and their curious manifestations baffled some of the shrewdest men of their day. John Fox, their father, was a hard-headed Methodist who found it difficult to accept the strange occurrences under his own roof as his daughters became the elite of the spirit world. It all began when he took a small farmhouse that was said to be haunted. Years earlier a pedlar was supposed to have been murdered on the premises, and now the neighbors believed that his ghost walked in the night. The farm was in Hydesville, thirty miles from Rochester, New York, in an area where such tales abounded.

The rappings were heard first on a March night in 1848. They came from the room where the girls slept. When Mr. and Mrs. Fox heard one of them cry out, asking for a certain number of raps, the response was instantaneous and correct. The sounds resembled the snapping of fingers, and the girls could give no explanation for what was happening. Margaret was twelve and Kate was nine. They were bright, attractive children, and soon the story of the rappings spread in the neighborhood and finally reached the metropolitan press.

Mrs. Fox summoned her friends for one of the most curious séances on record. They tested the girls from every angle. How many children did this man have? How old was another? How many deaths had there been in this family? How many births in another? Back came the correct number of raps in every instance.

"Here, Mr. Splitfoot, do as I do," said Kate, snapping her fingers three times. Three sharp raps came from the wall close to her.

Kate's thin face looked anxious. Her large dark eyes glowed with excitement. Margaret, also dark and pretty, was bland and uncommunicative. Their brother, David Fox, suggested that the raps be interpreted by way of the alphabet, and William Duesler, a neighbor, decided that the rappings spelled Charles B. Rosma, the pedlar who was supposed to have been buried in the cellar. As a result of all the excitement there were digging operations and a few relics were uncovered that might have been anything. The Foxes said that teeth, bones, and fragments of a broken bowl were found.

The girls' grown-up sister Leah Fish, a widow who was a music teacher in Rochester, took them back to the city with her and was soon exhibiting them. The poltergeist pranks around them became so pronounced that they had to move from one house to another. Tables rose in the air. Crockery was smashed. Mirrors fell down. Pickets from fences were tossed about, and rappings were produced to order. Wherever Margaret and Kate chanced to be, the rappings broke out. When Kate visited Auburn and her sister stayed in Rochester, they were heard in both places. The sisters had three public meetings in Corinthian

Hall, but the rappings were poor and infrequent, and at the third meeting a riot broke out in the hall and the girls had to flee. A committee appointed to study them at a hotel dinner were startled when the heavy dining table at which they all sat was lifted slowly above their heads. Skeptics concluded that the table legs were hollow and contained batteries.

The girls ran into trouble in Buffalo in the winter of 1850 when they gave exhibitions before three doctors who were professors at the university. Immediately afterward the experts wrote to the Buffalo *Commercial Adviser* that the rappings "could be explained by movements of the knee-joints." Leah challenged them to prove their theory at a personal interview. The girls were placed close together with their heels resting on cushions and their legs stretched out. Their toes were raised and their feet were separated from each other. Half an hour passed and there were no raps. When the girls resumed their usual position, with their feet resting on the floor, the knockings were clearly heard. In the second experiment their knees were firmly grasped so that any lateral movement of the bones would be perceptible to the touch. This was repeated for an hour and there was dead silence, but as the pressure was released the rappings came faintly, then with strength when the doctors let go altogether. This unofficial jury decided that the Rochester knockings emanated from the knee joints of the Fox girls. Leah explained that the spirits were chased away by such brutal treatment and would not perform.

But the trio flourished. The adverse evidence was not conclusive, and the believers increased in number across the country. Soon mysterious rappings were being heard all along the Eastern seaboard. In 1850 they were reported from Bridgeport, Auburn, Syracuse, and farther afield, as new mediums appeared. Two hundred cases were reported from Ohio, and others from New Jersey and South Carolina. "Have you heard any rappings today?" one young person would ask another, and the Fox sisters were as widely discussed in the 1850's as the Beatles in the 1960's. The entire field of psychic phenomena was being questioned. For two generations the induced trance had been studied in France, Germany, and elsewhere in Europe. Mesmerism was in good standing, and occult manifestations were being related to various electric, magnetic, and cyclic theories. The Shakers had claimed spiritualistic communications as early as 1837. The Swedenborgians and Fourierites developed strong associations with spiritualism, animal magnetism and hypnotism, which were tied in with a complex of other movements. But the Fox girls quickened and dramatized the subject, with their businesslike sister, Mrs. Leah Fish, exploiting them in the background while serving as a medium as well as their business manager.

This strange troupe went with their mother to New York in the summer of 1850 and stayed at Barnum's Hotel at Broadway and Maiden Lane. Every day they held séances in the parlor, charging the public a dollar a visit. They had already had so much publicity that people flocked in, including many celebrities. Horace Greeley, always attentive to a new and eccentric cause, was one of their first backers. He invited them to his house, commented favorably on them in the *Tribune*, and paid for some schooling for the untutored Kate. He told her seriously that she could develop into another Margaret Fuller if only she would concentrate on her studies. Both sisters had an elfish and stubborn disregard for education. They had gone to country schools, but now that they were child wonders, stared at by awed spectators as they evoked rappings from ceilings, walls, floors, tables, and other inanimate objects, they had neither the time nor the inclination to study.

The séance that established them with the intellectuals was held at the home on Broadway of Dr. Rufus W. Griswold in the spring of 1850. William Cullen Bryant, who had watched them a number of times and believed in them fully, was present, as well as Horace Greeley, George Bancroft, James Fenimore Cooper, N. P. Willis, John Bigelow, and other men prominent in the world of letters. Margaret and Kate put on their best performance. Dr. Griswold was completely skeptical when he called them in, but George Ripley, reporting for the *Tribune*, wrote:

"The raps were loud and distinct, and various members of the party conversed by means of the alphabet. . . . The manners and bearing of the ladies are such as to create a prepossession in their favor. They have no theories to offer in explanation of the acts of their mysterious attendants, and apparently have no control of their incomings and outgoings."

Cooper, who later became a spiritualist, was impressed with their answers about the manner in which his sister had died. Greeley, carefully studying their slow, languorous waits for the rapped answers; their fresh young faces; their honest-looking mother who was now more in evidence than Leah, was impressed and he later commented on them editorially in the *Tribune*:

> It would be the basest cowardice not to say that we are convinced beyond a doubt of their perfect integrity and good faith. . . . Whatever may be the cause or the origin of the rappings the ladies in whose presence they occur do not make them. . . . We believe that fully three-fourths are convinced, as we are, that these singular sounds and seeming manifestations are not produced by Mrs. Fox and her daughters nor by any human being connected with them.

Although Greeley backed them for many years, other editors were more skeptical, and many papers made gibes and jests about witches' brooms, dancing tables, and talking walls, in connection with the Foxes. But the time was ripe for their appearance; the public was attuned to novelty and eccentric demonstrations; and the girls reaped a rich harvest as they traveled. Leah, always ready to come to their defense, asked their medical critics how their joints could have stood years of constant manipulation if their theory was correct. In the end Margaret and Kate Fox provided the most sustained demonstration of mediumship in the history of the United States, and they became equally well known in England.

As they toured under Leah's wing their manifestations broadened in scope. Although their rappings were the prime attraction, they were soon doing automatic writing, drawing, and painting.

Kate was particularly adept at automatic writing. With her left hand she did mirror writing at high speed and poured out answers to questions almost before they were completed. For long messages this was faster than the rappings, and seemed to be less tiring for the girls. Again, a circle of eight or ten persons would hold hands and form a battery to magnetize the medium. Answers to questions would be spelled out in letters on a card. The phenomena had variety. Leah favored the poltergeist and was a medium herself. Ghostly hands were added to the mystic raps. When she was in action dresses were tweaked, pantaloons were pulled, and feet were patted. On one occasion these eerie sprites swarmed like bees around William Lloyd Garrison, the antislavery leader. N. P. Tallmadge, Governor of Wisconsin and an early convert, believed that he communicated with the spirit of John C. Calhoun through Margaret and Katie Fox. Another spirit invoked was that of Benjamin Franklin, and this caused a stir in Cleveland. John W. Gray, editor of the *Cleveland Plain Dealer*, was a friend of Horace Greeley's, and he saw to it that Leah, Margaret, and Kate received medals and watches as they toured Ohio. In Cincinnati there was great interest in the whole subject, and many circles were formed after their visit. Auburn, New York, became an active center and had 150 mediums in 1850, two years after the rappings had been heard in the little farmhouse.

In the winter of 1852 Leah, who was now married to Calvin Brown, moved permanently to New York, and the sisters came and went, depending on their engagements. They had their own fees as mediums, and their mother usually accompanied them on their tours. Greeley had them give several séances at his house, and Jenny Lind had a sitting at one. The messages came through to her in Swedish. Mrs. Greeley was deeply interested in the occult, mesmerism, or any spirit manifestation. Mrs. Fox lived for a time with the Greeleys, and her daughters one way or another met most of the celebrities who circled around the *Tribune* editor. There was great interest in the personalities of the sisters. Katie was still relatively untutored, except that she had become a fast and accurate speller as she coped with her mirror writing. But Margaret profited by her association with the learned Elisha K. Kane, whom she later claimed was her common law husband. They met in Philadelphia in 1852, when Margaret was sixteen and he was thirty-two. He had just returned in an exhausted condition from his first expedition to the Arctic in search of Sir John Franklin and his party.

For years Dr. Kane had been traveling around the world as a naval surgeon, making geological observations. He lectured and wrote on his expeditions and was well known in scientific circles. When he called for a sitting at the Fox parlors in Philadelphia, he found Margaret reading a French textbook. He was touched by her youth and the air of charlatanry that surrounded her. From the start he was skeptical about the rappings and made every effort to have her break away from the strange life she led. He visited her often and took her driving, along with her mother. Kate by this time was attending school in New York under Greeley's auspices, and Kane proposed to Mrs. Fox that he send Margaret to a good school since, although quick to learn, she was comparatively ignorant. He brought his friends to hear the rappings, but he would not let them laugh or scoff at her. However, he was quite severe and lectured her on her manners.

When the Foxes moved to Washington to hold sittings there he saw them again. He was preparing for his second expedition to the Arctic and read to her some of his letters from Lady Franklin. He sent her books, music, and flowers, and urged her to cultivate her mind, to present a ladylike appearance wherever she went in Washington, and never to indulge in any "spirit jokes" with the people there. "I am anxious that you two girls should be well dressed," he wrote solicitously to Margaret and sent her, toward this end, an ermine collar, some Honiton lace, and a smart bonnet.

Dr. Kane shuddered when Katie's name appeared in the papers in connection with a suicide in New York. "Oh, how much I wish that you would quit this life of dreary sameness and suspected deceit," he wrote to Margaret. "You should forget the r-pp-gs (I never mention the name now) and come out like gold purified from the furnace; a pure simplehearted trusting girl."

As he traveled about the country lecturing, he wrote that in Boston the spirits seemed to have friends. He had been to a sitting where the chairs had danced about the room and clothes had been twitched, but he still detested it all and showed his impatience to the Fox sisters. There was much affectionate banter back and forth, with Margaret believing him to be infatuated with her. She was introduced by his Washington friends as the "future Mrs. Kane," and he wrote to her on January 27, 1853: "It is that strange mixture of child and woman, of simplicity and cunning, of passionate impulse and extreme self-control, that has made you a curious study. Maggie, you are *very* pretty, very childlike, very deceitful, but to me as *readable* as a grandmother's Bible."

Dr. Kane was meeting with great success himself as he dined with the President, lectured to scientific gatherings on the Arctic expeditions, and drew around himself "all the wealth and beauty of this great city," as he wrote to Maggie. When they were in the capital at the same time he hired a carriage to drive her and her mother to country inns. He sent her briefly to Madame Barati's School in the capital and gave her a Newfoundland dog. As he was about to leave on the second expedition he told her that there would be no more investigating committees for her, no wiseacres studying her, for she was going away to school. He made vague promises: "If you really can make up your mind to abjure the spirits, to study and improve your mental and moral nature, it may be that a career of brightness will be open to you. . . . I sometimes doubt whether you have the firmness of mind to carry them through."

One remarkable thing about the Fox sisters was the importance of the people they drew within their circle. When Mrs. Franklin Pierce, the President's wife, arranged to call on Margaret at the request of Governor Tallmadge, Dr. Kane warned her not to do any rappings, for Mrs. Pierce was distraught over the death of her son in a railroad accident. In course of time his attitude toward the spirit manifestations had its effect on Margaret, and she came to loathe the sittings and to avoid them when she could. But her mother and Leah kept drawing her into the circle again, and Kate had never left it. Finally, three days before Dr. Kane left for his second expedition in search of Sir John Franklin, Margaret was enrolled at the Crookville School near Philadephia. She was left in the care of his aunt, and before they parted Margaret and Dr. Kane made a mutual compact of "truth and constancy." The newspapers announced that the "celebrated Dr. Kane would shortly lead to the altar Miss Margaret Fox, of spirit-rapping celebrity," a piece of news that his family promptly repudiated.

As she coped with her studies and forswore all rappings for the time being, Margaret waited for letters from the Arctic and followed Dr. Kane's adventures through the papers. He had commissioned an artist to paint her, and he carried this portrait with him on his travels. But when he returned in 1855 Maggie was staying with Leah on Clinton Place and was again working as a medium. Dr. Kane, ill with rheumatism, was disillusioned with his protégée and was not anxious to become involved with her again. His friend, Henry Grinnell, who had supplied the ships for the Franklin expeditions, tried to recover the letters that the scientist had sent to Miss Fox. Under pressure Dr. Kane finally visited her and told her that their marriage must be postponed because of the opposition of his family. "I must either give you up from this moment and for ever, or give up those who are very dear to me, and who hold my name and reputation as sacred," he wrote.

The Kane-Fox romance was so widely discussed in New York that the *Times* commented on November 6, 1855: "Whether they have been, are, may be, are not, or will not be, 'engaged'—can be nobody's business but their own and that of their near relatives. Then why should the press trumpet their names in connection with each other?" But in spite of his family's opposition, Kane and Margaret were reconciled. He told her he "cared no longer for the world's opinion or its sneers." They went driving and visiting, and Maggie was seen with him at the opera, wearing a blue silk gown and white opera cloak. Again he drew her away from the spirit circle and would not let her stay in a room where the subject was being discussed. The rappings were an affront to his scientific reputation.

He bought her a diamond bracelet at Tiffany's and gave her his books bound to order. Finally they went through what Margaret claimed was a common law marriage, with her mother, their servant, and a friend for witnesses. They never met again. He was leaving for England when they made their pact and seven months later, as she and her mother were planning to join him in Cuba, he died in Havana on February 16, 1857. She later incorporated his letters in a memoir, although she had been told that they would be taken from her by legal means. The publication planned for 1862 was held up when she made a compromise with Dr. Kane's brothers and executor, but when the agreement was not fully kept she reclaimed the letters and published them. From the time of the so-called common law marriage she was known as Mrs. Kane, both in England and the United States.

Margaret's life changed considerably after Dr. Kane's death. She had a temporary breakdown, and then in August, 1858, she became a Catholic convert. She was baptized in St. Peter's Church on Barclay Street with her father, mother, and Kate for sponsors. Dr. Kane had often urged her to take this step, feeling that it might break her link with spiritualism, and for the time being it did. Governor Tallmadge wrote to her sympathetically from Saratoga Springs: "I know how depressed and disconsolate you have been since your disappointment in a matter of the heart, to which we all look forward for happiness in this life. . . . Your pure and Christian life will assure you a blissful and happy future."

The governor, like countless others, had read in the papers the strange story of a medium recanting.

"Margaretta, do you renounce Satan?" the priest asked of the kneeling figure.

"I do renounce him," said the most famous Fox sister.

"And all his works?"

"I do renounce them."

The conversion followed a severe experience in Boston that had done the reputation of the Fox sisters little good. For three days in the summer of 1857 a group of distinguished scientists had assembled to appraise psychic phenomena, and their principal subjects were the most noted practitioners in the field—Katie and Maggie Fox. The Boston *Courier* had offered $500 if the spiritualists could prove any supernatural manifestations. The tests were searching and severe, and the girls seemed to be at a total loss. A chilly report issued by the committee warned the public "against this contaminating influence, which surely tends to lessen the truth of man and the purity of woman . . . any connection with spiritualist circles, so-called, corrupts the morals and degrades the intellect." Louis Agassiz told Leah privately that there was a time when he could have done everything that they did. He had been a mesmeric subject for the Rev. Chauncey Hare Townshend at Neuchâtel in 1839.

Leah was furious over the public snub that they had received. She wrote that Professor C. C. Felton, the newly appointed president of Harvard, "burned with angry zeal against spiritualism." The letter he published on the subject was sharply answered by Robert Dale Owen, a firm believer in the power and integrity of the Fox sisters. "I have known Kate Fox for years," he commented. "She is one of the most simple-minded and strictly impulsive young persons I have ever met; as incapable of framing, or carrying on, any deliberate scheme of imposition as a ten-year-old child is of administering a government."

However, carriages still came rolling up to Leah's door at 232 West Thirty-seventh Street with some of the most interesting persons in New York, all bent on communing with the spirits. Leah invited President Felton to spend a fortnight with them for a sustained demonstration of their powers but he declined. Her second husband, Calvin Brown, had died two years after their marriage, and she was now the wife of Daniel Underhill, a prosperous insurance man. Unlike her two sisters, Leah had a substantial, motherly look about her and a commanding air. Before long

she had Maggie back in tow. For a time this sister was the high
priestess of a psychic research organization established in Philadelphia by Henry Seybert. When he died he left money for
testing phenomena and his successor, Dr. Howard Horace
Furness, turned the tables on Margaret and pronounced her a
fraud.

The war years were prosperous ones for the sisters. Bereaved
relatives in great numbers sought comfort by trying to establish
communication with the dead, and clairvoyance was widely practiced across the country. In 1865, the last year of the Civil War,
Mr. and Mrs. Fox died within a few months of each other. Kate
then went to board at the Swedish Movement Cure establishment
run by Dr. George H. Taylor at Sixth Avenue and Thirty-
eighth Street. He was a Vermonter who had studied medicine at
Harvard and New York medical schools and had taken up phys-
iotherapy, a current fad, after visiting Sweden in 1858. His wife,
Mrs. Sarah Elizabeth Langworthy Taylor and he had become
interested in spiritualism after losing their two children. They
made detailed recordings of Kate's spirit writing over a period of
years and arranged sittings for her. The Taylor circle operated
from 1869 to 1892, and intermittently Kate was the star per-
former. The high-water mark of her career was the series of
séances held for C. F. Livermore, a well-known New Yorker. He
lost his wife in 1861, and she became "Estelle" of the spirit world.
At the first séance held that year the Taylors recorded a tremendous rap on the heavy mahogany table as it rose and fell. Then
the door "was violently shaken, the windows opened and shut; in
fact, everything in the room seemed in motion. Questions were
answered by loud knocks on the door, on the glass of the windows, on the ceiling—everywhere." Then, according to the
Taylor record, a substance like gauze rose from the floor, moved
about the room, became more distinct in outline, floated up toward the ceiling, and at one point Estelle even rested her head on
her husband's shoulder. Taylor held Kate Fox's hands tight during all these manifestations. He never had any doubt of her true
gift as a medium. Robert Dale Owen took notes on these curious

sittings. Benjamin Franklin was said to appear with a great rustling, and he sat in a characteristic pose and supposedly struck matches to show himself clearly. On his third visit his hat moved from his head to someone else's; then he and Estelle showed up together, but "Miss Fox became nervous and her exclamations caused the final disappearance of both figures."

Part of Miss Fox's trouble was that she had become an alcoholic, and Margaret had too, to a lesser extent. Katie at times had to be whisked out of sight in the middle of a séance when she was all too clearly tipsy. This indulgence had grown up over the years. Her sitters often brought liquor to sustain them during the long hours in the charmed circle, and Katie had fallen into the habit of drinking with them. Her father had been an alcoholic and had been separated from his wife for a number of years, but he had given up drink and had rejoined her shortly before Margaret and Kate were born. Kate had become so addicted to drink by the 1870's that she was kept for long periods in sanitariums. She was always thought to be the stronger medium of the two girls, for Margaret had a flighty approach to what she was doing and periodically would turn from it with disgust. She, too, found consolation in the bottle, but she was less notorious for this than Katie was. These habits, plus a large following of those who believed in free love, deepened the stigma surrounding mediums as a class.

Katie had dreamy eyes, and she both spoke and moved in a slow, languorous way. Sometimes her own revelations seemed to frighten her, and she had a pinched, anxious look. Her watchers occasionally were not sure whether she was drunk or in a trance, but the spiritualists insisted that she was "thoroughly and permanently magnetized." She was much esteemed by her fellow practitioners, who considered her more gifted than Margaret. But Margaret had great charm for her sitters. She was dark-haired, small and slight, with magnetic eyes that sometimes held a gleam of mischief. After her association with Dr. Kane she affected a degree of worldly knowledge and talked intelligently to the learned men who came into the charmed circle of the Fox family.

Katie remained more the simple, childlike type in manner, although she was an extremely complex woman. The Taylors recorded her work off and on from 1865 until she went to Europe in 1871, and then again in her later years up to 1892, when she died. The final score was 1,211 closely written pages with 1,367 different written "communications," in addition to accounts of the psychical phenomena surrounding the sittings.

Kate wrote the messages in pencil, backward, with her left hand, on long strips of brown paper, which were destroyed later as being too bulky for storage. They were read off by Dr. Taylor with a mirror and written down by his wife from his dictation. The first "message" came through in November, 1869, and the last on June 1, 1892. In spite of her unreliability, Katie did not go out of fashion, like many of the other mediums who were exposed or who faded into obscurity. She and Margaret had a firm hold on the public imagination, and they found fresh acclaim when they went to England. Sir William Crookes, the famous physicist who was interested in psychical research, took them up, and for a time they were great pets in Victorian drawing rooms. Katie married H. D. Jencken, a barrister of Dutch ancestry, and they lived on Brompton Crescent. Her oldest son, Ferdinand D. Loewstein Jencken, was born in 1873, two years after her arrival in England, and a story circulated that when he was one a pencil was put in his hand and he wrote in Greek "He Who Trusts in Me Shall Live."

Sir William Crookes used Kate in making his most exhaustive tests, and he announced that for "power and certainty" he had found no one to touch her. He worked with her for several months and was especially interested in the sounds that she could evoke. He found that the rappings came when her hands and feet were held, when she was standing on a chair, when she was enclosed in a wire cage, and, again, when she was in a faint on a sofa. Deeply impressed, he wrote:

> It seems only necessary for her to place her hand on any substance for loud thuds to be heard in it, like a triple pulsation, something loud enough to be heard several rooms

off. . . . I have heard them on a glass harmonica—I have felt them on my own shoulder and under my own hands. I have heard them on a piece of paper held between the fingers by a piece of thread passed through one corner. . . . I have tested them in every way that I could devise, until there has been no escape from the conviction that they were true, objective occurrences not produced by trickery or mechanical means.

Sir William also told of seeing materializations—of a luminous cloud hovering over a heliotrope plant, breaking off a sprig, and carrying it to a sitter as the cloud condensed itself into the shape of a hand. A séance at the home of Thomas Carlyle, in which the spirit of the wretched Jane, his wife, was invoked, was the talk of England, and Katie's ministrations became more popular than ever. On her return to the United States a second son, Henry, was born at Mrs. Underhill's home in New York in 1875. Katie returned almost at once to England after a brief stay at the Taylor sanitarium where the water cure, dieting, and massage helped to restore her equilibrium. There she did some more spirit writing.

Margaret by this time was fully committed to the plushy comfort of Victorian London, and to the dinner tables of some famous men and women who regarded spiritualism as a religion. Her own disillusionment was becoming complete, and she wrote angrily and revealingly on the subject after Katie, on a return trip to the United States, had her sons taken from her by E. T. Gerry, head of the Society for the Prevention of Cruelty to Children. She was accused of drunkenness and idleness and of being an unfit mother. A wave of anger and incredulity swept the leading lights of the spirit world when the famous Kate was labeled in this disastrous fashion. Margaret was dining in London with Hensleigh Wedgwood, the mathematician whose grandfather, Josiah Wedgwood, founded the famous pottery firm, when the news of Katie's disgrace reached her. She promptly faked a message from Edward Jencken, the children's uncle and their guardian after the death of Kate's husband, demanding that the children be returned at once to their mother, and that all three be sent to join him in England. The fact was that Jencken was in Russia at the time and knew nothing about the matter. But American friends raised $15,000 for Katie and put it in a London bank to her credit. She and her sons sailed in triumph, with masses of flowers from well-wishers. They were soon reunited with Maggie in London.

But Maggie chose this time to send the editor of the New York *Herald* a strange letter that caused much talk in New York. Was a Fox sister turning her back on the cult that had brought her world-wide fame? It was dated May 13, 1888, and read:

> Spiritualism is a curse. God has set his seal against it. I call it a curse for it is made use of as a covering for heartlessness. . . . No matter in what form spiritualism is permeated it is, was and always will be a curse to those who meddle with it. No right minded man or woman can think otherwise. I have found that fanatic area as plentiful among "inferior men and women" as they are among the superior and more informed. . . . They cannot hold their fanaticism in check and it increases as the years increase. All they will ever achieve for their foolish fanaticism will be loss of money, softening of the brain and a lingering death.

The fact was that mediums at this time were on the run in England. There had been some sensational exposures, a few jailings, and a rising tide of skepticism. The Fox sisters decided to return to the United States. Kate had been back and forth several times, usually staying at Dr. Taylor's sanitarium and doing more spirit writing. Now they were home to stay. Both were broken down and in need of funds. Margaret was determined to capitalize on their history, renounce spiritualism, and expose the trickery of the rappings. Kate was less convinced of the wisdom of this course, but she gave public assent to Margaret's dramatic act. The older sister talked wildly to reporters on her arrival, and word soon spread that the Foxes were going to tell all. A public meeting was arranged for them, to be held at the Academy of Music in October, 1888.

A *Herald* reporter found Maggie beforehand in dingy lodgings on West Forty-fourth Street. He pictured her as a "small, magnetic looking woman whose face bears the traces of much sorrow and a worldwide experience." She was carelessly dressed, seemed distraught, and "told a story of as strange and fantastic a life as has ever been recorded." She repeated over and over again that she would balance the account that the world of humbug-loving mortals held against her by making a clean breast of all her former miracles and wonders. She spoke with great bitterness of the arrest of Katie for neglect of her children and vowed that she would meet Gerry face to face and "take his life's blood." She added: "I don't suppose I'd kill him, but I'd look at him," and the intense glance she gave the reporter at this point reminded him of a Medusa.

Maggie was equally vengeful about Leah, blaming her for having Katie arrested. She charged her older sister with forcing them into the life they had led, with encouraging the hoax and persecuting them when they would not go her way. "She's my damnable enemy," Maggie screamed. "I hate her. My God! I'd poison her! No, I wouldn't, but I'll lash her with my tongue. . . . I loathe the thing I have been. . . . I was too honest to remain a medium. That's why I gave up my exhibitions."

She said that she had honestly tried to get some authentic sign of communication, even going to graveyards in the dead of night, but no amount of experimentation had brought her any enlightenment. "No," said Maggie firmly. "The dead shall not return, nor shall any that go down to hell." She disclosed that for some time before leaving England she had carried her séances to a certain point in the process of delusion, and had then enlightened her sitters, convincing them of the ease with which they could be practiced upon.

Leah, now a highly respected matron, took refuge in the country while Maggie ranted, but her husband told of helping both sisters. He thought they might still be doing well if only they would stay sober. He was convinced that both were tipsy when they forswore their allegiance. Other spiritualists shared this belief. They could scarcely credit the fact that their great leaders, who had upheld spiritualism for so many years, had abandoned them.

"Maggie can be as nice as you please or as vicious as a devil," Underhill commented. "I don't think she is in her right mind. I have seen her produce some effects when too drunk to realize what she was doing." He insisted that even when lying ill in bed he had known her to evoke rappings in various parts of the room—upon ceilings, doors, and windows several feet from where she was.

Maggie said that she had thought of committing suicide on the ship coming home. Katie was also in a scornful mood when she arrived with her children, all ready for the great exposé. "I do not give a fig for spiritualism," she announced on her arrival, "except in so far as the good will of its adherents may affect the future of my boys. Spiritualism is a humbug from beginning to end. It is the greatest humbug of the century. And yet Maggie and I are the founders of Spiritualism. I certainly know that every so-called manifestation produced through me in London or anywhere else was a fraud. . . . We ought not to leave that base fabric of deceit behind us unexposed."

With these preliminary statements the public was prepared for the day of revelation. In forty years the rappings had never been satisfactorily explained. The Academy of Music was crowded with believers and nonbelievers. The spiritualists swarmed in, a strange lot in all kinds of curious garb. Some of the mediums summed up the essence of grotesquerie in their bearing. Katie sat in a box while Margaret, dressed in deep mourning, was the focal point of interest on the stage. She put on her glasses, curtsied to the audience, and read her confession slowly, and in a trembling voice. "Many here will scorn me, but if they knew the sorrow of my past life they would pity, not condemn," she said.

The rappings, said Margaret, were made with the joint of her big toe. Three doctors came up to the stage to observe while she poised herself on a pine table with nothing on her feet but stockings. As she stood, seemingly motionless, loud rappings were heard distinctly, first from the floor, then from behind the scenes, and finally from the gallery. Excitement swept through the audience. A whirlwind of applause followed. Maggie clapped her hands, danced about, and cried: "It's a fraud. Spiritualism is a fraud from beginning to end. It's a trick. There's no truth in it. . . . That I have been chiefly instrumental in perpetrating the fraud of spiritualism upon a too confiding public most of you doubtless know. . . . I am now however telling the truth, the whole truth and nothing but the truth, so help me God. . . . I am here tonight as one of the founders of Spiritualism, to denounce it as an absolute falsehood from beginning to end, as the flimsiest of superstitions, the most wicked blasphemous treason of the world today."

After a detailed apologia and explanation she went down into the audience and placed her foot on the instep of a well-known man. He felt and acknowledged the series of tiny raps that followed. The demonstration was complete. Katie applauded from her box. There were cries of disbelief and protests from the spiritualists, but next day the papers spread the news far and wide. The Fox sisters had "undone the infamous work of many years," said the *Herald*. Mrs. Kane, its founder, had publicly confessed it to be a fraud—"her big toe did it all."

The answers now came thick and fast. Kate and Margaret readily admitted that the tale of the haunted house had amused them and caused them to frighten their parents by dropping apples on the floor and snatching them back under the sheets by means of strings. Then, while pushing their feet against the footboard of the bed, they discovered that they could make the same sounds by snapping the first joint of the big toe. When Leah learned how they got their effects she frightened them into expanding the phenomena, said Margaret. Table rappings were easily produced by putting a foot at the base of the table. The same technique was used with doors, with the rappings seeming to come from the top. They used simple psychology, too, and stared at distant points when the rappings were supposed to come from the ceiling or walls.

But their halo still surrounded the Fox sisters among the professionals. The facts they offered did not seem to be conclusive, and Katie later recanted. The faithful continued to believe that they were authentic mediums, and those who knew them best decided that the mood of confession was an alcoholic whim. They needed funds, and this was a fresh sensation. Sir William Crookes's faith in them was not shaken. Years later, in his inaugural speech as president of the British Association for the Promotion of Science, he said that he held to his conclusion of 1874 about the Fox sisters and in no whit relaxed his belief in the veracity of the metaphysical phenomena. But Sir William had come under fire himself for his sponsorship of Florence and Kate Cook, two sisters who were exposed as frauds. They were the most famous mediums in Britain in the 1870's, just as the Fox sisters were in the United States. Browning, Dickens, John Bright, and other British celebrities had moved in the charmed Cook circle, where the sitters were touched by invisible hands, tambourines were shaken, and stringed instruments were plucked. Semiluminous figures draped in veiling and carrying bunches of roses flickered through darkened rooms, and lights hovered in the air.

The Fox sisters found that the Cook girls had introduced more variety into their manifestations, but the British were impressed with Kate Fox's versatility as a medium. Camille Flammarion commented in particular on her automatic writing, but Michael Faraday and Ernst H. Haeckel, who had followed the manifestations in America with interest, did not agree with him or with Sir William Crookes about the Fox sisters. Professor J. H. Hyslop, secretary of the American Society for Psychical Research, commented in his book *Contact with the Other World* that the confession of Margaret Fox deprived the movement of both its scientific and religious interest. He did not believe that they had supplied the complete answer, for "there were other and mental phenomena which were well attested, and there was testimony that raps had occurred in localities where action of the toe joints could not be effective. . . . There can be no doubt in the mind of the present writer that the phenomena of the Fox sisters . . . whose early manifestations were the very basis of the whole metaphysi-

cal revival in the world . . . never received their deserved recognition. . . ."

Not only did Margaret verbally renounce spiritualism—and
with more conviction than Kate—but a booklet, *The Death Blow
to Spiritualism*, was circulated as the true story of the Fox sisters
"revealed by authority of Margaret Fox Kane and Catherine Fox
Jencken." But when all the excitement had died down there was
little left for the Fox sisters, and they drank more heavily than
ever and were a seedy pair when glimpsed in their own haunts.
They continued to pick up a penny when they could by acting as
mediums. Katie sometimes called on the Taylors to have tea and
be paid a dollar for a sitting. They considered her trustworthy
when sober, and sweet-tempered at all times, but her decline was
rapid. She was fifty-three when she died on July 2, 1892, in a
shabby room at 609 Columbus Avenue. Her second son, Henry,
had died when young and Ferdinand, who dabbled in spiritualism, would live only until 1908.

Margaret was ill and penniless during the last two years of her
life. She lived off charity and was rarely sober. She was fifty-
seven when she died on March 8, 1893, at the home of a friend in
Brooklyn. Both sisters were buried in Greenwood Cemetery, and
the famous rappings were heard no more. The Foxes were known
around the world, wherever psychic phenomena came under discussion, and were taken more seriously for a longer stretch of
time than any other mediums. But in the end they had the faded
and sordid look of two eccentrics who had dabbled in something
beyond their ken, and had found it bitter and empty.

Victoria Woodhull and Tennessee Claflin

Ninety-two years before Margaret Chase Smith decided to run for the office of President of the United States, a nineteenth-century siren threw her bonnet into the ring. Victoria C. Woodhull was the nominee of the National Equal Rights party in 1872, but hers was a lost cause from the start. Ulysses S. Grant was the winner, and Horace Greeley, his leading opponent, went down to defeat as well as Mrs. Woodhull, whom nobody seemed to remember on election day.

All the stray radicals, eccentrics, and necromancers who flocked to her banner were of little use to her, and neither Vicky's fluent tongue nor her good looks, her flamboyant ways nor her suffrage support, availed her in the big arena of national politics. Before she had thought of the White House for her ambitious self she had tarnished her own image in the public eye. Her causes were many. She upheld the dark powers of spiritualism and spoke openly for free love. She was one of the leading suppliants for woman suffrage.

Vicky's effects had some of the largeness of her own personality. She and her sister Tennessee Claflin, who closely matched her in fame, were hard to classify, either as journalists or human beings. They were magnetic, eerie, raffish, triumphantly heralding the freedom of women, basking in the counsel of the great financiers of the period, and using the honest craft of journalism for their own questionable ends. The 1870's was a decade rich in possibilities for the two mysterious sisters who founded their own bank, launched their own weekly paper, charmed such financiers as Cornelius Vanderbilt, Jim Fisk, and Jay Gould, and swaggered around town as the Lady Brokers of Wall Street. Victoria even wrung support from suffrage leaders. Susan B. Anthony felt that her able championship of suffrage outweighed her dedication to strange gods. But the sisterhood in the homes watched the lady brokers through lace curtains as they drove past in their dashing equipage, until interest turned to suspicion, suspicion to censure, and censure to howls when their machinations were uncovered. This did not bother the Claflin sisters, who had been fighting the forces of law, order, and respectability all their lives.

They were born in Homer, Ohio, the children of Reuben Buckman Claflin and Roxanna Hummell Claflin. "Buck" was a stableman, tavern keeper, farmer, and promoter—a man of many occupations and of dubious reputation. He looked the sport he was, with his plug hat and diamond studs, his quick tongue, gold glasses, and auburn hair. He was equally adept at trading horses or gambling on the river boats. His wife, Roxanna, communed with the spirits and attended religious revivals. She went into trances and insisted that she heard spirit voices. Vicky, born in 1838, and Tennie, born seven years later, were the victims of family hysteria. Tennie was a willing disciple but Vicky, proud and disdainful, held herself aloof from the strife and frenzy that surrounded her, although in later years she insisted that she had spiritual visions at the age of three. Another sister, Utica, grew up to be a scoffer. Spiritualism was sweeping the nation in the 1840's. In Ohio the Millerites were out on the hills, awaiting the end of the world. Margaret and Kate Fox were stirring up excitement in Rochester with their eerie rappings. Tennie and Vicky were to batten for years on the craze for spiritualism, hypnotism, and magnetism.

But they grew up to be beauties in the midst of all the uproar in their squalid, storm-ridden home. They ran about wild, wearing tattered clothes, whispering gibberish to the spirits, and wailing loudly when they were whipped with braided withes. Vicky came out of it all with style and strength. She had a delicately modeled face, deep blue eyes, and masses of tawny hair. She had force and depth and always gave the impression, even while she practiced the Claflin brand of spiritualism, that she knew it to be charlatanry. Tennie, on the other hand, was deeply committed to the spirit world. She was a delicate sprite in looks, with fair hair and china-blue eyes. Her wayward spirit was cloaked with the look of innocence. She was trivial and frivolous, whereas Vicky was striking, a forceful personality who throughout the years could always command the attention of intelligent men and women.

When the people of Homer could no longer endure the Claflin ménage, Buck and his disorderly family embarked on a wandering life, stopping at small towns, picking up odd jobs, and eventually touring in a covered van, with a ball-fringed top. Tennie, a mere child, was already the star, with her childish face on bottles of lotion containing "Miss Tennessee's Magnetic Elixir for Beautifying the Complexion and Cleansing the Blood." Roxanna mixed the brew and Buck promoted it, plastering his van with signs and scattering circulars. The customers were offered the further inducement of the séance. In 1859, at the age of fourteen, Tennie was billed as the "Wonderful Child who could cure the most obstinate diseases, including cancer, and in the course of a trance travel to any part of the world, and establish communication between the dead and the living."

Vicky pulled away from all this trickery at the age of fifteen when she married Dr. Canning Woodhull. He was a gentle, scholarly man whom she soon discovered to be a hopeless alcoholic. They lived in California, where for a short time she was on the stage, besides also working as a cigar girl and a seamstress. But during the eleven years of her marriage she picked up some worldly flavor and sophistication. Her speech improved, and her husband tutored her in manners. She had two children, Byron and Zula Maud, and she flowered into a genuine beauty. Finally Roxanna ordered Tennessee to send the spirits to bring Vicky back into the family fold. She joined them in the "cancer infirmary" they ran in Ottawa, Illinois, during the Civil War, but Tennie got into difficulties when one of the patients died under treatment. They moved on to Cincinnati where they abandoned medicine and concentrated on clairvoyance. But again Tennie landed in trouble—this time she was charged with blackmail and adultery.

They stormed into Chicago like a traveling circus, with a band blaring and outriders preceding their gaily decorated van. Their pitch now was animal magnetism, which was becoming a popular craze. Cards went out that "Miss Tennessee the Wonderful Child has Established a Magnetic Infirmary at 265 Wabash Avenue, Chicago." By this time Vicky had abandoned Dr. Woodhull in favor of Colonel James H. Blood, who had commanded a Missouri regiment during the war. He joined the traveling troupe and toured the Western and Southern states with Vicky. She was Madame Harvey, a mystic who told fortunes; he was James Harvey, the entrepreneur. But Mrs. Blood pursued them and agreed to a divorce in exchange for the profits from their tour. Vicky divorced Dr. Woodhull in Chicago, and from then on the able and handsome Colonel Blood played a large part in her history and fortunes. Tennie had married a man named John Bartels, but she kept this secret, lest it interfere with business.

The sisters were now ready for New York. Vicky announced
that Demosthenes, her guiding spirit, had summoned her to a
house on Great Jones Street. The entourage arrived quietly and
set up quarters in the appointed place. The medicine cult was
now abandoned. Spiritualism and magnetism, being in good standing, made a respectable cloak for their operations. Colonel Blood
kept out of sight, and Vicky exploited with discretion her views
on women's rights, free love, prostitution, divorce, and other
social issues. Tennie was the siren in the combination, and her
first visit was to Cornelius Vanderbilt, who had spent a fortune
trying to cure his ills, and was susceptible to the wiles of the
mystic, the faith healer, the fortuneteller. Because of this Buck
Claflin, acting as Svengali in the wings, had no difficulty in getting to the financier and setting up an appointment for Tennie.
Soon she was giving magnetic treatments to the commodore.
Eventually she even claimed that he asked her to marry him.

With this promising start Vicky and Tennie soon had access to
Jay Gould, Jim Fisk, Henry Clews, and other financiers. They
took parlors in the Hoffman House and talked knowingly of
stocks and bonds. There was much discussion of silver mines, and
gold took on fresh magic for them when they made a killing on
Black Friday. The commodore's tips on railroad securities were
helpful to the sisters, although he gave them credit for aiding him
by their clairvoyance. Soon they had opened Woodhull, Claflin &
Company, their own banking house at 44 Broad Street. Businessmen, impressed with their influential backing, arrived in numbers
to play the market under their guidance. Inevitably they were of
interest to the press, and made such headlines as "The Lady
Brokers," "The Queens of Finance," "The Bewitching Brokers,"
and "The Lady Financiers." In their office they moved about
with authority, gold pens behind their ears, their broadcloth
costumes severely tailored to their graceful figures. Buck Claflin,
now tricked out in race track clothes and highly polished boots,
kept a watchful eye on the business end of the combination, and
saw to it that "Little Sparrow," the commodore's name for
Tennie, did not fail to cultivate the men of Wall Street.

From Jones Street the family moved up to Murray Hill and settled at 15 East Thirty-eighth Street in a house deep in Victorian plush and marble. The sisters inevitably were drawn into the salons of the day, for they provided novelty and were much discussed. They soon came to know Horace Greeley, who usually took note of new movements in public life, and surrounded himself with the eccentric leaders of odd causes. One of his friends was Stephen Pearl Andrews, a strong Abolitionist who had taught in the South, practiced law in Houston, and was a follower of Swedenborg and Fourier. Vicky found Andrews, who had a degree in medicine and who also spoke Chinese, a gifted lion to add to her entourage. Like Colonel Blood, he believed in freedom of expression, free love, and a free society. He had written *The Science of Society* and was more learned than Blood, who was a philosophical anarchist in his political outlook. Andrews was handsome, worldly, and obstinate, an extremist on every front.

He and Blood became the two smart "ghosts" who functioned behind the sisters when they took a headlong plunge into journalism. Neither girl was noted for her literacy, although Vicky had a flaming intelligence that overrode her lack of education. Her ghosts gave her a halo of learning that had little to do with the facts. She was born for a headline role—one of the naturals of her generation. She could have led an army or swayed a mob—as, in fact, she sometimes did. And with these two men in the wings she was ready for action. On April 2, 1870, the New York *Herald* announced: "Victoria Woodhull, the Balmoral Broker, to Race for the White House." She was described as a "petticoat politician" and in her "First Pronunciamento," written by Andrews and Blood, she claimed the right to speak for the "unenfranchised women of the country":

> While others argued the equality of woman with man, I proved it by successfully engaging in business; while others sought to show that there was no valid reason why women should be treated, socially and politically, as being inferior to man, I boldly entered the arena . . . of business and

exercised the rights I already possessed . . . and believing as I
do that the prejudices which still exist in the popular mind
against women in public life will soon disappear, I now
announce myself as candidate for the Presidency.

Americans sat up and took note. Who was Victoria Woodhull?
How did she dare? Was she a woman or a witch? The hour had
scarcely struck for a woman to think in terms of the Presidency,
least of all a woman with a history as lurid as Victoria Woodhull's. The air blew cold around her, but her pronunciamento
was followed within a month by the first issue of *Woodhull &
Claflin's Weekly*, published on May 14, 1870. Its avowed purpose was to back Mrs. Woodhull in her campaign, and its front
page spread the news of her platform: *Upward and Onward!
Progress! Free Thought. Untrammeled Lives. Breaking the Way
for Future Generations.* The weekly was to function without
party or personal considerations; it would advocate suffrage
without distinction of sex—or so its editors promised. Cunning
Tennie had already rounded up a lavish display of financial ad-
vertisements through her Wall Street friends. The five-cent
weekly was printed on good paper and was found to be "handsome and readable." The text was mild at first, since its editors
moved with caution. Soundings were taken on such subjects as
birth control, sex hygiene, prostitution, free love, and other social
problems. But when circulation lagged its editors switched to
unabashed muckraking.

At the end of 1870 Victoria, in a purple gown with a white
rose at her throat, arrived in Washington with a memorial that
swung the support of the leading suffrage women to her side,
however much they might disapprove of her views on social
problems. The National Woman Suffrage Association, which had
been snubbing her, was holding a convention in Washington
when the news broke that Mrs. Woodhull would be heard by the
Judiciary Committee of the House, which was more recognition
than had come to any of them. Susan B. Anthony and Isabella
Beecher Hooker conferred on what to do. Should they back her
and get the benefit of her enterprise? In the end they went to

hear her speak in the committee room. She was trembling as she read her memorial in a deep, melodic voice. Her plea was not for a new amendment but for the right to vote that was already inherent in the Fourteenth Amendment. Benjamin Butler and William Loughridge supported her, but the memorial was rejected.

Immediately afterward Victoria and Tennie were asked to attend the suffrage convention. They had earned their stripes and had changed the course of the suffrage fight. Instead of battling for new rights, the suffrage leaders now proposed to assert those already in the Constitution. The Woodhull Memorial became the most discussed event in suffrage circles. Mrs. Woodhull alone among women had stormed the Capitol and had even made an impression on the men who had heard her. She was something new in the suffrage ranks—a siren as well as an advocate. "Bravo!" Susan Anthony wrote to her, as she went west to deliver a lecture, "The New Situation," based on the Woodhull Memorial. Elizabeth Cady Stanton became her champion on the platform, and when Victoria's morality was assailed she quickly came to her defense: "Cast the first stone who is pure among you," she said, arguing that women had crucified Mary Wollstonecraft, Fanny Wright, George Sand, Fanny Kemble, and now men mocked them and said that women were cruel to one another. "If Victoria Woodhull must be crucified, let men drive the spikes that plait the crown of thorns," said Mrs. Stanton. "This woman stands before us today as an able speaker and writer. Her face, manners and conversation all indicate the triumph of the moral, intellectual and spiritual."

Susan Anthony took a similar stand. She said she would welcome all the infamous women in New York if they spoke for freedom, and she added that Mrs. Woodhull's antecedents were as good as those of most of the Congressmen. The women who disapproved of suffrage, under all circumstances, were skeptical of this whitewashing of the daring Mrs. Woodhull. There were other suffrage gatherings at which the air was frosty, skirts were pulled aside, and Mrs. Stanton had to plant Vicky firmly between

Lucretia Mott and herself to proclaim her place in the sun. This was at a meeting held in Apollo Hall in 1871, and in the end it proved to be a triumph for Mrs. Woodhull. Flinging out her arms, she promised "to overthrow this bogus Republican Government" if Congress did not grant women their rights. "We mean treason, we mean secession, we are plotting revolution," she exclaimed. Impressed with her manner and intelligence Horace Greeley wrote in the *Tribune*: "This is a spirit to respect, perhaps to fear, certainly not to be laughed at."

But while the town was still talking about her fiery address, her entire family was suddenly in the middle of a police-court brawl, and much of their early history was brought to light in the papers. Roxanna ran through Murray Hill, shouting and cursing at Colonel Blood who, she insisted, had tried to kill her. He retorted that he had only threatened her with a well-deserved spanking. She took him to court and embarrassed her daughters with her revelations. Wild doings were commonplace in this curious ménage, but so far the Claflin troupe had managed to stay clear of the law in New York. In the police-court proceedings that followed, evidence was offered that Victoria's discarded husband, Dr. Woodhull, was living under her roof, as well as Colonel Blood. She insisted that she had merely done a humane act in taking him in when he arrived penniless, helpless, a total wreck. In fact, to Victoria it seemed one of the most virtuous acts of her life. She announced with dignity: "I was divorced from Dr. Woodhull for reasons which to me were sufficient, but I never was his enemy. He continued to need my friendship and he has had it. My children continued to prize and need his affection and presence, and they have had them."

But Roxanna would not keep quiet. She called heaven to witness that a gang of free lovers lived in the house. Tennie testified that since she was fourteen she had contributed to the support of more than thirty family deadheads. Before the hearing ended Mrs. Woodhull was called a "trance-physician" and a "brazen, snaky adventuress." This incident crystallized much of the shadowy gossip that had surrounded the sisters, and the suffrage

workers who had been won over by Mrs. Woodhull were chagrined to find her in the midst of this vulgar situation. Susan
Anthony was criticized for sponsoring her. The *Independent*
launched an attack, which was promptly reprinted in the Woodhull weekly, with the bold comment that "Daniel Webster and
William Pitt were bon vivants but they were also great statesmen, and if Mrs. Woodhull had valuable ideas, what did her past
history have to do with them?"

She now went further and threatened to publish the private life
histories of a number of prominent men. Her paper became recognized as an instrument of blackmail when veiled threats appeared in its columns. She wrote to the editor of the New York
World on May 22, 1871:

> I know that many of my self-appointed judges and critics
> are deeply tainted with the vices they condemn. I advocate
> free love in its highest, purest sense as the only cure for
> immorality. . . . My judges preach against "free love"
> openly, and practise it secretly. . . . I know of one man, a
> public teacher of eminence, who lives in concubinage with
> the wife of another public teacher of almost equal emi-
> nence. . . . I shall make it my business to analyze some of
> these lives, and will take my chances in the matter of libel
> suits.

Mrs. Woodhull had fired the first arrow in her deadly assault
on the Rev. Henry Ward Beecher as the intimate friend of Elizabeth Tilton, wife of Theodore Tilton, an elder in Plymouth
Church and a well-known man of letters in New York. He was
then editing the *Golden Age,* and Vicky called him in after
writing to the *World* and showed him her letter. They had never
met before. Tilton was a tall, languid poet, with aquiline features
and long auburn hair, who had worked on the *Tribune* and
haunted the parlors of the intellectuals. He had moved from extreme Calvinism to free thinking and was deeply involved in
liberal reform drives. His wife, who had been a Sunday school
teacher at Plymouth Church, had fallen under the spell of Dr.
Beecher. She confessed to Theodore and he forgave her, but he

then proceeded to spread the tale among his women friends. Mrs. Stanton heard it and told Miss Anthony, who had seen the Tiltons quarreling and was easily convinced. Mrs. Woodhull heard the story from Mrs. Stanton, who later bitterly regretted her indiscretion in giving her this weapon of attack. But Vicky also claimed that she heard it from Tilton himself, when they came to be friendly. He later insisted that in seeing so much of her he was only trying to placate her, but Vicky chose to view him as one of her conquests. She saw no obliquity in Dr. Beecher's acts but deplored his hypocrisy, since she preferred to see people following their instincts grandly, gloriously, in the candid Woodhull manner.

Tilton took Vicky to call on his wife, a gesture that did nothing to clear the air, although Elizabeth gave her a book of poems and smiled at her sadly. She had a thin, pointed face and a meek but persistent manner. It was clear to all of them by this time that Mrs. Woodhull meant business and must be mollified. Harriet Beecher Stowe and Catharine Beecher were attacking her openly in the *Christian Union*, and were even circulating letters about her. Vicky wrote to Dr. Beecher, warning him that this must stop, and she tackled Miss Beecher herself during a carriage drive through Central Park. But Catharine was cold and unresponsive, the "hapless victim of malignant spirits." As they parted she said: "Remember, Victoria Woodhull, that I shall strike you dead," to which Vicky replied: "Strike as much and as hard as you please, only don't do it in the dark so that I cannot know who is my enemy."

Tilton wrote an extravagantly flattering sketch about Mrs. Woodhull for the *Golden Age* that did neither of them any good. Due to speak at Steinway Hall on November 19, 1871, Vicky demanded an interview with Dr. Beecher at the last minute, and in a threatening manner asked him to preside at her meeting. She later claimed that the famous pastor, well versed in the histrionics of the pulpit, knelt on the sofa on his knees, took her face in his hands, and with tears streaming down his cheeks, begged for mercy. According to her story, he admitted that he was a moral coward on the subject of free love, though "he agreed with nearly all my views on the question." He asked her for twenty-four hours' warning if she intended to air her charges, and she promptly told him that if she had to go alone on the platform she would begin by telling her audience why he was not there.

In the end Tilton introduced her that night, appearing in impromptu fashion and giving her an ambivalent send-off: "It may be that she is a fanatic; it may be that I am a fool; but, before high heaven, I would rather be both fanatic and fool in one than to be such a coward as would deny a woman the right of free speech." Her subject was "The Principles of Social Freedom, Involving the Education of Free Love, Marriage, Divorce, and Prostitution." Vicky held three thousand people spellbound. She was her most dynamic self, with flaming cheeks and blue eyes ablaze, as she traced the fight for freedom from the sixteenth century and argued that in marriage it was better to break a bad bargain than to keep it. Free love, she said, would be the religion of the future, the natural sequence to social freedom. She was heckled, hissed, and applauded. Her sister, Mrs. Utica Brooker, who detested Vicky, asked her nippily from a box how she would like to come into the world without knowing who her parents were.

"Are you a free lover?" came a shout from the audience.

"Yes! I am a free lover," Vicky shot back.

A fresh tea rose was pinned to the neck of her plain black dress. A watch chain pendant hung from her neck. Large placards were carried around, creating excitement. Circulars were distributed with "Freedom! Freedom! Freedom!" spattered over them.

Dr. Beecher had a brief reprieve, but Tilton had reason to regret this appearance. He lost ground with the Plymouth Church congregation, and many doors were closed to him. His invitations to speak fell off, and his defense of Vicky in the *Golden Age* as the Joan of Arc of the suffrage movement did not help him with his friends who sought the vote. Three months after her Steinway Hall meeting she spoke at the Academy of Music on "The Impending Revolution." She made her usual dramatic appearance, with her hair hanging long on her shoulders and her flounced black dress showing off her tiny waist. As always, she wore a rose close to her neck and presented an appearance of feminine charm. Tennie, with gaiters on her trim ankles, whisked from box to box with murmurs of assent as she listened to her sister's speech. But this time Vicky introduced a sacrilegious note that shocked her audience. "Christ was a Communist of the strictest sort, and so am I, and of the most extreme kind," she exclaimed. She attacked A. T. Stewart, John Jacob Astor, and other men of property.

Vicky made one public gesture after another in 1872, the year in which she ran for election to the Presidency. She and Tennie carried red banners and red ribbons in the memorial demonstration of the International Workingmen's Association to honor the men executed at Versailles by the Thiers Government. Colonel Blood had implanted the theories of Marxism in fertile soil, and Vicky soon published an English translation of the Communist Manifesto. She was under a heavy cloud when she appeared at the National Suffrage Association meeting held in Washington on January 11, 1872, although she looked serene and trim in her blue broadcloth suit and chinchilla coat. The New York *Herald* called this the "Cackling Convention" and noted that Mrs. Woodhull made a speech that "bristled with points and was well delivered."

But she faced fresh ructions with the suffrage forces later that year when she tried to have the People's Party convene jointly with the National Woman's Suffrage Party in Steinway Hall. This time she had overstepped the bounds and Susan Anthony said no. Vicky then tried to swing the suffrage workers over to Apollo Hall, where her own nomination for the Presidency was due to take place. The People's Party, or the National Equal Rights Party as it was also known, had a motley membership of Communists, spiritualists, free thinkers, and suffragists who had deserted Miss Anthony. Andrews drew up the platform, and Vicky promised that from the convention a tide of revolution would go forth and sweep over the whole world. There were sobs, shouts, and high excitement when she was nominated by Judge A. Carter of Cincinnati on May 10, 1872. Frederick Douglass, the Negro reformer, received the nomination for the Vice-Presidency, and Tennie announced that she would run for Congress. Meanwhile, the Victoria League, created by the Woodhull weekly, beat the drums for the candidate, while silence surrounded her elsewhere.

Victoria had always felt that some mystical influence tied her to Queen Victoria, and now she had taken to wearing royal purple. Her parents' choice of a name gave her great cause for optimism. She envisioned a twin sisterhood of Victorias presiding over the United States and Britain, and wrote in her weekly that "as the great Napoleon believed in the star of his destiny . . . I believe also in the fatality of triumph as somehow inherited in my name."

The country was little aware of Victoria's drive for the White House, but the sum of her personal woes mounted as the year wore on. Her magazine had become notorious, with its scandals, its threats, its advocacy of lunatic theories, its strong suggestion of blackmail. The Claflins had to move away from Murray Hill, where they had caused such commotion. The Hoffman House would not take them in. The brokers of Wall Street no longer beamed on the beautiful sisters. They were locked out of their office but climbed over the transom and slept there for several weeks until they finally were accepted at the Gilsey Hotel. They had to find a new office, and on June 22 their weekly was suspended. They had run out of funds and reputation. Nor had the great champion of woman's rights played the game in her own office. A woman compositor complained in another paper that Mrs. Woodhull employed six male clerks and turned her down with the brisk remark: "We can't have our paper spoiled by women."

Clearly something drastic had to be done to whip up their failing fortunes, and Victoria turned again to the Beecher-Tilton situation. For the first time she told the entire story in September

1872, at the meeting of the National Spiritualistic Association in Boston. Her audience was stunned, and the papers did not dare to use it. One suggested that she had slandered a clergyman, and another described her speech as objectionable. She repeated the story to New York reporters, but again the press sat tight on the issue, although the situation had been a matter of dinner-table discussion for months. Finally she revived her weekly and printed the entire tale on November 2, 1872. Little was left to the imagination as Vicky insisted that Dr. Beecher held substantially the same views as she did but had permitted himself to be overawed by public opinion.

"The fault with which I therefore charge him," said Vicky, "is not infidelity to the old ideas, but unfaithfulness to the new. . . . I am prone to denounce him as a poltroon, a coward and a sneak . . . for failing . . . to stand shoulder to shoulder with me and others who are endeavoring to hasten a social regeneration which he believes in." She added that every great man of Dr. Beecher's type "had had in the past, and ever would have, the need for, and the right to, the loving manifestations of many women."

Victoria had launched one of the major social scandals of New York history in eleven columns of sizzling copy based on this unusual triangle. That night she and Tennie and their two ghosts had a celebration, but Anthony Comstock, founder and secretary of the New York Society for the Suppression of Vice, soon clipped their wings. They were arrested on a charge of transmitting obscene literature through the mails, after being rounded up in a carriage on Broadway, sitting haughtily on five hundred copies of their weekly. They went quietly to Ludlow Street Jail, where their bail was set at $8,000. Meanwhile Luther Challis, a former friend of Tennie's, sued them for libel, and he included Blood and Andrews in his charges. William F. Howe, of the firm of Hummel and Howe, was a picturesque figure in court, wearing plaid pantaloons and purple vest as he defended the sisters. Victoria acknowledged that their weekly had been started with money from Vanderbilt, that Blood was the broker, and that she and Tennie were the editors. Tennie was furious when the papers described her as a woman who cursed and smoked vile cigars.

Their weekly caught the high winds of publicity, and the Beecher issue sold for forty dollars a copy. Victoria announced that she would tell the full story at Cooper Institute on January 9, 1873. Comstock took action again by having a letter enclosing money sent to them from Greenwich, Connecticut, for a copy of the controversial issue. They responded at once, and grand jury action followed for sending obscene matter through the mails. Blood was arrested and warned the sisters. Tennie jumped into one washtub and had another clapped over her, and Vicky fled to Jersey City with her bondsman. She stayed there in a hotel until it was time to cross the river and deliver her address.

Cooper Institute was jammed. All around the building were marshals and policemen with orders to arrest Mrs. Woodhull on sight, since no one knew where she was, and she had promised that she would speak. "She can't appear tonight lest she again be thrown into the American Bastille," Laura Cuppy Smith announced from the platform a little prematurely. "Is this a free country? Have we free speech? Have we a free press?"

Soon a muffled figure moved down to the front of the hall. Then Vicky sprang onto the platform, casting from her shoulders the brown plaid shawl that had covered her head and disguised her. She looked flushed and excited, and the audience jumped to its feet and roared. This was Victoria resplendent, her blue eyes blazing, her clear voice repeating what was now a familiar refrain. The policemen and marshals were spellbound as she held her ground for an hour and a half, repeating every detail of the Beecher-Tilton scandal. Comstock, she said, was only Beecher's agent. But when her story was told a marshal moved into action with his writ. He mounted the platform and led Vicky away. Her hour was over.

After a night in jail she appeared again in court. Howe quoted from the Bible, Smollett, Shakespeare, and Richardson in his effort to prove that the story, as presented in the Woodhull weekly, was not obscene. Tennie walked into court, jaunty in a blue jacket with velvet facings and an Alpine hat. She shook hands with Vicky and offered to give herself up, but this time no one wanted her. The verdict was not guilty, and the impression prevailed that the sisters were being persecuted by Beecher supporters. The tide was now turning against him.

Vicky rehashed the story again in her weekly in May, 1873. But things were getting worse for her. The suffragists, who had forgiven her much, were not able to condone her performance in the Beecher-Tilton case. Although the charges against her had been dismissed, they had left an ugly echo. But she stirred up a fresh storm with a speech she made in Vineland, New Jersey. She called it "The Scare-Crow of Sexual Freedom," and it startled her audience. "They say I have come to break up the family," she announced boldly. "I say amen to that with all my heart." She turned to Colonel Blood and said that he was her lover. The colonel took it calmly and smiled faintly when she added: "When I cease to love him I will leave him, though I trust that will never be."

The Scarecrow speech stirred up so much dust that she repeated it in other parts of the country, but she had a cold reception from the American Association of Spiritualists, meeting in Chicago in September, 1873. They, too, had deserted her over the Beecher exposé. And she, in turn, resigned from the organization with mutterings about paraffin hands, fraudulent materializations, and cabinet hoaxes. After this her course grew ever more stormy. She was in poor health during 1875 and 1876, and she did not know which way to turn for money. Tennie appealed to Commodore Vanderbilt, but he had abandoned the sisters and all that they represented. He had switched from faith healers to the authentic world of medicine, and he no longer attended séances.

Victoria now took a fresh tack, interpreting the Bible through sex symbolism, with the aid of Colonel Blood. She appeared on lecture platforms with a Testament in one hand and a white rose in the other. She wore smart gowns with brief trains and draped a lace veil over her shoulders. In this new incarnation she became the champion of marriage, purity, and motherhood. She had been warned that she could not hire a hall unless she eschewed immorality in what she had to say. But in the small towns she was still the scarlet woman, and husbands forbade their wives to attend her lectures. Tennie was the advance agent for her tour. Colonel Blood opened the meetings, and Vicky's daughter, Zula Maud, usually read a poem before her mother spoke.

Her name sprang into the headlines again when the Beecher-Tilton trial began in January, 1875, to end in July with a hung jury. Largely because of Victoria's exposé, and the talk that followed, Tilton had finally sworn out a complaint against Dr. Beecher, charging him with alienating his wife's affections, and demanding damages of $100,000. The pastor was in the White Mountains nursing his hay fever when the news reached him. The case was heard in Brooklyn City Court, and the public was well aware of the details before it came to trial. It ran for 112 days and was one of the most discussed trials in American jurisprudence. Upwards of three thousand persons were turned away from the courthouse each day. Diplomats, politicians, and social leaders jockeyed for places at this three-ring circus, and tickets sold for five dollars apiece.

Both sides were afraid to call Mrs. Woodhull, although Tilton's attorneys subpoenaed her three times, but she insisted on making a brief statement in court. The most brilliant lawyers of the day were in action, and Beecher's side called ninety-five witnesses. All the tricks he practiced so ably in the pulpit were forgotten by Dr. Beecher when confronted with the painful questions put to him, and he was a conspicuously poor witness in his own behalf. His wife, Eunice Beecher, who disliked Tilton intensely, sat grimly watching her husband squirm. Elizabeth, with her sharply pointed profile and dark ringlets, was a mournful figure as she studied the two principals in action. She rose in court and waved a paper, saying that she had an announcement to make. The judge would not let her read it, but it was made public several days later and in it she protested her innocence of the charges brought against her and contradicted her earlier confession. But before long she had recanted again. Dr. Beecher, evasive and contradictory on the stand, sniffed the flowers his admirers sent him and jested with his counsel when he was not testifying. He preached regularly at Plymouth Church while the trial lasted and was at a prayer meeting the night his case went to the jury.

Andrews testified for Tilton and compared Mrs. Woodhull's house to the salon of Madame Roland during the French Revolution. Tilton acknowledged that he had done favors for Mrs. Woodhull, but only to keep her quiet. Mrs. Stanton resented this and wrote sharply to a newspaper that Tilton need not have shirked acknowledging his friendship with Mrs. Woodhull, who had "faced and dared men to call her names that make women shudder, while she chucked principle, like medicine, down their throats."

When all was said and done more than two million words were embedded in the record, fifty-two ballots were taken in eight days, and nothing was proved. Crowds sobbed and cheered on the sidewalk outside his church when Dr. Beecher returned to preach after the jury had disagreed. He then left for his New Hampshire home, where he treated his summer parishioners to a mock Beecher-Tilton trial. His life went on as before, although a shadow had crossed the sun. Victoria later apologized to him for her interference in his affairs. When he died of apoplexy in 1887, one of the largest turnouts in New York history attended his funeral. Tilton left the United States in 1883 and outlived the pastor by twenty years. In a shabby room on the Ile Saint-Louis he wrote poems and novels and became a familiar figure playing chess at the Café de la Régence. His wife went on to a lonely existence with one of her daughters.

Victoria's weekly suspended publication in June, 1876, and ironically enough the advocate of free love dismissed Blood from her life for infidelity. Roxanna became a Roman Catholic, and Vicky turned into something of a *religieuse*. When Commodore Vanderbilt died in 1877 the impression prevailed that she and Tennie were paid by members of his family to leave the country. Both were in straits, and Vicky was so ill that she could scarcely mount a platform, but a new life opened up for her in England, and she turned her back forever on the irregularities of the past. She lectured on "the Human Body, the Temple of God" and other subjects with the social hygiene slant of a later period. Her approach had changed, and she renounced free love, communism, and sundry other causes that she had espoused, but she could not altogether obliterate her past.

When John Biddulph Martin, a banker and scholar, heard her lecture he was so impressed that he decided to make her his wife, but her past sins were resurrected in the press and several years elapsed before they were married. It was all too easy for the British correspondents to unearth the sensational facts of Victoria's life, and the Martin family put every obstacle in the way of this union. Their son was well-off and of excellent social standing. He had taken both classical honors and athletic trophies at Oxford, and he was still a strikingly handsome man when Victoria met him. She found him kind and considerate after her life of turmoil.

But instead of lying low she answered the newspaper charges and drew more fire. In January, 1881, she brought out one issue of her old journal for the express purpose of appealing to the press to run down her traducers. Threatening legal action, she denied that she had written the Beecher article, but the discarded Colonel Blood did not uphold her in this contention. He insisted that she had written her own lectures and books, and was entirely capable of sustained composition. Vicky now turned on both her ghosts. Blood traveled for a time with a show, functioning as a hypnotist. He was a barker at Coney Island, did newspaper work in Maine, and finally went to Africa to dig for gold.

The glow that had at first surrounded the suffrage queens from across the sea faded under these attacks, but Victoria, well aware of the prize within her reach, did everything she could to push through the marriage. She drew up an ancestral history for herself that went back to the early kings of England. By degrees she won over the Martins and was established in Hyde Park Gate as Mrs. John Biddulph Martin. She now played the role of great lady for which she had always hankered, entertaining on a lavish scale and scattering bounty. Victoria had become austere in looks and bearing, whereas Tennie remained the china doll, with big blue eyes and fluttering manners. She, too, married well in the worldly sense. Her husband was Sir Francis Cook, an importer who collected antique rugs as a hobby. Although wealthier than Martin, his family was not as solidly entrenched in England, but he had a large estate and considerable prestige in Portugal, where he was known as the Viscount de Montserrat.

Both sisters now had substantial homes, unlimited money at their command, and admiring husbands. Roxanna, faded, heavily powdered, and much subdued, lived with Tennie, who had not entirely divorced herself from the familiar spirit world. "Buck," aged eighty-nine, had died at the time of Tennie's marriage. Dr. Woodhull's end, from alcoholism and drug addiction, had been a miserable one. But few traces of their past life were evident in the two fashionably turned out women who joined in the afternoon parade in Hyde Park, using fine horses and the smartest of victorias. Although they were not received in the inner circle, they had a certain degree of social standing, and visiting Americans shunned them more than the English did. But from time to time Martin was outraged when certain women refused to sit with his wife at dinner parties, or checked her name off charity lists. Tennie gave large garden parties at Richmond, a ravishing sight herself in gossamer gowns and wide-brimmed hats. She was aging gracefully, if also somewhat frivolously. In Portugal she was received by everyone of account, for Sir Francis Cook was known there as a philanthropist.

The publication of *A Biography of Henry Ward Beecher* in 1888 caused a fresh flurry of talk. The Beechers were well known in England, and in this instance Victoria was labeled a black-mailer by the authors, William C. Beecher and the Rev. Samuel Scovill. Things became so uncomfortable for the two sisters that their husbands offered a large reward for information about those who were defaming them. This had little effect, except to cause more talk and raise more questions. Finally they took to publishing pamphlets about themselves that were both defensive and laudatory. In 1892 the Martins visited the United States, and while there they asked the help of the New York police in rounding up the culprits. In the course of this investigation Victoria's husband learned many things that he had not known about her, but this did not lessen his great devotion or weaken his efforts to clear her name. The revelations about Tennie were even more disturbing, but the sisters dusted it all off as a tissue of lies.

Victoria's chief objective on this trip was to run again for the Presidency, feeling that this might improve her status in Britain. Her "humanitarian platform" included better housing, labor tribunals for arbitration, tribunals of health, free courts of justice for the poor, analysis of impure foods and liquors, woman suffrage, revenue and tariff reform, encouragement of arts and sciences, and, finally, the "aristocracy of blood."

Victoria announced that she had come to America to lead the Woman's Movement and to arrange for a national convention in Chicago at which she would be nominated for the Presidency. She revived the Victoria Leagues and stressed the humanities rather than suffrage. "I am no fanatic," she announced. "We can appeal to man through his brain and his sense of justice." But the spirit forces were still at work in Vicky and she added: "I am a woman of destiny. It has been known to me for more than a score of years that in the year 1892 I should be chosen to govern my people."

But Chicago gave the Martins a hot welcome. A blazing attack on the Claflin sisters, unearthing every ancient charge against them, was made by one of the newspapers. Martin struck back with threats of libel until Vicky, more experienced in such matters, persuaded him that it would be useless to fight back in the courts. They sailed for England, leaving a trail of indignant protests that Victoria should presume to speak for American womanhood. But they soon returned and fifty women nominated her for President and Mrs. Mary L. Stowe for Vice-President, in the Willard Hotel in Washington. Lucy Stone indignantly denied that the National Woman Suffrage Association was behind this nomination. She said that she did not know one of the women backing Mrs. Martin.

The Martins took a house at 142 West Seventieth Street, New York, and Victoria gave out interviews on what she would do in the White House, as her husband listened admiringly. But the hailstorm of protests continued. Frances Willard said that it was her own business if Victoria wished to be President, but her name should not be linked with such saints as Susan Anthony. However, she gave Victoria her due when she added: "Victoria Woodhull has stood more pelting than she deserved. I was right glad when she married an English gentleman and had someone to defend and care for her."

On election day Victoria took her defeat with equanimity. Not one vote was cast for her, and by this time she was ready to admit that she had not really expected to be elected. She worried more about the social snubs she received than she did about her political defeat. She was soon on the platform in Carnegie Hall speaking on "The Scientific Propagation of the Human Race." She had become an enthusiast for stirpiculture, the breeding of special races, or the "aristocracy of the blood." A great crowd gathered to hear her speak and to study Victoria Woodhull in her new guise. She wore purple and had violets at her throat, instead of the rose that had once been her trade-mark. It was the first time in seventeen years that her voice had been heard from an American platform. She had aged visibly and now used glasses as she read her manuscript. Her boast that twenty thousand people had waited in the streets of London to hear this lecture had little effect on her audience. Her talk fell flat. She was upset as the meeting ended, and her husband insisted that she cancel the tour she had planned. Instead they went on to Chicago, where he served as a British Commissioner at the Columbian Exposition of 1893. After her earlier experience there Victoria dreaded a return trip, but this time the papers let her alone. They had done their worst.

On her return to England she caught the headlines again by bringing a unique suit against the British Museum for harboring books and pamphlets unfavorable to her. In February, 1894, she and her husband took action against the Museum trustees to recover damages for libel and to seek an injunction against the distribution of two books dealing with the Beecher-Tilton case. There was much hilarity in the British press over this, the first libel action ever brought against the British Museum. Sir Charles Russell, a trustee of the Museum, appeared for the defense, but he found Mrs. Martin a fluent and tricky witness. She brought her ancient spirit, Demosthenes, into the proceedings when he questioned her about her spiritualistic practices. And she took time to expound her newest theories on stirpiculture. The prestige of the British Museum remained undisturbed and the verdict was for the defendants, with costs.

At this point Victoria decided to write her autobiography, and the first chapter appeared in pamphlet form, but it never went any further. She began:

> Sitting here today in this north room of 17 Hyde Park Gate, London—dreary, smoky, foggy, insulated as you are in the customs and prejudices of centuries—I am thinking with all the bitterness of my woman's nature how my life has been warped and twisted out of shape by this environment, until, as I catch a glimpse of my haggard face in the mirror opposite, I wonder whether I shall be able to pen the history of this stormy existence.

This would suggest that Victoria was not completely at peace in England. The sisters simply could not stay out of trouble. Their next complication was a breach of promise suit brought against Sir Francis Cook by an elderly woman named Mrs. Holland. Victoria was dragged into the case, for she was charged with buying love letters from the plaintiff for thirty pounds. There was further trouble over the *Humanitarian*, a publication launched by her in 1892, to be published simultaneously in London and New York. Her daughter, Zula Maud, was associate editor, and Victoria wished her to run a literary salon at the house she shared on West Seventy-second Street with Dr. and Mrs.

Charles S. Welles. This combination soon broke up, and court battles followed over smashed possessions and failure to pay rent. Mrs. Welles was a niece of Victoria's, and she and Tennie were tired of staking relatives. The *Humanitarian*, which was Mrs. Martin's mouthpiece, was published until 1901. Although it dealt with social issues it avoided the sensationalism of *Woodhull & Claflin's Weekly*. Vicky had renounced communism, saying: "I am convinced that the internationalists and communists whom we have so welcomed are only adventurers, who ruin the laborers with their big philanthropic talk."

Before his death in 1897 Martin, by that time president of the Royal Statistical Society, wrote *The Grasshopper of Lombard Street*, a history of his family's bank. Victoria was not with him when he died of pneumonia at Las Palmas in the Canary Islands. He had been sent there for the sun after an earlier illness, and it was his first separation from Vicky in many years. His friends agreed that he was worn down from the constant strain of defending his wife and fighting her endless battles. But theirs had been a harmonious marriage in spite of all the trouble that the Claflin sisters had brought into the staid Martin orbit. Inheriting a fortune of $850,000, Victoria gave up her London house and lived at her country place, Bredon's Norton in Worcestershire.

Here she lived the life of the lady bountiful, fostering the Flower Show, pushing the Froebel kindergarten system, installing trained kindergarten teachers in the village school, staging Christmas parties with carols sung by the village choir, and arranging lectures and other entertainment in an old barn on her property that she turned into a hall. Her surroundings were idyllic, and Victoria made the most of them. She contributed generously to the purchase of Sulgrave Manor, the home of George Washington's family in England, and bought antiques from time to time for its various rooms. There were occasions when she spread the impression that she alone was responsible for the purchase of this historic house.

Zula Maud finally settled with her mother, and Victoria no longer made trips to America, although Tennie continued to cross the Atlantic at every opportunity. Her husband died in 1901, and she was so upset over the whispers that she had murdered him that she applied for an order to have his body exhumed, but Sir Francis' relatives persuaded her to abandon this plan. Tennie inherited the house at Richmond and approximately a quarter of a million dollars. Sir Francis had given her a great deal of money during his lifetime and, like her sister, she had established schools, sent girls to convents, and made provision for clothing the poor and caring for the sick. When she proposed building a home for unmarried mothers at Richmond, the townspeople objected, and Tennie promptly announced that she would found a bank instead. She called it "Lady Cook & Company," but she did not repeat the smashing success she had had on Wall Street, and before long it closed. England was scarcely ready for a lady banker. Victoria was impatient over these whims of Tennie's and thought her undignified, particularly when she paid a visit to Ludlow Street Jail on one of her trips to America. But Vicky made a return trip of her own to Homer, Ohio, a great lady from across the sea. However, her visit was marked by restraint, whereas Tennie took reporters with her when she visited the jail and some of her other old haunts. It was a question which sister hankered more for publicity; both had acquired the headline habit.

They were not in close sympathy in their later years. Victoria had become stately and conservative in looks and dress. Tennie continued to wear ruffled pastels through the English rains, and she used an excess of make-up. With money and a title, she had managed to pick up a new set of friends in the United States and circulated freely among suffrage workers. Tennie even managed an interview with President Theodore Roosevelt on behalf of the suffrage cause, and she drove around Washington with "Votes for Women" banners on display. She took up the prevailing fad for collecting art, and posed as a connoisseur. Like Vicky, she talked eugenics, which was becoming a fashionable topic, and advocated the legal recognition of illegitimate children.

Both sisters threw themselves into patriotic effort when the

First World War began. Lady Cook again visited the United States, this time to lecture on stricken Belgium. She tried unsuccessfully to see President Wilson and at every opportunity advocated an amazon army in khaki. The Flaming Twenties were getting under way when Tennie died in 1923. From that time on Victoria, full of fears, slept each night in a chair lest she die if she went to bed. Strange furies drove her as her old spiritualistic fancies took the ascendancy again. Day after day she motored madly through the countryside, lying prone in her car, and urging her chauffeur to greater speed. She was interested in aviation and through the Women's Aerial League of Great Britain she offered $5,000 to the first man or woman to fly the Atlantic. Victoria lived to know that Charles A. Lindbergh had performed this feat, for she was found dead in her chair on June 10, 1927, three weeks after his dramatic landing at Le Bourget. She was ninety years old and her history had been strange beyond belief. By her own wish she was cremated, and her ashes were scattered at sea. Her fortune went to her daughter, Zula Maud. Byron had died years earlier. In his memorial sermon the rector of Bredon said that the parish had been privileged "to have one of the world's greatest personalities among us." But in the United States she was remembered more for her transgressions than for her courage and good deeds.

Mrs. Jack Gardner

In the words of Henry James, her life was a "dense splendid tissue of adventure." Isabella Stewart Gardner lived it to the full, the inspiration of famous men, a discriminating patron of the arts, a cinquecento figure among the Puritans of Boston. She lived from 1840 to 1924 and left her own romantic memorial in Fenway Court, her Venetian palace in Back Bay. Ninety thousand visitors pass through it each year, and by the terms of her will everything is as it was in the days of Mrs. Gardner—even to the fresh violets placed daily before Giorgione's "Christ Bearing the Cross," her favorite, if not the best, of her paintings.

Over the entrance is her motto *C'est mon Plaisir*, and traces of her imperious will are evident in her creation, with its mingling of Roman, Byzantine, Romanesque, and Gothic influences. The central courtyard blazes with seasonal flowers, and nasturtium vines dangle in long festoons from balconies. John Singer Sargent's famous painting of her revives her image for posterity.

Without beauty, she was one of the great romantics of her era. Not born to the Puritan tradition, she lived freely and willfully among the austere. For years she scandalized Bostonians, but by the turn of the century the magnificence of her gestures, the importance of her acquisitions, and her own dominating personality had washed away the memory of her eccentricities. She ranked with the great collectors and had become a legend—Mrs. Jack Gardner of Boston, well known to the art lovers of two continents. She was as famous for her friends as for her collection of Italian masterpieces. There were few celebrities in contemporary art and letters whom she did not meet at one time or another, and she chose to back and encourage struggling young artists, giving them financial aid and promoting them with finesse. Established writers valued her judgment, and Henry James read some of his manuscripts to her before they went to his publishers. F. Marion Crawford also sought her advice and studied Dante with her. She backed Bernard Berenson in his student days and he, in turn, helped her to assemble some of the finest Italian art in the United States. Sargent found her a constant inspiration and was her devoted admirer for a lifetime.

Although a brilliant conversationalist in her own right, Mrs. Gardner was a quiet and responsive listener when artists discussed their work with her. She could lift their spirits when they felt depressed, and her own vitality conveyed itself to those around her. She had many male friends but wasted little time on women, although those she liked best had achievement behind them— Ellen Terry, Edith Wharton, Nellie Melba, Emma Eames, and Julia Ward Howe, among others.

Mrs. Gardner was plain to the point of ugliness, with a face suggestive of her Scottish ancestry. Her sandy hair was laced with red; her blue-gray eyes had a blurred look and were not symmetrically set in her blunt, combative face. She had a cold, distant look, and Sargent always had trouble painting her rudely fashioned mouth, as he did her eyes. Her delicate skin flushed easily, and her figure was superb. She moved with ease and grace, and her Worth gowns played up her curves in the era of the hourglass figure. Artists commented on the beauty of her shoulders and arms. In 1908 she went walking on Boston Common in a sheath so tight that a policeman came to her rescue when a crowd gathered to watch her. Dr. William Sturgis Bigelow, a good friend and famous surgeon who exchanged witty notes with her, wrote jestingly on one occasion: "There seems to be no alternative but to sit on the top of Oak Hill and think of the way your dress fits." He called her a "gloom-dispeller, corpse reviver and general chirker up."

There were so many facets to Mrs. Gardner's personality, so many startling incidents in her life history, that she never ceased to make headlines. She could be both ruthless and extravagantly kind; her strong nature allowed no compromise or evasion. She was widely quoted as saying that the only person she envied was the Empress of China, who could give the order "Cut off his head." Sometimes those who worked for her could almost feel the ax. Actually, her life was full of contradictions—of anger and remorse, of worldliness and piety, of opulence and, at the end, excessive frugality. She was a snob and also a penitent, equally at home with kings and laborers, with poets and peasants. There was a strong strain of earthy strength in her own nature, although she insisted that she had the blood of kings in her veins. Mrs. Gardner claimed descent from Mary Queen of Scots and found genealogical proof that her family belonged to the Invernahyle branch of the Appin Stuarts. She cherished Stuart relics, and there were times when she dressed like Mary, usually for Christmas mass in her private chapel at Fenway Court. She felt a strong affinity for the Isabellas of Spain and Italy, and Berenson catered to this fancy in the choice of some of her paintings. Her friends had many names for her—Donna Isabella, Ysabella, Piccolina, Bianca, Queen, Wonderful Lady, or the Presence. Mrs. Howe's name for her was Kepoura, Greek for gardener.

Mrs. Gardner lived three lives—as a delicate but enterprising girl brought up in conventional surroundings; as a dynamic woman who flowered in an atmosphere of art, travel, love, and pleasure; as an aging recluse counting pennies, all passion spent, living on her memories but still as bright as quicksilver in her mental responses, even after she had a stroke and was carried around Fenway Court in her Venetian sedan chair. Her mother was Adelia Smith, whose ancestors came to Boston from England in 1650. Her father, David Stewart, settled in New York before he was seventeen and in time built up a fortune, first as an importer of fine linens, then with iron and mining interests in Pennsylvania. Her paternal grandfather, James Stewart, was a Scot who married a Connecticut girl named Isabella Tod. Through him Mrs. Gardner was descended from two early governors of Connecticut—Thomas Welles and Robert Treat.

The Stewarts lived on University Place in New York, and there Isabella was born on April 14, 1840. She had a sister Adelia, who died at the age of twelve, and two brothers, David and James. They passed their summers at their maternal grandmother's farm in Jamaica, Long Island, where Isabella ran about like a small fury, whipping imaginary horses. Her childhood pleasure in driving and lashing others was never outgrown, in the opinion of Morris Carter, her official biographer. In her old age she recalled running off to the circus and being caught by the family butler as she crawled under the canvas. "Don't spoil a good story by telling the truth," she was apt to comment when one of the apocryphal tales about her was brought to her attention. If she liked it, the story stood uncontradicted.

Isabella attended Miss Mary Okill's School and then St. Mary's Convent, where she stood apart from her fellow students because of her love for sports. She swam, rode well, and liked athletic contests. All through life she disciplined her body and took strenuous gymnastic exercises before this custom had become fashionable. Her interest in art was first in evidence when her parents took her to Paris for a year at a finishing school. One of her classmates was Julia Gardner, a quiet Boston girl who was drawn at once to the fascinating Isabella Stewart. All four parents were with the girls. Their fathers, both rich and successful men, became close friends. But Mrs. Gardner had little in common with Mrs. Stewart. She was Catherine Elizabeth Peabody of the Salem Peabodys, where the tradition prevailed that there you were a Peabody or a nobody.

When the Stewarts moved on to Italy, Isabella studied Italian with Ida Agassiz, who later became Mrs. Henry Lee Higginson and was always one of her closest friends. They saw Venice together for the first time. Isabella was entranced with the Italian scene and after going through the galleries of the Poldi-Pezzoli Palace in Milan, she said to Ida in her positive way: "I mean to make a collection of the best pictures in the world and hang them in a palace worthy of them."

On their return home in 1858 the Stewarts settled in a house at 27 East Twenty-second Street. Isabella was invited to visit the Gardners in Boston, where she and Julia skated, went sleighing, danced, played Fox and Geese, and attended simple tea parties. Jack Gardner, her friend's brother, fell madly in love with her the moment he saw her. He proposed as they walked by the river on a bitterly cold day. She told him that he would have to follow her to New York for his answer, which he did. Both families approved, and the young pair were married in Grace Church on April 10, 1860, with Amy Gerry and Julia Gardner among the bridesmaids. Although this romance was one of propriety from beginning to end, when Mrs. Gardner's dashing ways became more familiar to Bostonians the story spread that she had jumped through a boarding-school window and eloped with Jack Gardner.

From the start her husband adored her and viewed her impulsive acts as part of her charm. When things got snarled up, as they sometimes did, he was always there to restore order and redeem his beloved Isabella. He was a proper Bostonian in every sense of the word, a young man of impeccable ancestry whose family fortune had been made in the East Indian trade. Ellery Sedgwick, editor of the *Atlantic Monthly*, observed that Mrs. Gardner "lent an unaccustomed shimmer to a staid and respected

family, solid as the rock of Beacon Hill. . . . Among the ladies of
the Renaissance you might have found her exact parallel, but
hardly, I think, since. . . ."

This impression was confirmed in 1899 by Henry James, who
said of her that she had everything, she did everything, and she
enjoyed everything. "I think of you," he wrote, "as a figure on a
wondrous cinquecento tapestry—and of myself as one of the
small quaint accessory domestic animals, a harmless worm, or the
rabbit who is very proud and happy to be in the same general
composition with you." But her success in Boston was hard won
and took time. From the moment she and her husband settled at
152 Beacon Street she was regarded as an exotic, a discordant
note in the charmed circle of the self-righteous. Isabella Gardner
did nothing to reassure them. It was clear at once that she had
wit, intelligence, and vivacity, but her health was poor and she
spent her mornings in bed—a pampering of self quite alien to the
New England spirit. She did not welcome the chance caller, an
inhospitable touch not understood in these surroundings.

When she drove to Danvers to visit the Peabodys she was so
lacking in strength that at times she had to be carried in and out
of the house. Jack's relatives decided that he had married an
invalid. Meanwhile she played backgammon by the hour with
him and charmed him with her clever conversation. She had no
small talk but she was a shrewd observer of men and world
affairs, and she showed keen interest in her husband's business. In
the summer of 1863, while the Civil War raged and the antislavery agitation was strong in Boston, she bore a son who resembled her closely. Her pride in him was such that she showed him
off in their bay window and took him out of his cot at midnight
to display him to friends. The two Gardners watched the torch-
light procession for Lincoln in November, 1864, but life clouded
over for them soon after, when little Jackie died before reaching
the age of two. For years afterward Mrs. Gardner went into
retreat on the anniversary of his death. She never referred to him,
but she kept a miniature with a lock of his hair on her father's
writing table.

For the next two years she lived obscurely, ill and deeply depressed. Finally she was sent abroad for her health in the spring of 1867. She was taken to the wharf in an ambulance and was carried aboard ship on a mattress. A tour of Europe seemed to revive her completely, and she returned to Boston with her health restored and her spirits more exuberant than they had ever been. All of a sudden she had become strong, vital, and reckless, and soon she was startling her husband's friends with her daring ways. She ran a salon on Beacon Street after they bought the adjoining house, No. 150, and cut through the walls, creating an effect of different levels linked by small flights of stairs. Her drawing room was furnished with eighteenth-century French pieces, and the walls were bright yellow, diffusing light on the dingiest day. Jack Gardner was a knowing host, and he chose to arrange the dinners and engage the servants. But when his wife walked into a room she took over. Her personality was overpowering. She filled her bay windows with a display of flowers so distinctive that people walked past especially to view this show.

Mrs. Gardner used the smart Binder carriages, narrow and luxurious, with small black horses always driven at high speed by Deacon, her coachman. She had two liveried footmen on the box, which was one more than the other ladies of Boston approved. And when visiting Dr. Bigelow one day after attending a symphony concert she ordered her driver to run the sleigh over the sidewalk and close to the front door, so that her gown and shoes would not be wet by the snow. Her Worth creations and her jewels were much discussed, particularly the two large diamonds on gold springs that rose some inches from her reddish hair and glimmered like antennae as she moved. These shimmering headlights were the most talked-of jewels in Boston. She called them "The Rajah" and "The Light of India," and she was wearing them one night as she drove to Mrs. Howe's through a crowd of strikers. The mob closed in on her carriage, and Mrs. Gardner realized that her diamonds might be an irritant to the angry men. But suddenly a large hand was held up to hold them back, and she heard a voice saying: "Don't be afraid, Mrs. Jack, I'll see you get through all right."

She leaned forward and asked who he was. "John L. Sullivan," said the warrior. After that she was to know several prize fighters, and she always had great admiration for outstanding athletes. She enjoyed fights and attracted almost as much attention as the star of the evening when she sat in a box and watched James Corbett give an exhibition bout in a Boston theater. When Eugene Sandow was the man of the hour, exhibiting his bulging muscles, Mrs. Gardner walked up to him and felt his biceps, to the horror of other Boston ladies who were content to look. But Mrs. Potter Palmer did the same thing in Chicago. Isabella was a baseball fan and appeared at times with a Red Sox cap perched on her hair. All through her life she was interested in horse racing and in 1923, a year before her death, she clipped pictures of the international race at Belmont Park when Zev defeated Papyrus, winner of that year's Kentucky Derby. But she could not endure cruelty to animals, and she cowered on the floor of her box at a bull fight in Spain. Although fearless in most respects, she had a horror of the dark, which became so intense in her last years that she would not lie down at night, but slept sitting up in a chair. She always snapped on a flashlight when lights went out in the theater. If this was impossible, she walked out into the corridor.

Mrs. Gardner swung from feasting and high living to penitence and humility. She was a *religieuse* as well as a worldling. On her fourth wedding anniversary in 1864 she was confirmed at Emmanuel Church by the Rt. Rev. Manton Eastburn, Bishop of Massachusetts. From then on she favored high Anglican ritual and eventually, in her own private chapel at Fenway Court, there was little to distinguish the services from those of the Roman Catholic faith. She went into retreat after her most worldly flings, and Bostonians were somewhat skeptical of her annual gesture during Lent. It was her custom to drive to the Church of the Advent in the Gardner variation of sackcloth and ashes, go down on her hands and knees and scrub the stone steps. Afterwards she handed the bucket to her footman and drove off. But this act of devotion did not keep some of the dowagers from telling their daughters that Mrs. Gardner was "fast." Well aware of their attitude, she remarked, when asked to subscribe to the Charitable Eye and Ear

Infirmary, that she did not think there was a charitable eye or ear in Boston.

One of her most discussed acts was hiring a locomotive when she and her husband missed a train out of Boston while on their way to join a coaching party on the North Shore. Their fellow guests had given them up when the toot of a whistle drew all eyes to a solitary locomotive steaming into view. Mrs. Gardner stepped down from the cab, fresh as a daisy in a white Paris gown and swinging a ruffled parasol. Her husband catered to her impulses, even when he thought them childish. After the death of his parents they used the Gardner country place in Brookline, known as Green Hill. Mrs. Gardner had large trees cut down to make way for an Italian garden, with a baroque statue of Neptune and other statuary displayed in the grounds. There were wide walks with pergolas and seasonal flowers massed for color effect. At the Alhambra, their farm in Beverly, she sought to reproduce a courtyard of Seville. The low stone wall around the lawn was smothered in nasturtiums, the flower that she chose to use so effectively in Fenway Court. Many of her ideas for gardens, as in art, were picked up on her travels.

"It was Mrs. Gardner's rule to select and acquire the best," Morris Carter commented on this period. "If she were attending a polo game, she would be escorted to her seat by the best player of the day, the best tenor of the opera, the best painter, the best art critic, the best judge of horses—these, each for a special purpose, were her friends." She had already chosen one of the best businessmen of Boston for a husband, and Richard S. Fay, a family friend and popular man about town, became her favorite cotillion partner, since he was the best dancer. She had taken dancing lessons in Paris before her marriage, and when she settled down on Beacon Street she haunted the studio of Lorenzo Papanti to perfect her steps. In her early married days she arrived at the City Assemblies with her arms filled with flowers from admirers. When other young matrons followed suit, she walked in with none, for instinctively she was the individualist.

Like other Americans of the period who had wealth, the Gardners went abroad with regularity. In 1874 they wintered in Egypt, and in passing through London Jack Gardner bought Isabella her first string of pearls. Each time they went abroad he bought another until she had seven, which she sometimes wore in a long rope that fell to her knees. Her pearls, in course of time, became almost as famous as her paintings. While touring Europe she picked up some stained glass and objects of art, the start of her collection. Although always deathly sick at sea, living solely on champagne and Huntley & Palmer biscuits, Mrs. Gardner revived quickly when she stepped ashore, and did thoughtful, meticulous sightseeing. "Busy Ella," her husband called her, as he followed her over cobblestones and through miles of corridors in picture galleries and museums. Long before she began to buy her masterpieces she had filled albums with reproductions of the pictures she liked best so that in the long run she had a working knowledge of what she wanted.

While they were abroad in 1874 Jack's brother, Joseph Gardner, died, and his three orphan sons came to live with Jack and Isabella on Beacon Street. After that Mrs. Gardner was seen at concerts, in church, and at sports events with her young nephews. She read the classics to them and encouraged them to ride, sail, and swim. Two of the boys toured England and France with the Gardners in 1879. Henry James took them all to Hatfield House, and he introduced them to Edward Burne-Jones, who was then living in the house where Samuel Richardson wrote *Clarissa Harlowe*. Mrs. Gardner's visits to Henry James became almost annual events, and he took her to the studio of John Singer Sargent, a significant meeting. Sargent, in turn, led her to James Abbott McNeill Whistler, and she bought some of his early pastels.

In 1883 the Gardners went around the world, driving to the dock in Boston behind two carriages smothered in flowers from Isabella's admirers. The Orient gave her fresh vistas, and in after years she dwelled most often on her trip to Cambodia as the most exciting episode in all her travels. From Saigon they took bullock carts to Cambodia, where she ate her first peacock flesh and

Nellie Bly ready for her trip around the world in 1889. (New York Public Library)

Portrait of Madame Jumel with grandniece and grandnephew. By Alcide Ércole, 1854. (Courtesy, Jumel Mansion)

Aaron Burr and Madame Jumel, who became Mrs. Aaron Burr in 1833. (New York Public Library)

dame Jumel in early girlhood. Engrav- by Saint-Mémin, captioned: Madame de Croix.

e Jumel Mansion in colonial days. (New rk Public Library)

Hetty Green in the familiar garb of "The Witch of Wall Street." (New York Public Library)

Hetty Green in meditative mood. (Brown Brothers)

Home of Mr. and Mrs. Edward Henry Green (Hetty Green) at Bellows Falls, Vermont. (New York Public Library)

Hetty Green at the marriage of her daughter Sylvia to Matthew Astor Wilks in 1909. (Brown Brothers)

Hetty Green with her Skye terrier, Dewey. (Brown Brothers)

The Fox sisters—Margaret (left) and Kate—and the house in Hydesville, near Rochester, where they first heard mysterious rappings.

Sample of Kate Fox's "spirit writing," a communication that she claimed came from Benjamin Franklin.

Lady Cook during her aging days in England.

Victoria Woodhull, first woman to run for the Presidency of the United States. (New York Public Library)

Victoria Woodhull nominated for President, Apollo Hall, New York, May 10, 1872. (New York Public Library)

Mrs. Jack Gardner in her twenties. (Copy of a photograph in the Boston Athenaeum. Courtesy Isabella Stewart Gardner Museum)

John Singer Sargent portrait of Mrs. Gardner. (Isabella Stewart Gardner Museum)

Courtyard of the Isabella Stewart Gardner Museum in Boston showing part of the Venetian palace and statuary in the garden. (Isabella Stewart Gardner Museum)

Carry Nation, aged eighteen.
(Yale Photographic Service)

Carry Nation with Bible.
(Brown Brothers)

"I Cannot Tell A Lie. . . . I Did It With My Little Hatchet!", a cartoon in the Utica *Globe*, February 16, 1901.

Isadora Duncan, 1910. (From Irma Duncan papers, Dance Collection, New York Public Library)

Sketch of Isadora Duncan by Jules Grand'Jouan. (Dance Collection, New York Public Library)

Isadora Duncan in 1912 with her children—Patrick (left) and Deirdre—who were drowned in the Seine. (From Irma Duncan papers, Dance Collection, New York Public Library)

Irma Duncan, Isadora Duncan and Sergei Essenine on Isadora's and Sergei's wedding day, 1922. (From Irma Duncan papers, Dance Collection, New York Public Library)

Aimee Semple McPherson preaching in Angelus Temple, Los Angeles.
(New York Public Library)

Postcard showing Aimee Semple McPherson arising from the sea, widely sold after her disappearance in 1926. (New York Public Library)

Angelus Temple, where she presided as a noted evangelist. (New York Public Library)

Mrs. Frank Leslie, publisher and noted journalist. (New York Public Library)

Mrs. Frank Leslie at her desk on Fifth Avenue in the 1890's. Bust of Frank Leslie on mantelpiece. (New York Public Library)

played after dinner with a tiger—"a dear, wild, savage little thing." The King of Cambodia received her—"I, in my dirty old white and black foulard and black lace bonnet, but to make a glitter, my diamond and pearl dog collar, my two white diamonds in my bonnet strings, and my yellow diamond on the front of my dress!" she wrote home. In Java she wore native dress and from then on was insistent when she entertained Orientals—as she often did—that they wear their native costume. Her footmen would be similarly garbed, serving them the dishes of their countries. The religious rites had fascinated her and in her later years she deplored the Americanization of the Orient. On their way back from the East the Gardners stopped in Venice. This was Isabella's first visit there since her school days, but she was never again to go abroad without returning to her adored city.

Her walks, drives, and dinners in London and Paris with Henry James in the early 1880's gave him the "happy faith that we shall Europeanize together again in the future." On January 29, 1881, he wrote to her: "Look out for my next big novel; it will immortalize me. After that, some day, I will immortalize you." In the following year he was touring the United States. So was Oscar Wilde, and James wrote to Mrs. Gardner from Washington that he had gone to a dinner party there and had found "the repulsive and fatuous Oscar Wilde, whom, I am happy to say, no one was looking at."

James considered Washington a village in the material sense, but "socially and conversationally bigger and more varied . . . than anything we have." In some respects it seemed "too rustic and familiar." He was struck by the energetic type of man to be found in the capital, although few were "accomplished gentlemen." When he met President Arthur at a dinner given by Secretary of State James G. Blaine he thought him a "good fellow— even attractive" and also a gentleman. James took note of his well-tailored coat and carefully trimmed whiskers, but since "he told me none of the secrets of state I couldn't judge of him as a ruler of men." James considered New York both brilliant and beautiful. He dined out several times a week and found the talk and the entrées equally good. His dinner partners often asked him about Mrs. Gardner and her original ways. "I gave a sketch—with a few exquisite touches—and then they sighed and said to each other: 'Ah, if we only knew how to be like that!' But they don't," he wrote to Donna Isabella.

Back in the Reform Club on Pall Mall, with the "black broth of the London atmosphere" around him, he wrote tenderly to her of their farewell before he sailed: "That final interview—that supreme farewell—will however always be one of the most fascinating incidents of life. I think with extraordinary tenderness of those two pretty little evenings when I read you my play."

The play in question was *Daisy Miller*. Mrs. Gardner went through every phase of Henry James's agony over the production of this play on both sides of the Atlantic. "Poor little Daisy Miller, in the comic form, has been blighted by cold theatrical breath, and will probably never be acted," he wrote after this visit to America. "She will in that case only be published. But she had two evenings' success and that amply satisfies your very faithful friend." However, the play was produced eventually with success in London and New York. In 1891 he refused the "most glittering American offers in order to elicit still more glittering ones on the basis of the triumph in *this* place."

James freely exposed his special sensitivities to Mrs. Gardner and wrote to her of the lacerating pain he suffered over printers' errors in the publication of his magazine material. A misplaced comma was torture to him. He also worried about the criticism he encountered for alienating himself from the American scene. After breakfasting in Paris with the "good and clever John Hay," he wrote to Donna Isabella: "You see I am very national; do insist on that to people when you hear them abuse me—even when it's you yourself, who have before."

All through the 1880's, Mrs. Gardner moved more deeply into the world of art and letters. She attended the classes given in his Shady Hill study by Charles Eliot Norton, the medievalist who had returned from Cambridge to teach the history of art at

Harvard. In England Norton had come to know Ruskin and Carlyle, Darwin and Dickens, and the pre-Raphaelites Edward Burne-Jones, William Morris, and Dante Gabriel Rossetti. He diffused their culture to the group that attended his classes, among them Oliver Wendell Holmes, James Russell Lowell, Mrs. Howe, and her nephew, F. Marion Crawford. Mrs. Gardner and Crawford were fellow members of the Dante Society, and this became a lifelong bond between them. Surrounded by rare manuscripts and paintings, Isabella now conversed with William and Henry James, Henry Adams, and a curly-haired young man named Bernard Berenson, whose career as one of the world's leading art experts would be indissolubly linked with her own great collection. She was his inspiration and his backer in his early days, and his own fame grew as he masterminded her choice of pictures.

Her early association with these poets, authors, and artists affected the course of Mrs. Gardner's life. Although an indifferent correspondent herself, she had a large view of the world of letters through her frequent communication with gifted men. She collected rare books, manuscripts, and autographs, and in 1903 Dr. Norton sold her his Venetian manuscripts. Her particular treasures were her 1481 Dante, with plates after Botticelli, and her Book of Hours, which had belonged to Mary Queen of Scots but may now be seen in Fenway Court. In reading Dante together she and Crawford used two copies that were interleaved and bound by Tiffany. He watched for rare editions of this poet's work in Italy to send to Isabella.

Fascinated by Mrs. Gardner's good sense as well as by her charm, Crawford usually asked her to read his manuscripts before he sent them to his publishers. They came in a constant stream, for he wrote popular books that were serialized in the magazines. After writing six novels in fourteen months, he told her that he must decide between selling his soul to meet the serial requirements, or settling for the austere life of the true artist. As Isabella watched him develop into a highly successful author, she listened to stormy confessions of inner woes, for Crawford was an unhappy man. All through the 1890's and the early part of the twentieth century he wrote to her, most often from Santagnello di Sorrento, his home in Italy, which he considered the most beautiful spot in the world. She consoled him, both in moments of triumph and despair. "A little encouragement freshens the blood at the end of a long race," he wrote after working ten hours a day for a long stretch until life seemed "like a long straight line of rail." When he sent her a copy of *The Ralstons* he wrote: "Your blessing I value. I think you know it, for I do believe that it is a wholehearted blessing and so it must be good." On another occasion he wrote from Sorrento: "I hope you are enjoying everything, as you always do. People envy you for many reasons, but you are most enviable for that marvellous power of getting grapes from thorns—and sugar plums out of paving stones."

Her interest in music was almost as keen as in art and letters. When the Gardners joined their two houses on Beacon Street they designed a spacious music room. Wilhelm Gericke, director of the Boston Symphony Orchestra, and Charles Martin Loeffler, first violinist, became friends and protégés. Her most stiff-necked critics were somewhat chastened when Gericke led his orchestra in her house; this was major entertainment for Beacon Street in 1888, and it was also free. She held morning recitals, and Clayton Johns gave talks in her music room. On concert nights Gericke would not raise his baton until Mrs. Gardner was in her seat. Her love of music is honored today at Fenway Court, where William Mason directs a musical program that includes Sunday concerts, often with chamber music, and on open days recitals and concerts in the Tapestry Room. Now, as in Mrs. Gardner's day, background music, a wealth of flowers, and an air of intimate charm make Fenway Court a museum without the customary chill and conventionality.

In her many encounters with famous musicians and composers Mrs. Gardner assembled a choice collection of signed manuscripts. At Ischl she strolled with Brahms and Johann Strauss, who gave her a photograph of Brahms on which he scrawled a few measures of the "Blue Danube." She was in Bayreuth in 1886 when Liszt died, and she led his funeral procession with his daughter, Frau Cosima Wagner. At the last moment she threw a shovelful of earth on his coffin, and her wreath inscribed "Homage de l'Amérique" was placed beside the one sent by Queen Victoria. She made a point of visiting the graves of Mozart, Haydn, Beethoven, and Schubert in Vienna, and during this period she and Emma Eames became close friends. In Paris Massenet played his new opera *La Navarraise* for Mrs. Gardner. She persuaded Jean and Edouard de Reszke to break their rule not to sing at private musicales, and later she studied the scores of Wagner's "Ring" with Jean, and fed him his favorite apple pie for lunch. At one of their performances her dramatic appearance drew newspaper comment, when she sat with her face swathed in a cobwebby white veil edged with black and white lace. The ends were drawn up in winglike effect on top of her coppery hair, and were stabbed with long turquoise pins. Paderewski thought he was playing for her alone, but Mrs. Gardner had seen to it that several of her friends were concealed behind screens to share in this treat. She always treasured the program that he scrawled hastily on a scrap of paper; it included three of his own compositions. Later she engaged him to give a concert in Bumstead Hall and sent tickets to all the musicians of Boston. She liked to hand out programs herself at concerts given by any of her protégés. It was characteristic of her that she also attended the summer pop concerts in Boston and drank beer in public.

Mrs. Gardner's interest in art became concentrated around 1886 after Henry James took her to Sargent's studio in London to see the portrait of Madame Gautreau, which is now in the Metropolitan Museum in New York. It was the most discussed picture of the year, and Mrs. Gardner was never to like it, although it was considered one of Sargent's best. She was drawn at once to the handsome young artist of thirty, with blazingly bright blue eyes, a pointed beard, and the look of a Van Dyck subject. Isabella was then forty-six. He visited and painted in the United States in 1876, 1887, and 1890, and almost every year from 1895 on, finally establishing a studio in Boston in 1903. Sargent who, like Henry James, was American-born, remained a close friend until her death in 1924. They met on both sides of the Atlantic and corresponded constantly. In *The Happy Profession* Ellery Sedgwick recalled Sargent's chasing Mrs. Gardner through a gymnasium in a New England country house on a summer morning. Sedgwick was a mere boy at the time. He was hidden away reading *Ben Hur* when he witnessed this scene:

> The pursuer was much younger than the pursued but that did not affect the ardor of the chase. The lady raced to the stairway leading to the running track above. Up she rushed, he after her. She reached the track and dashed round it, the ribbons of her belt straight out behind her. . . . For me that race was forever lost and forever won. The figures go flying motionless as on the frieze of the Grecian Urn.

This was the year in which Sargent painted his famous picture of Mrs. Gardner. He made eight attempts and was ready to give up when she reminded him that nine was Dante's mystic number. So he tried once more, and this time with success. She wore a severely plain black gown, closely molded to her figure. It had a deep décolletage, and her magnificent shoulders and arms were shown to full advantage, with her hands symmetrically clasped before her. A black shawl was draped tightly around her hips to accentuate her curves, and he persuaded her to take her pearls with the ruby pendant from her neck and loop them around her waist. Mrs. Gardner always insisted that it was Sargent's finest portrait. He refrained from public comment on this conclusion, but she quoted him as saying that it was "so imbued with her personality that if it were cut up into pieces one inch square and the pieces were scattered on the Charles River, the finder of one piece would know it came from a portrait of her." After this she was never without a plain, tight-fitting black gown similar to the one in which Sargent had painted her. "No old master had left a more puzzling personality upon canvas," wrote Morris Carter, who had come to know her well and to enjoy her eccentricities as well as her graces.

The portrait was exhibited at the Saint Botolph Club, and the comments on its obvious charms were so disturbing to the tolerant Jack Gardner that he said it must never be exhibited again as long as he lived. His wife observed his wishes, and even after his death it was kept in a room never opened to the public. But she decreed that after her own death it might be shown, and today thousands stroll past it and study the plain face and stunning figure of the creator of Fenway Court. For background Sargent used a piece of material subtly suggestive of a halo around her head. "She's had herself painted as a medieval saint," one passerby commented. A Unitarian minister, hearing this, replied: "Leave off the 'medi' and you will describe it."

In the spring of 1888 the Gardners were in Spain, and Henry James was addressing her as a "wonderful Jack-in-the-Box, popping out with all sorts of graceful effects and surprises . . . in the most unexpected parts of the universe." Later that summer they visited Daniel Curtis at the Palazzo Barbaro in Venice, which Isabella later took over and enjoyed for years. When Henry James heard of this he wrote to her from Garmisch on June 24, 1890: "The Palazzo Barbaro is divine, and divinely still; don't make it spin around."

This warning went unheeded, and it became one of the liveliest salons in Europe as artists, musicians, writers flocked to enjoy her hospitality, her cuisine, and the attentive ear that she lent to their visions and works. The established artist and the novice were welcome, but only if they had talent. Mrs. Gardner disliked the amateur touch in anything, and she was as sure in her instinct for promising talent as she later proved to be in her choice of paintings. "Her taste was infallible," Ellery Sedgwick observed. "Of course she had the advantage of the wisest advisers of her time, Whistler, Sargent and Berenson among them, but to take the best advice is as rare as to give it, and in the making of every choice she was the guiding spirit."

Few mistakes were made in her ultimate selections. Sedgwick asked her once whether her first purchases were still among her favorites.

"I asked that question of Mr. Frick," she replied. "His are in his cellar. Mine are on the wall."

She bought her first old picture in Seville—Francisco Zurbáran's "Madonna and Child." This hung in her bedroom on Beacon Street and later above the chapel window in Fenway Court. Finally it became the altarpiece of the Spanish Chapel which she designed as a memorial to her little boy Jackie. While in Spain she developed a strong interest in Isabella, and some time later Berenson induced her to buy paintings of the Infanta. Again he recommended one that represented "the greatest and most fascinating lady of the Renaissance—your worthy precursor and patron saint—Isabella, Marchioness of Mantua."

Berenson was her friend and adviser from 1884 to 1906, when he tied his fortunes to Joseph Duveen. Before he was thirty-two he had bought two dozen masterpieces for Mrs. Gardner within the space of two years. After graduating from Harvard in 1887, he did not return to the United States except for brief visits. Bearded, auburn-haired, with gray-green eyes, the young Lithuanian progressed rapidly from lunching off chestnuts and coffee in Paris, and deploring the "horrible solitude" of the French capital, to days of luxury and authority as one of the great art experts of the world. He had violent likes and dislikes and abhorred the Mona Lisa—"a woman beyond the reach of my sympathies or the ken of my interests . . . watchful, sly, secure, with a smile of anticipated satisfaction and a pervading air of hostile superiority." The Last Supper was another of his strong dislikes.

Berenson never spoke to Mrs. Gardner of his great love, Mary Pearsall Smith, until he visited her at the Palazzo Barbaro in 1897, when his patron was fifty-seven and he was thirty-two. He told her then of Mary, who belonged to a well-known Fabian family in England and had deserted her children and husband, Frank Costelleo, to live with him in Florence. When her husband died they were married at the Palazzo Vecchio, and Berenson then wrote to Mrs. Gardner: "She understands me and my needs and my interest as no other person, and I am sure she will try to make me happy." Eventually they settled at I Tatti, the Tuscan farmhouse that was to become a shrine for art lovers. Mrs. Gardner's name was never mentioned to Mary either, but in the end they became good friends, and Isabella left one of her rubies to the woman who had exercised such influence over the young art connoisseur.

When Berenson visited the Palazzo Barbaro as the guest of Cole Porter in 1923 he wrote to Mrs. Gardner, who had only a few more months to live: "If I ever sigh for anything in the past it is for those days." She had helped to enlarge his circle of buyers, and at one point he wrote to her: "We want Americans to have as many good pictures as possible. You have had the cream. Other collectors will only enhance the superiority of yours." Although their correspondence throws much light on their art transactions, Berenson made only passing allusion to her in his writings as "Boston's first pre-cinema star" and "The Serpent of the Charles." But Mary spoke for him, and with affection, when she wrote: "It is not only that when he was young and unknown you confided to him many honourable responsibilities—it is the way you did it—as different from most people who have sought advice, as a Queen from a petty Merchant. He loves the splendid way in which you have carried out your ideas and is proud that you associated him with them."

In 1891 her father died, leaving her $2,700,000. Her husband had another $3,000,000, so that between them their fortune was never a great one in the comparative sense, and the Gardner collection, priceless today, was assembled for something like $3,000,000. Eventually Mrs. Gardner refused to sell it to Duveen for $15,000,000. Twenty years before Andrew Mellon came into the field she was picking up bargains that are legendary today. While in Paris in December, 1892, she made one of the most notable of all her purchases—"Le Concert" by Jan Vermeer, a gem in her collection at Fenway Court. It fell to her for $6,000. She used her favorite technique for controlling the bidding, holding her handkerchief to her face and then dropping it as a sign to her agent that he must go no farther. On this occasion officials of the National Gallery and the Louvre were eager to get the Vermeer, but each decided as a matter of courtesy not to bid against the other. They were appalled to find that it had gone to Mrs. Jack Gardner of Boston.

Although she made her purchases with steady judgment and taste, she was apt at times to follow a whim, and she picked up "A Young Commander" by Justus Suttermans in Venice in 1892 because its subject, the Duke of Monmouth, chanced to be a Stuart. She wanted Whistler's "Harmony in Blue and Silver: Trouville" when she saw it hanging in his bare studio on the Rue du Bac. It was not finished, and in any event he could not bear to part with it, but with the collusion of T. Jefferson Coolidge, she virtually took it off the wall and carried it away. She told him he could finish it at her hotel, and he finally put the Butterfly seal on it there, and let her have it. There was no denying Mrs. Gardner when she wanted a work of art, as Norton, Sargent, Whistler, Henry James, Paul Bourget, and Berenson all found out at one time or another.

She had the same enthusiasm for other treasures. On this trip abroad in 1892 she bought the famous ruby that she later wore in her hair, at her neck, at her waist, in her shoe buckle, or wherever the fancy struck her. It had belonged to an Indian prince and was kept in the Bank of England. She bought it in memory of her brother David, with a legacy he had left her. In the same year she acquired her final string of pearls. Earlier that summer she had held court at the Palazzo Barbaro, with Henry James and Joseph Lindon Smith visiting her. On the Fourth of July a Venetian serenade was staged outside her palazzo, and then they all floated along the canals with "the music accompanying us and the moon sinking into the lagoon." One of her protégés at this time was Pier A. Tirindelli, the violinist, and she attended all the rehearsals of his opera *Atenaide*. Since she was wise in the ways of publicity and wished to help him with official backing, she asked the London *Times* correspondent in Rome to cover his concert. However, he could not leave his bureau, so Mrs. Gardner telegraphed her own critique and was always proud of her payment—the only money she ever earned in her life.

She loved the diversity of travel, from the Derby and Henley to the Passion Play and the Palio at Siena. Both she and her husband felt much at home at the races in Victorian England. In the Gainsborough era Mrs. Gardner outdid the most extravagant in the size of her hats and her Worth creations. Coaching to the races one day in a downpour her husband begged her to use an umbrella. "Who ever heard of anyone carrying an umbrella on the way to the Derby!" she exclaimed, as her plumes drooped around her neck and her wide brim flopped over her face. Full of good cheer, she persuaded the rest of the party to bet on a horse that seemed doomed to lose, but with her customary good luck he came in the winner.

Soon after her return from this trip, Anders L. Zorn came into Mrs. Gardner's life at the Columbian Exposition held in Chicago in 1893. She had given Paul Helleu's "View of the Abbey of St. Denis" for the loan collection. When she arrived in Chicago for a preview of the fair, two of the great dowagers of America—both superb hostesses, both patrons of the arts—met for the first time. Mrs. Potter Palmer entertained Mrs. Gardner at her mansion known as the Castle, on Lake Shore Drive. Neither was deeply impressed with the other. Mrs. Gardner was patronizing, and Mrs. Palmer had her own opinion of the vivacious Mrs. Gardner from Boston, but each recognized style in the other. Mrs. Palmer's French Impressionists were causing a great deal of talk, and Isabella looked them over, both at her house and at the Exposition. When Honoré Palmer showed her some of his mother's gold plate and fine china, telling her that she had fifty of everything, Mrs. Gardner inquired briskly: "What does she do when she has a really big party?"

Zorn attended the Exposition as Swedish Commissioner. Mrs. Gardner noticed his painting of a group of people on an omnibus and thought it good. She bought the picture and immediately made him one of her protégés, suggesting an exhibition of his work at the Museum of Fine Arts in Boston. He did an etching of her that she disliked intensely, but they became fast friends, and she entertained Mr. and Mrs. Zorn later at her palace in Venice. Like Sargent, he kept on doing sketches of her and hoping to catch her elusive personality. Then one night he saw her pushing open the French doors and stepping in from the balcony to the drawing room. Her beautiful arms were outstretched, and he was struck at once by the joyous spontaneity of her pose. "Stay just as you are!" he exclaimed. "That is the way I want to paint you."

And thus he painted her, all in yellow, with her rope of pearls, held by her ruby, swinging to her knees, and the Venetian scene behind her. When the picture was exhibited in Paris the critics found it wonderfully expressive and one of Zorn's best. Mrs. Gardner liked both the portrait and the painter better than Mrs. Palmer did hers. Zorn had a broken collar bone when he painted her, and he worked with his left hand, never putting the finishing touches to the portrait. The final effect was too much the sparkling princess of the fairy tale for Mrs. Palmer's discriminating taste. There was more of the breath of life in Mrs. Gardner's portrait. "Your letters make me love life," Zorn wrote to her on his return to Sweden. Both he and Mrs. Zorn had floated about in gondolas with the Gardners. Occasionally wives looked apprehensively at Mrs. Gardner, although without much cause. When the Paul Bourgets arrived in the United States in 1894 with introductions from Henry James and Paul Deschanel, Madame Bourget was in a panic at the thought of her husband being exposed to the gorgeous Mrs. Gardner. She was twenty-five and had been married only three years to the highly sophisticated Bourget, who was forty-one. They were taken to Newport on a yacht and Madame Bourget spent all her time weeping in one of the cabins, but when the two women met all was harmony and they became good friends. Mrs. Gardner arranged a luncheon at which they met Oliver Wendell Holmes, then eighty-four years old, and at Green Hill she introduced them to Mr. and Mrs. William James, Edith Wharton, and other well-known writers.

In the following year, 1895, she was received by Pope Leo XIII. She wore her pearls in one long string as she knelt before him, and he picked them up and studied them thoughtfully. She never ceased to be interested in the Catholic Church, which she associated with the royal Stuarts. At her own request she attended a mass celebrated by the Pope in his private chapel. But she created a diplomatic crisis by impulsively sending yellow roses to the King of Italy after a court ball. It was his birthday, but this unconventional gesture immediately caused an uproar. Her husband, always able to counteract a malapropism, asked Wayne MacVeagh, the United States Minister to Italy, to explain that his wife had no idea that she was violating protocol and was merely following an impulse. She always sent flowers to others after being entertained. Why not to the king? She laughed over the incident herself, but the papers whipped it up into a storm.

Before going home she bought the halberd now in Fenway Court that had belonged to Paul V, the Borghese pope, as well as copes, iron *torchères,* and the stone hawk that surmounts the court. Sargent had persuaded her to buy a magnificent Persian rug that is now one of the treasures of her museum. It belonged to a Turk whose shop was too small to hold it unrolled, and he sent it to Sargent's studio in Chelsea. Sargent was painting Ada Rehan at the time and decided to use it for background. "Whenever I put my model on it, she covered up something infinitely more beautiful than herself, so I merely did a sort of map of the carpet for the pattern," he reported to Mrs. Gardner, who paid $1,750 for this priceless sixteenth-century Ispahan rug. It was another of her sensational bargains.

Berenson's first purchase for her was Botticelli's "The Tragedy of Lucretia," which he got for $17,000. From this time on they worked together, Berenson suggesting various paintings as they came on the market and Mrs. Gardner deciding on some she wished for herself. She insisted on buying Giorgione's "Christ Bearing the Cross," which had hung in the Casa Loschi in Venice. She had studied it often and had come to love it. Berenson was cool to this purchase and its attribution was questioned. He wrote that it was not the "kind of picture he thought of for her." But she bought it and later spent more time looking at it than at any other in her collection. She saw to it that fresh violets were always in front of it. Mrs. Gardner grew her own violets and appeared with them often; they were her favorite flower.

There were times when Berenson considered Mrs. Gardner greedy in her intense wish to own a certain painting. The seal on her letters was *Man Sabar Safar*, Arabic for he who waits will attain. He warned her that she must not expect to own *all* the great paintings that came on the market. For a time he jockeyed her between the masterpiece of her collection—Titian's "Rape of Europa"—and "The Blue Boy," Gainsborough's painting acquired eventually by Henry E. Huntington. Berenson had offered the Titian to Mrs. S. D. Warren, of Boston, feeling that since Mrs. Gardner had her heart set on "The Blue Boy" she could scarcely afford both. But Isabella was furious at being outmatched by one of her Boston neighbors, and as soon as Berenson learned how she felt about it, he slowed up the negotiations with Mrs. Warren. He assured Mrs. Gardner that the Titian was a much greater work than "The Blue Boy" and that Dr. Wilhelm Bode wanted it for the Berlin Museum. Mrs. Gardner immediately telegraphed her offer to forestall Mrs. Warren's letter, and the Titian was hers—now one of the major Italian masterpieces in the United States. It had extra significance for her since it was given to Charles I, a Stuart, when he went to Madrid to seek Philip III's daughter in marriage. After this plan fell through, the painting was kept in its wrappings for many years, and eventually came into the possession of Lord Darnley, from whom Berenson bought it. It was in exceptionally good condition because of its long immurement, and Rubens pronounced it the greatest picture in the world when he made the copy of it that is now in the Prado. Van Dyck later copied Rubens' copy, and Mrs. Gardner added this to her collection, too.

Actually 1896 was her great buying year, although from 1894 to 1900 she picked up one art treasure after another. In 1896 she landed Rembrandt's "Portrait of the Artist as a Young Man," his own painting of himself, just as the National Gallery in London was about to get it. Berenson described it to Mrs. Gardner as "one of the most precious pictures in existence!" Late that year he bought Velasquez' "King Philip IV of Spain," for her, although its attribution was later questioned. Before leaving Rome she bought the mosaic pavement from the Villa Livia which she used for the center of her court, and in Paris she picked up her finest tapestry, "The Ladies Tournament." Her summer in Venice that year was like a Renaissance dream as she and Berenson bought objects of art almost on a wholesale scale. Poets and artists lounged at her feet and read their poems to her. Her cuisine was exotic; her parties were famous. She had a piano on board her own barca, and music floated from the Palazzo by night and day. Antonio Mancini painted her and F. Marion Crawford lounged on a sofa, reading *The Divine Comedy* aloud.

She became almost as well known in Venice as in Boston, and one of her own favorite stories about herself concerned a Venetian girl who found one of her friends at the railroad station and asked her what she was doing there. She said she was waiting for the arrival of a train.

"Why?" she was asked.

"Because Mrs. Jack Gardner of Boston is coming on it, and I want to see her."

"Why do *you* want to see *her*?"

"Because she's so wicked."

"How wicked is she?"

"More wicked than Cleopatra."

Mrs. Gardner liked to make selections of her own, and a case in point was Lippo Memmi's "Madonna and Child," one of her favorite paintings. Berenson persuaded her to buy the picture that he liked better than any in her collection—Carlo Crivelli's "Saint George and the Dragon." Another of his favorites was Fra Angelico's "Death and Assumption of the Virgin," which he described as one of the loveliest pictures ever painted. Although she did not go abroad in 1898, she added to her collection Raphael's portrait "Count Tommaso Inghirami," Rubens' "Thomas

Howard, Earl of Arundel," which had hung in Warwick Castle, and two Rembrandts—"Storm on the Sea of Galilee" and "A Lady and Gentleman in Black." A Giotto, "The Presentation of the Child Jesus in the Temple," added luster to her growing collection, and Henry James wrote to her from London on April 3, 1898: "Goodby, daughter of Titian. Is the Pope going to sell you one of the rooms of the Vatican?"

At this time she also bought Benvenuto Cellini's famous bust of Bindo Altoviti, and while prowling around Florence she picked up the marble doorway, with St. George in relief, that leads into her museum today. Norton bought for her the sarcophagus with figures in high relief that stands in her chapel. Her acquisitions in the 1890's gave her an unquenchable taste for Italian masterpieces. Nothing but the best would satisfy her after that, and she stopped buying English eighteenth-century paintings. Her house on Beacon Street became known as the Musée Gardner, and she now thought in terms of an art gallery to house her valuable possessions. She was discreet about her purchases and never talked of them until they were installed in her home. It sometimes took months to get them out of Europe, and upon occasion they were shipped in roundabout ways.

When they were hung she gave small private showings, inviting her friends in relays to view her treasures. Long before the turn of the century she had become a sensational figure on the American scene, and her comings and goings were recorded as if she were royalty. Van Wyck Brooks thought that she quite outglittered the magnates of Nob Hill in San Francisco. She made headlines in a variety of ways, and none that pleased her more than her adventures at the Zoo. She often said that she liked animals better than she did human beings, and the wilder they were the better she liked them. In the winter of 1896 she took two cubs from a lioness when they were six weeks old and drove them in her carriage along Beacon Street. She tied a red ribbon round the neck of one, who was known thereafter as "Mrs. Jack" or the "Society Lion." She terrified visitors at the Zoo when she walked about, leading a young lion named Rex by the mane. She was an ardent antivivisectionist, and made trouble for anyone who threatened the animal kingdom.

Although Bostonians sometimes thought that Isabella treated her devoted husband with all too little consideration, he continued to back her on every issue and to show great kindness to her assorted friends, as well as to her. In 1896 they both began giving serious thought to a museum site to house their treasures. Each agreed that the other would carry out the plan, in case of death. They had architectural plans drawn up and were considering a site when Gardner had a stroke at the Exchange Club in December, 1898. He died the same evening. With the faith he had always shown in his wife's judgment and business ability, he left her the bulk of his estate in trust, with the proviso that she could demand principal at any time she wished.

Many tributes to the genial nature of Jack Gardner reached his widow. Berenson called him the "dearest fellow in the world." F. Hopkinson Smith wrote: "His sterling integrity of *thought*—his sound common sense and his unfailing courtesy and good fellowship made a rare kind of man of him." Henry James added his tribute: "I haven't a memory of him that isn't delightful or mixed with delightful things."

Almost at once Mrs. Gardner bought the land at Fenway and Worthington streets where her museum stands today. The fens were a barren waste, and the piles had to be on stilts when the building operations began. She sold her Beacon Street houses, taking carved woodwork, her fireplaces, and other treasures for her private apartments at Fenway Court. Her friends soon noticed that she had undergone another change in personality, for now she became as parsimonious as she had been extravagant in the past. Most of her staff were dismissed, and she reduced her scale of living. Guests commented on strange party combinations, such as champagne and doughnuts, or tea, bread and butter, with apple sauce. Whispers got about that she did not have enough to eat, but others scoffed at this, knowing that peaches and nectarines, hot-house grapes, dairy products, and vegetables were brought in from her farm. It was all relative, but her economies startled those who had been familiar with her spendthrift habits. She had never done anything by halves, and now she seemed to be aping Hetty Green. But she had strong purpose behind these measures. Every penny must be saved for Fenway Court, and she could still find substantial sums for a worthy work of art, although her buying tapered off after 1900. But it included two portraits by Holbein, "Sir William Butts, M.D." and "Lady Butts," and her Fra Angelico. Berenson advised her to buy Simone Martini's five panels, making an altarpiece considered unique in the United States. She added the Chigi Botticelli "Madonna and Child of the Eucharist" getting it for $70,000, at this time, and bought a pair of choir stalls and more sculpture.

As the foundations for Fenway Court were being laid she went abroad to the Palazzo Barbaro, and all summer she roamed about in Italy, buying columns and capitals, reliefs and frescoes, pilasters, arches, fountains, balconies, and mirrors. On her return she went into dynamic action, going each day to the fens, keeping the same hours as the workmen, knocking off for lunch with them, and contributing her ten cents for oatmeal to clear the drinking water. As huge cases arrived from Italy they were unpacked in orderly fashion under Mrs. Gardner's direction. She knew the whereabouts of every item, from the convent grill she had bought in Florence, to her staircase from Dorigo and the Fior di Persica columns that the tourists perambulate when they visit her museum today. Her architect insisted on a steel frame, but Mrs. Gardner told him that if marble columns could support a palace in Venice they could do the same in Boston. When she ran into trouble on building requirements she told the visiting inspector: "If Fenway Court is to be built at all it will be built as *I* wish, and not as *you* wish." But for once she was wrong and her columns had to be reinforced.

Nothing discouraged her. She cherished the four-leaf clover she had found on her first visit to the site on which she built, and preserved it in a crystal locket, believing it to be an omen of good luck. But her sudden rages startled the workmen, and she had little patience when they made mistakes, firing them at a moment's notice. When oak for the floors did not arrive on schedule she switched to hard pine. Experts from a shipbuilding firm were hired to work on the ceiling of the Gothic Room, which was to be supported by huge beams. Mrs. Gardner decreed that the beams should be hewn by hand. When she did not like the effect the workmen were getting, she seized a broadax and swung it herself, to show them how it should be done.

When the painters failed to get the shade of pink she sought for the walls she climbed on their ladder, dipped a sponge alternately into a bucket of white and a bucket of pink paint, and sloshed it on with a lavish hand. By chance she caught the pink marbled effect that was later greatly admired. She had already picked up the blend of paint for the Boldini blue of her corridors while she was in Italy. Her chief helper was Tibaldeo Travi, an Italian known as Bolgi, who handled each precious item with a knowing touch. He worked out a system of signals on his cornet, so that Mrs. Gardner could summon the mason, the steam fitter, the plumber, carpenter, plasterer, or painter by the prescribed number of toots. They all came running in response to their particular signal.

The men were all sworn to secrecy, and Mrs. Gardner was so silent herself about the work going on that the "Eyetalian Palace," as some of the neighbors described it, became a house of mystery. A blank wall had gone up that frustrated spectators. Early in 1902, however, Mrs. Gardner gave small private "showings" of what lay within. She let Henry Irving and Ellen Terry view it, but another friend, Mrs. Edith Wharton, did not rise to the bait. The secrecy annoyed her, and when Mrs. Gardner invited her to call at twelve minutes past eight in the morning to take a look at Fenway Court, she replied that she never got up that early. The favored few were admitted through a side door known as a postern, and if they did not arrive punctually the entrance was closed.

The acoustics of the Music Room gave her much trouble, and when she sought to make a final test before the opening she invited the children from the Perkins School for the Blind, knowing that they would be the best possible judges of sound. But a nightmare followed. The day was snowy, and after they had lined up their rubbers in orderly fashion a servant scooped them all up in a sheet. When the children were ready to leave, the confusion was heartbreaking as they tried to find their own rubbers. Mrs. Gardner flung herself on the floor and worked frantically to help them, but she never forgot this experience.

The grand opening of Fenway Court was held on New Year's night, 1903, and it was an unforgettable event in Boston's history. Mrs. Gardner stood at the top of a horseshoe staircase in a severe black gown, like the Sargent model, with her diamond antennae glittering above her hair. Those who had cherished her and those who had snubbed her among Boston's élite climbed the stairs to be received by the regal figure in command. Her favorites remained beside her; her critics were steered down the other side of the horseshoe. To the more cynical observers it seemed that she was demanding an act of homage. Fifty members of the Boston Symphony Orchestra, led by Gericke, and nine singers from the Cecilia Society played Bach, Mozart, Chausson, and Schumann. Then Mrs. Gardner had her moment. A huge mirror was rolled back, and the courtyard that had been guarded by her high wall was revealed in all its glory, with flowers blooming around its mosaic floor, nasturtiums streaming from its balconies, lanterns and candles flickering through windows and arches. Morris Carter wrote that it seemed to Bostonians as if the "Venetian Renaissance had been reincarnated in twentieth-century Boston."

Her guests quickly saw that in spite of the magnitude of her art this was no formal gallery that housed her great paintings. They found warmth and life as they moved from room to room, admiring the sculpture, the tapestries, velvets and assorted works of art, as well as her paintings. Characteristically, Mrs. Gardner had ignored the conventional rules for hanging pictures and had given full play to her own tastes, knowing the rules well, but breaking them freely. Above all, it was to be *her* creation. Dr. George L. Stout, who became director of the Gardner Museum in 1955, found that by the usual standards of propriety the installation was "peculiar, irregular, ungainly and confusing," ignoring category, history, and geography. He saw it as a sturdy refusal "to go along with the neat index of all history and all art that was the guide of conduct in museum affairs at the turn of the century." Clearly it was an attempt, he added, to let the work of art hold all that it could of its individuality. By degrees the museum had acquired the flavor of a home where people had lived and where the things around them had added to the fullness of their lives.

The museum was opened to the public in February, 1903. Visitors paid a dollar then but enter free today. They came from far afield, and Bostonians recognized the fact that Mrs. Gardner had given them something of enduring value. William James described it as "aesthetic perfection . . . a gospel miracle . . . a very extraordinary and wonderful moral influence." Henry Adams called it a "tour de force" and Mrs. Gardner a creator, standing alone. Sargent wrote to her from Madeira soon after the opening: "The only thing I have seen worthy of Fenway Court is a piece of wood carving, out of a church. . . . I think it would look very fine in your Gothic Room." F. Marion Crawford wrote to her from Kent in the summer of 1907: "Your place is grave and calm—as a Venetian Senator! . . . When I shut my eyes and see it again, I feel that I should not wish anything to be different. . . . It is so altogether yours, the form of your thought, that you and it are one—like light and air—you are at peace with it and ever newly refreshed by it." Whistler wrote to her from the Rue du Bac: "There was a time when I thought America far away—but *you* have really changed all that—and this wonderful place of yours on the Bay ends by being nearer to us than is the Bois to the Boulevard on a summer afternoon." And again he wrote to her from Ajaccio, signing himself "Butterfly": "No one is so *immediately* nice and charming in the doing of a kind thing, as your own delightful clear-headed and sympathetic self!"

Mrs. Gardner made her last trip to Europe in 1906, and this time she visited Monet at Giverny, an experience that she found "perfect in every way." From then on she summered at Gloucester, nearer home. Sargent was now quite often by her side, and when he was away he wrote to her regularly. Her correspondence with him and others was filled with allusions to Fenway Court. By this time she had six Sargents, eleven Whistlers, and twelve Zorns in her collection. Her final score for the Isabella Stewart Gardner Museum of today was 290 paintings, 280 pieces of sculpture, 240 items of ceramics and glass, and 250 miscellaneous items, as well as her manuscripts, rare books, and the architectural treasures embedded in the building itself. Her letters in themselves express the versatility of her tastes, coming from such men as George Santayana, Gilbert Murray, Richard Mansfield, Owen Wister, William Dean Howells, Richard Harding Davis, and Theodore Thomas, among others.

She let Sargent use the Gothic Room as a studio and the public was not admitted there or to the chapel. Loeffler rehearsed his "Pagan Poem" in her Music Room. Melba sang in the Dutch Room, and on this occasion Mrs. Gardner gave her a huge yellow diamond. "This was coveted by the King of Cambodia but I have saved it for the Queen of Song," she said as she hung it around Melba's neck. Isadora Duncan danced for her, and Lady Gregory had the Irish Players stage a performance in her Music Room. In 1905 Sir Charles Wyndham and Mary Moore gave the duologue "Mrs. Hilary Regrets." Two years later Mrs. Gardner had her last big concert with the Boston Symphony Orchestra.

In 1908 she was deeply depressed when she was accused of smuggling in some of her art treasures. Lippo Memmi's "Madonna and Child" was in this consignment, and it had all been shipped through Mrs. Emily Rockwell Crane Chadbourne, the divorced wife of the well-known New York lawyer, Thomas L. Chadbourne. Treasury agents were in the habit of watching Mrs. Gardner's imports. She had given them trouble before. Five years earlier she had wrangled with them over whether or not she should pay on art treasures destined for her museum. There was no seizure then but she was told that she must pay the full duty, since Fenway Palace was not a public museum. This time, however, she was accused outright of a smuggling plot and had to pay a $40,000 penalty and $30,000 in duty on works of art valued at $80,000. The tapestries in the shipment were as well known in their field as a Titian in the art world. One was "Boy in Tree in

Springtime," and there were four tapestries catalogued as "Rebecca's Story."

Mrs. Gardner and Mrs. Chadbourne were known to be close friends, and the customs men were tipped off from Paris that the "household goods" addressed to Mrs. Chadbourne in Chicago and passed through New York in bond, might be Gardner treasures. Isabella was known to have $250,000 worth of tapestries, marbles, oil paintings, and armor stored in Paris at this time. Government agents picked up the trail when a large shipment of her art treasures was sent from Paris to London. Mrs. Chadbourne landed in New York from England with several large cases labeled "household goods" that were sent straight through to Chicago. But government officials were ready for her there. Art experts were called in to evaluate the contents of the boxes, and the case was laid before the Department of Justice. Mrs. Chadbourne's father, Richard T. Crane, president of the Crane Manufacturing Company, explained that his daughter had acted in good faith and in ignorance of what was involved. She did not stand to gain one penny in the transaction. After being interviewed by government agents Mrs. Gardner clammed up but was angry. It was an old issue with her, since she stoutly maintained that treasures going to a museum should not be dutiable.

That same year she was in the headlines in a less controversial way when she helped her watchman drag a drowning man out of Muddy Creek, close to Fenway Court. When the *Titanic* went down she had a tablet installed in the corridor of Symphony Hall to the musicians who kept on playing as the ship was sinking. She gave many benefits and invariably had a birthday party for herself, usually with a play, a Japanese dancer, or a novelty of some kind. In 1912, at the age of seventy-three, she was learning Russian dance steps. She had a physical fitness program quite her own, and she kept it up until her final illness. When she had a broken leg she insisted on being taken to a Boston theater on a stretcher to see Harry Kellar, whom she had met some years earlier in India. It amused, but did not greatly surprise her, to have a post office clerk write "Try Mrs. Jack" across a letter addressed merely to "Mrs. Gardner, Esq., Well known lady in high life,

Boston Mass." A mountain peak in the state of Washington had been named for her, and she was fast becoming a legendary figure.

By this time she was being identified in various books, and Crawford made no secret of the fact that he was thinking of her when he wrote *To Leeward*. This was not dismaying to Mrs. Gardner, who relished publicity, in spite of her passion for veiling many of her acts in mystery. "The Boston woman who is getting columns upon columns of free advertising out of her love of privacy is a genius in her way," a Floridian wrote while Fenway Court was being built. She continued to look young and vital. Her hair was bright and springy. Her gait was full of vigor, and the icy winter winds stirred color in her aging cheeks. At seventy she rose at six in the morning to catch a football train for New Haven to watch her nephew play. She attended the hockey games with great enthusiasm and seemed as well adjusted to the cold Boston winters as to the warmth of the Adriatic. Ellery Sedgwick watched her with close interest in her declining years, observing that she was without a worldly scruple and what she wanted, that she would have. He wrote of her:

> There was no sacrifice she would not make to Beauty. She would pinch herself to the extremity of economy. She would go without her carriage; she would live on the top floor of her house almost on a diet of herbs, but the magical canvas, the inspired bust, the glass of Chartres, the ruby that men must have died for, and the three great ropes of pearls which hung to her waist, these things she enjoyed, she adored, and out of the fullness of her joy would thank God for them.

In 1914 the great mirror was removed, and the Music Room was demolished to make way for the completion of Fenway Court, as she had always planned it. A Spanish Cloister was designed to show off Sargent's "El Jaleo," a picture owned by T. Jefferson Coolidge. It was hung in a special alcove with electric lights illuminating it from below, like footlights. When Coolidge saw how successful the effect was he let Mrs. Gardner have the picture, and it gives a dramatic, stagelike touch for visitors entering the museum today. In 1917 when Sargent was painting Woodrow Wilson he wrote to Mrs. Gardner:

> It takes a man a long time to look like his portrait, as Whistler used to say—but he is doing his best, and has been very obliging about finding time for sittings. He is interesting to do, very agreeable to be with, and the conditions are perfect as he allows no interruptions and does not hold levees as Roosevelt used to do—and his wife approves and does not even think there is just a little something not quite right about the mouth.

In 1919 Mrs. Gardner persuaded Morris Carter to leave his post as assistant director of the Museum of Fine Arts to work for her at Fenway Court. She made him the first director of the Isabella Stewart Gardner Museum. By this time she had sold Green Hill and spent all her time in her Venetian palace on the fens. But late in 1919, after she had been dining out with Sargent and some other friends, she had a stroke. Her right side was paralyzed, and she could never walk again. She wrote with difficulty, but she was carried about in her sedan chair and spent long hours among the gorgeous flowers, with her flaming nasturtiums, a brick wall bordered by petunias, a willow tree, and a world of memories. There was always music in the background, friends to visit her, old letters and papers to burn. She kept up a front to the end, and when she drove through the streets of Boston, she was quickly recognized. She wrote to Hans Coudenhove on November 15, 1922:

> I am trying to keep up my courage. I'm quite an invalid, but cheerful to the last degree. I think my mind is all right and I live on it. I keep up a lot of thinking and am really very much alive. I have music, and both young and old friends. The appropriately old are too old—they seem to have given up the world. Not so I, and I even shove some of the young ones rather close. I really have energy.

Sargent had just done a water color portrait of her—his last portrayal of Donna Isabella. She was swathed all in white, with a wraithlike air, and her eyes staring comprehendingly at the world she was soon to leave. She had a heart attack and died on July 17, 1924. For two weeks she had been taking Communion every day, for she seemed to know that the end was near. Her coffin was placed beside the Spanish Chapel, and over it was the purple pall that had been used for her husband. A crucifix was hung at her feet and candles burned around her bier. Nuns mounted guard at prie-dieu and a requiem was sung for her. The funeral service was held at the Church of the Advent, and she was buried in the Gardner tomb at Mount Auburn. By her will she established Fenway Court as a "museum for the education and enjoyment of the public forever." Her gift was in perpetuity, with everything to remain as it was, down to the last detail.

In spite of her passion for Italian paintings in the great tradition, Mrs. Gardner did not turn her back on modern art. Corot's "Noonday" was an early purchase. She bought Henri Matisse's "Terrace, St. Tropez" and "The Flax Spinner" by Jean François Millet. She had Edouard Manet's "Madame Auguste Manet" and six paintings by Degas, including "Madame Gaujelin," a lady who had disliked her portrait and regretted that it should be exhibited in the United States. Charles Norton helped Mrs. Gardner in her selection of French Impressionists, and Berenson occasionally stepped out of his own field to buy her a Dürer or a Degas that she fancied. She was competitive to the last, and in offering her hand at a dinner party to Paul J. Sachs, who had trained many museum experts at the Fogg Museum of Art, she remarked: "This hand I offer is the hand of friendship. In the Renaissance it would have held a dagger. You outbid me for the Spanish fifteenth-century St. Michael I coveted."

"My dear lady, it is yours," he said, and he sent it to Fenway Court.

Today art experts rate Mrs. Gardner's collection as one of the choice ones of the world, and its fame is intensified by the legends that surround the dazzling but eccentric woman responsible for its existence.

Carry Nation

Carry Amelia Nation's mother thought she was Queen Victoria and drove around in a coach and four, wearing purple velvet and sometimes a crystal crown. The seeds of madness lay deep in Carry's inheritance and her subsequent history. There was little but tragedy in her own life. Her first husband died an alcoholic's death seven months after the birth of their child, and her second avoided her for years and then faded out of her life altogether. Her daughter became a mental case and Carry, as the years went on, heard voices and thought that she communed with spirits. She blazed with frenzy when she went "hatcheting," and her own tempestuous life came to an end in an institution.

This nineteenth-century reformer, swinging a hatchet in saloons, smashing glass with shrieks of triumph, stirred up a storm wherever she appeared. Whiskey, tobacco, Masonry, sex, and sin were her points of attack; the saloon her particular focus. She worked with fervor rather than strategy, rage instead of common sense, for Carry considered herself one of the Lord's anointed as she pushed her way like an avenging angel through the swinging doors of saloons. She might not be a mystery to the twentieth-century psychiatrist, but she baffled her own generation and was one of the most eccentric of the reformers.

With a hatchet in one hand and a Bible in the other, Carry became a national nuisance, the delight of the cartoonists, the scourge of the liquor dealers. The meek little Kentuckian turned into a fury soon after her first husband's death, and in course of time she was challenging President Theodore Roosevelt on the liquor question, storming Congress and various state legislatures, destroying property, lecturing in any shelter from a burlesque house to Carnegie Hall. She would knock a cigarette from a man's mouth, tear a Masonic pin from his lapel, dash a glass of whiskey to the floor, or insist on a nude statue's being draped. "I never saw anything that needed rebuke, exhortation or warning but that I felt it was my duty to meddle with it," Carry admitted in her autobiography. Since so many things she saw seemed to need rebuke and exhortation—even a lover's kiss as he sat with his girl on a bench—she became by all odds the most meddlesome woman in the country. Yet in the long run she was credited with focusing attention on flaws in state liquor laws, with stirring women to action over the grosser aspects of the saloon, and with helping the temperance movement in general. No one could discount Carry Nation as a force in public life, humbug and fanatic though she might be.

She first appeared in the headlines at a time when reformers were busy with many causes. The antislavery agitation of the Civil War period had touched off a wave of social protest. The temperance crusade was making progress under the skillful direction of Frances Willard. The women suffrage workers were locked in a high-pitched campaign, and the rights of man were in debate on every level. The nineteenth century was waking up to economic and social ills, and the voices of the apostles, confused though they seemed, were heard by a multitude. Carry, an outright fanatic, stood alone, causing more violence than any of the others and leaving fewer traces when she had gone. She made people angry. She also made them laugh, for she was unique, even in her generation, an eccentric whose symbol was the shining hatchet.

When Dorothy Dix interviewed her in her old age she found her a "queer, frowzy, fat, unromantic Joan of Arc who heard voices and saw visions, and who made no move unless she was spiritually guided." Even in her earlier years Carry was one of the least engaging and, by all odds, the most crude and destructive of the forces let loose on the nation in an era of extravagant protest. She did as much physical damage as a small army. The absence of feminine charm, of genuine persuasive power, were marked as she battered her way across the country with the impact of a steam roller. Jail held no terrors for her, and she was in and out of prison with regularity at the turn of the century. The more conservative temperance advocates gave her a clear berth. Yet Carry's childhood was peaceful and pleasant enough until her mother's aloof and pretentious ways became too disturbing. Her face suggested a sweet nature before the gathering years and her own furies scored deep and angry lines over its surface.

Carry chose to claim descent from the Duke of Argyll and often burst into a saloon singing "The Campbells Are Coming." Her maternal grandfather was James Campbell, a Virginian whose parents came from Scotland. He kept hounds and hunted in Mercer County, and although a Baptist deacon, he enjoyed a mint julep with his fellow huntsmen. Carry found him intimidating when she visited him as a child. Her father was Martin Moore, of Irish and Scottish descent, who farmed in Garrard County, Kentucky, where Carry was born on November 25, 1846. Their ten-room house was built of hewn logs, plastered over to a smooth finish. Red plush upholstery and gold-leaf paper gave the parlor a cheerful air. A water mill stood behind the house and slave cabins were nearby. Carry played in an old-fashioned garden with jasmine flowering at the picket fence, and purple flag, calamus, and thyme lining the graveled walk, while rose and althea bushes grew close to the cedar trees that flanked the approach to the house. The family cemetery, with flat grave-stones, was on their land. Dick's River ran close to the Moore property, and Carry spent long summer hours sitting on ledges of rock in the cliffs rising from the river banks.

Because of her mother's eccentricities, she spent much of her time in the slave cabins, listening to ghost stories and picking up eerie impressions of a phantom world. She followed the slaves to the fields, or tagged after her father, a bad-tempered but just man whom she adored. Because he was rabidly opposed to the use of liquor she heard much about the evils of drink in her childhood days. Carry was willful and often disposed to brood and storm, and the brightness of childhood seemed to pass her by. She was eight when her father moved his family to Woodford County, settling on a farm between Midway and Versailles. Their next home was in Belton, Missouri, where Carry became ill with a severe intestinal complaint that made her more or less of an in-valid for the next five years. She attended school intermittently as they moved from place to place, and her literacy was always at a low pitch. At the age of thirteen she attended a boarding school in Independence, Missouri, but was soon sent home because of her poor health.

Carry was fifteen when the war began, and her family mi-grated again with a great train of ox-drawn wagons—this time to Texas, because Moore believed that Missouri would be a battle-ground. They had no sooner settled on a farm in Grayson County than typhoid fever decimated their retinue of slaves. Many of the animals had died along the way. Discouraged by these reverses, Moore soon sold his Texas land and returned to Missouri. The backwash of war was visible as they journeyed north, and Carry never forgot the wounded men she saw along the way. They gave bedding and all the supplies they could spare to soldiers as they passed through Arkansas to Kansas City, where they stayed until the war ended.

With the restoration of peace, her father moved them back to Belton. His lands were ruined, his stock was scattered, and his slaves had disappeared. Now one of the impoverished Southerners, he took in boarders to raise a little income. Mrs. Moore's eccentricity had become so pronounced that Carry took over the management of the household. She tried hard to improve herself, for she had always longed to be smart, reading the poets and studying mythology along with the Bible. At this time she became letter-perfect in the Scriptures, an accomplishment that was to serve her well in her saloon-smashing days. She taught in Sunday school, and church and prayer meetings loomed large in her life. But she was allowed to attend an occasional country dance, provided she was careful not to engage in the round dance with a man. "I cannot think this hugging school compatible with a true woman," she observed. She was almost pretty in her adolescent years. Her dark hair fell in ringlets on her neck; she had keen eyes and a strong mouth; her complexion was fresh and her figure good. There was nothing uncouth in Carry's upbringing, for she was accustomed to comfortable surroundings, fine furniture, and the manners on which her mother insisted in her more lucid moments. On the whole she was a quiet girl, showing enthusiasm only when singing hymns. In moments of self-reproach she recalled that in her earlier years she had been a liar and a thief—a child who had rifled drawers and made up fantastic stories to cover her transgressions. Now religious services, prayer meetings, and hymns gave her a sense of virtue.

But a new element came into her life when Dr. Charles Gloyd, son of one of their boarders, kissed her in a darkened hallway. This seemed like the end of the world to Carry, who later described it in her own way: "I had never had a gentleman take such a privilege and felt shocked, threw up my hands to my face, saying several times: 'I am ruined.'" Dr. Gloyd was both handsome and kind, but he had become a drinker during the days of the war. When he asked Carry to marry him her father protested. He had already selected the son of a substantial farmer living nearby as a suitable husband for Carry but by this time she was madly in love with Dr. Gloyd. Their courtship was carried on surreptitiously. Lovesick Carry had only to open the volume of Shakespeare's plays that he left beside her on the breakfast table to find love notes tucked between the pages.

The marriage was held in Belton on November 21, 1867, and Dr. Gloyd wavered and reeled as he took his wedding vows, a circumstance that Carry never forgot. In her autobiography she refrained from detailing the miseries of her short married life, but it was Dr. Gloyd who made Carry a hatcheteer. His drinking grew steadily worse until the day he died. He smoked, too, and was a Mason, and Carry wrapped up all these elements in his nature in her large-scale warfare with the social body. While waiting for their child to be born she tried to waylay him in the saloons, but his Masonic friends conspired to hide him from the avenging goddess of the home. The Gloyds had no money for food or clothing, and Carry was in a wretched state when her father took pity on her and insisted on bringing her home. "The world was like a place of torture," she recalled. But she could not forget Gloyd, and from the family home she sent him letters imploring him to sign the pledge, so that they could live together again. He visited her twice at Belton, but her mother treated him with disdain and no one let him know when their baby, Charlien, was born. When the child was six weeks old Carry and one of her half-brothers drove to Holden, where Dr. Gloyd lived, and arranged for a final separation. He lived only six months after that, and Carry collapsed when she heard of the death of the "man I loved more than my own life."

Feeling she could no longer stay at the Moore home, she decided to support her baby, her mother-in-law, and herself by teaching. Within a year she had a certificate from a normal school and was teaching a primary grade in the Holden public school. Little was heard of Carry for the next four years, but at that time she was dropped, and blacklisted for future work in the schools. She insisted, among other things, on a curious form of calligraphy for her pupils, and she would not conform or obey the rules. She had become a disruptive force, and her eccentricities were beginning to show. Carry decided that there was nothing for her to do but to marry again. Her strong sense of sin and damnation had become overpowering. The wreck of her first marriage had hardened her, but when she was almost sixty she wrote complacently in her autobiography: "I was a great lover. I used to think a person never should love but once in this life, but I often now say, I would not want a heart that could hold but one love."

The man to whom Carry entrusted her fate the second time was David Nation, a minister of the Christian Church who had a smattering of legal training and some knowledge of journalism. He had fought with the Confederates and had edited the Warrensburgh *Journal*. She had first noticed him standing in a doorway in Holden, and when he turned and spoke to her a "peculiar thrill passed through my heart," she recalled. He was nineteen years her senior, but she thought him handsome as she studied his long, flowing whiskers and his grave face with dark eyes fixed attentively on her. They were married six weeks later, in the year 1877, and Carry knew little happiness after that. To the end of her days she insisted that David Nation had stirred up the combative elements in her nature. "I had to fight for everything I kept," she noted. She disliked him as much as she had loved Dr. Gloyd. There was little on which they could agree. He was jealous and suspicious, and although their marriage lasted for twenty-four years, their home was a battleground until they decided to live apart. Nation could see no virtue in Carry's passion for reform. "My Christian life was an offence unto him," she wrote.

Two years after marrying they traded their Missouri property for 1700 acres of land on the San Bernard River in Texas, where they grew cotton, but they had so much trouble with their stock that Nation went to Columbia, the county seat, to resume his practice of law. Carry was ill and penniless when she finally swallowed her pride, loaded her family into a wagon, and followed him there. She found her husband also without funds, so she took over the Columbia Hotel, brought her furniture from the farm, and staked the family for a time by running the hotel. She was up at dawn, cooking, doing laundry and housework, at the same time worrying desperately about Charlien, who did not seem to be developing in the normal way. "Why did the birds sing, the sun shine?" she asked in despair, staring at the blank face of her child. Her own prayers and cries could be heard for blocks as she shut Charlien behind closed doors to conceal her awesome tantrums. The child had a succession of operations to enable her to open her mouth after a severe infection in one of her cheeks. For eight years Carry suffered over her handicapped daughter, who grew up to marry a man named Alexander McNabb, to be in and out of state asylums, to be adjudged insane in 1904, and finally to repeat history by becoming an alcoholic.

Nation worked at anything that came to hand and while corresponding for the Houston *Post* he was deeply involved in the feuding on the Negro question among the Populists, the Bushwhackers, and the Jayhawkers. Finally Nation moved to Kansas, where he preached in a Christian church at Medicine Lodge. Here Carry had what she called her great conversion, with "divine electricity pouring upon her head and permeating her entire body." She went running from house to house, proclaiming her salvation and shouting: "I have this from God, this divine gift." She laughed, she cried and prayed hysterically. After this visitation she became critical of her husband as a preacher, deciding that he was not a true convert and had no right to be in the pulpit. At the same time she became convinced that she had a mission in the world, and the first outward manifestations were her loud interruptions in church, where she broke in on the sermon, burst into prayer or song, and contradicted the preacher as he spoke. When he announced one hymn she demanded another. She defended a woman accused of adultery and insisted that she be seated beside the preacher, to the horror of the congregation. The elders pronounced her a disturber of the peace.

In suing her ultimately for divorce Nation said that Carry had been all right as a wife up to the time of her conversion. At that point she seemed to go completely off the rails and soon turned

her ferocious energy to investigating the dives and saloons of
Medicine Lodge. The temperance cause was strong in Kansas, but
all too often for Carry's taste a bar operated full tilt behind the
saloon. She would march in singing:

> Who hath sorrow? Who hath woe?
> They who dare not answer no.
> They whose feet to sin incline,
> While they tarry at the wine.

As a member of the Woman's Christian Temperance Union she
was appointed evangelist of the jail, which kept her in touch with
the town drunks, since nearly all the prisoners were locked up on
charges of intemperance. She considered this an absurd condition
in a prohibition state, and she rallied the men around her while
she sang, with tears pouring down her cheeks:

> Touch not, taste not, handle not;
> Drink will make the dark, dark blot,
> Like an adder it will sting,
> And at last to ruin bring,
> They who tarry at the drink.

The prisoners found it good entertainment, but the constable
protested. Carry appealed to the mayor and soon one of the
leading saloons was closed down. Her next move was to go from
one saloon to another, praying loudly as she knelt outside in the
street. She threatened the barkeepers, talked to the women of the
streets, and assailed men of wealth. "The time is coming when the
millionaire will be the despised of all people," said Carry. "I wish
for the poor often to make the rich take back seats."

Aside from her more extravagant gestures she did much good
work. She rounded up the crippled, blind, and impoverished at
her house for Thanksgiving and Christmas, collected clothes to
distribute to school children who were badly off, and was super-
intendent of two Sunday schools and president of the local
W.C.T.U., in addition to doing all her own housework. These
good deeds flowed from the fact that she had married David
Nation, Carry insisted. "Had I married a man I could have loved,

God could never have used me. The very thing that I was denied [a home] caused me to have a desire to secure it for others." She turned her face against luxury in any shape or form, wearing an ugly black alpaca dress and a black poke bonnet. "I used to delight in cut-glass, china, plush, velvet and lace," she wrote. "Now I can say vanity, all is vanity."

When she found that saloonkeepers were disposed to laugh in her face and continue their operations, she adopted a technique of her own and went forth with rocks and bricks wrapped in paper, which she heaved through windows. This was followed up with an assault on barroom mirrors, bottles, and glasses. "I felt invincible," she wrote. "My strength was that of a giant. God was certainly standing by me. I smashed five saloons with rocks before I ever took a hatchet." But once having found the hatchet, Carry could use no other weapon. It give her a new sense of power. She fought and kicked policemen and sometimes they handled her roughly, too. When told that a saloonkeeper was threatening to shoot her Carry exulted: "O, I want to be shot! How glorious to be a Martyr to the cause." After making some sensational raids in Kiowak she turned up in Wichita, where she stormed a dozen saloons and observed men drinking at the bars with the police standing nearby. In one hotel she noticed a life-size picture of a nude opposite the mirror. Next day she hid an iron rod, a cane, and some rocks under her cape and, throwing it back with a dramatic gesture, she flung the rocks at the nude, then smashed the mirror, and finally used both rod and cane to wreck the bar itself. After this triple assault she rushed across the street to another dive, where she was chased away by the police.

But this was the last time that Carry bothered with rocks. The hatchet had become her weapon. Topeka, Wichita, and Kansas City felt the full fury of her hatchet. She had found a true occupation, a religion, in what she liked to call her "hatchetation." It was exhilarating work, and she scarcely heeded the assaults made on her person. One woman belted her with a broomstick, a saloonkeeper threatened her with a pistol, another grabbed her hatchet as she was about to smash a door. She was frequently cut by falling glass, but nothing would deter her from entering a saloon, and usually on her knees praying—her established form of approach. Topeka, which had many saloons, caught the earliest and fiercest onslaught, and she met with such success that the W.C.T.U. for the first time gave her recognition. Frances Willard's legions had been slow to approve such violent tactics, but now members of the State Temperance Union and the W.C.T.U. paraded in Topeka carrying miniature hatchets and the white ribbon, their symbol. At the same time they flourished full-size hatchets, crow bars, and even axes.

The businessmen were stirred up to the point of voting to clean up the city by closing its dives. The saloonkeepers were warned, and a circular was broadcast urging a general uprising throughout the state against the saloons. "We must smash these murder mills," cried Carry. "If we let them take away their poison they will sell it somewhere else and continue to murder souls."

Carry was not at all displeased to find herself in jail in Topeka. This gave her a chance to send out a clarion call from her cell on February 19, 1901:

> Organize, home defenders, and jump for the hatchet, and run to the dive and smash the murder shop. Delay only means more souls in hell; more girls in houses of prostitution; more naked children; more crushed hearts and homes; more devils; more hell; less of virtue, more of vice, less of heaven, less of life and more of death.

Within a month after this the *Review of Reviews* pointed out that tens of thousands were endorsing Mrs. Nation's stand and that it would be absurd to find any fault whatever with these determined women. The spirit of the Kansas crusade seemed to be so intense and uncompromising that we "shall not be in the least surprised to hear of the smashing of private houses whose owners are suspected of having dispensed alcoholic beverages in the entertainment of their friends." The Springfield *Republican* called Carry a "robust woman of simple character, with an unerring instinct for the moral law." The Rochester *Democrat* commented that whatever else might be thought or said of Mrs. Nation, she was "serving a good purpose as a stirrer up of dry bones."

But the wily saloonkeepers of Topeka, whose bars had been closed because of Carry's influence, had stored their liquor and bar fixtures in barns around the city. This called for fresh tactics, and she brought up heavy reinforcements to wreck the woodwork, now that the bottles were gone. The students of Washburn College made a battering ram, and Carry, with two crossed hatchets held above her head, led them, all singing "Onward Christian Soldiers." A crowd of five hundred gathered and joined in the chorus. More followers were picked up as Carry's army moved through the streets. Ministers who sympathized with her tactics were in the line of march.

"Smash, smash, for Jesus' sake, smash!" shouted Carry, and this was picked up as a marching chorus. White handkerchiefs waved, as the crowd moved forward unimpeded. Although they had orders to check any rioting, the police had been warned not to use revolvers or clubs. Vehicles and pedestrians scattered before the advancing horde. Shop shutters were closed, but watching eyes peered from behind curtains at the spectacle of Carry Nation in her poke bonnet and black alpaca dress, a white handkerchief knotted around her throat, and in each hand a red-bladed hatchet with the white ribbon of the W.C.T.U. dangling from its haft. The tide of excitement rose as Carry approached a restaurant where policemen stood beside a padlocked door. With one swift move she sent a hatchet flying clear through a window and shouted "Smash! Smash!"

The college youths drove their battering ram against the building. Glass splintered and window frames were loosened with axes as the crowd followed Carry. Once inside they let their leader make the first move. Triumphantly she smashed a mirror, and then her followers went to work, wrecking furniture, breaking china and glassware, cutting great holes in the walls and floor. But before their work was finished Carry had been dragged into the street, fighting and pummeling the two policemen who held her.

As she was taken off to jail she shouted back "Smash! Smash! Don't stop while I'm gone."

She was freed on her own recognizance at police headquarters and rushed right back to a pile of wreckage. Her lieutenants had done their work with dispatch, but once finished they did not know how to proceed without her guidance. Carry snatched two hatchets from a woman, swung them over her head and yelled: "Praise God. Another joint gone. Follow me. I know another place." This time she stopped at a livery stable where liquor and bar fixtures had been stored. Again doors and windows were smashed to smithereens. Carry was hauled off but was freed in time to lead her third assault of the day—this time against a cold-storage plant that sold ice to saloonkeepers and handled whiskey and beer in wholesale lots. Smash went the hatchets, but no liquor was found on the premises. Half a dozen policemen escorted caterwauling Carry to jail, but like a slippery eel she was out again to attend a mass meeting late in the afternoon, at which plans were made for further raids.

Next day fifty men with handkerchiefs tied like masks over their faces wielded their sledge hammers, crowbars, and the battering ram against another storage warehouse, wrecking its supplies. This time shots were fired and Carry was taken to court, along with some of her supporters. She was held on a charge of malicious mischief and entered jail on her knees, after singing and praying in the courthouse corridor. All night long she kept this up in what she called Jeremiah's Dungeon. Gripping the iron bars she shouted: "You put me in here a cub, but I will go out a roaring lion and I will make all hell howl."

In jail she tried to convert her prostitute companions. Her bed was the cement floor, with a blanket and no pillow. The newspapers reported that Carry Nation was in a padded cell, insane and abusive, but this was just her usual way of campaigning. She appealed to the governor for release. Finally she was freed in January, 1901, on a writ of habeas corpus, and went back to her smashing tactics. Crowds now followed her to watch the fun and applaud her, but eggs were thrown at her, too. In spite of all the destruction the show Carry had staged won her further official support from the temperance forces, and the *Union Signal*, the official paper published by the W.C.T.U. in Chicago, was ordered to print as many good things as possible of Mrs. Nation, for "she certainly has accomplished much."

By this time she was a national sensation, and excitement in Topeka ran high as her defenders and her critics fought it out. The New York *World* called her that "crazy woman from Kansas," but the New York *Journal* defended her, and predicted that "some day the mothers of this country will burn all the saloons, and never a man in all the land will dare to check them." To the Topeka *State Journal* she was a "furious driving Jehu." In general, the religious papers defended her, although they deplored her use of the hatchet. But for the time being women across the country were more stirred up by Carry Nation's antics than they were by Miss Willard's more disciplined course of action. The saloon became the kind of bugaboo that the speakeasy was in the 1920's. Heartrending tales were whipped up about the wives and children of the drunkard. John P. St. John, twice governor of Kansas and a candidate for the office of President of the United States on the ticket of the National Prohibition Party, wrote to a friend that Mrs. Nation was all right. "She is not crazy, nor is she a crank, but she is a sensible Christian woman and has the respect of our best people." He compared her campaign to John Brown's isolated act on behalf of the slaves.

But Carry had a rival in high-powered tactics. Mrs. Mary Sheriff had her own Flying Squadron. Her girls carried heavy pickaxes on their shoulders like muskets. Wherever Mary went she was trailed by five men and fourteen veiled women, with an assortment of hardware ready for action. As she wrecked drugstores for medicines charged with firewater, she pronounced herself the original smasher. Carry, she said, was merely a copy. But in the end she was glad to hold high office under Carry in the National Hatchet Brigade.

After her success early in 1901, Carry published *The Smasher's*

Mail for a year, assisted by Nick Chiles, a Negro supporter who had helped to bail her out of jail. It appeared twice a week and was chiefly a compilation of letters, with some rambling editorials by Carry. Most of the correspondence was from the wives and mothers of drunkards, and the letters were filled with lurid details. Carry was sometimes addressed merely as the "Commander-in-Chief of the Hatchet Army," and many of the notes were grouped together as "Letters from Hell."

Soon after Carry started her hatcheting operations her mother was committed to the State Hospital for the Insane in Nevada, Missouri. Her earlier delusions had become full-fledged mania. First she had believed herself to be a lady-in-waiting to Queen Victoria; then she imagined herself the queen herself. She added a crystal and cut-glass crown, to wear with her purple velvet robes. Her family were expected to bow and scrape to her, and her husband humored her to the extent of buying her a rubber-tired carriage upholstered with plush. Her gray horses had silver-mounted harness, and she drove through the countryside, ordering Negro boys to open gates for her carriage. One tall Negro in a scarlet hunting jacket, a relic of her Virginia hunting days, blew a trumpet to herald her arrival, and other Negroes flanked her carriage like outriders. The masquerade came to a sudden end. Mrs. Moore lived only three years after being committed, and Carry's distress over the mental state of her mother and her daughter deepened her own degree of excitation. She believed that Charlien's condition was due to Gloyd's drunkenness.

After her campaign in Kansas she was now ready for the lecture circuit and was obviously prime material for her promoters. Her fame had spread from coast to coast. But Chicago gave her the cold shoulder. Mayor Carter Harrison was ready for Carry. He declined to receive her, and she was warned not to smash in the Windy City. Carry piped down and announced that she was on a paid lecture tour and had not even brought a hatchet with her. However, she had not forgotten the uses of publicity, and she took up a new theme, ordering a saloonkeeper to drape a nude figure displayed in his bar. He considered this good advertising, and wrapped his girl in pink netting and hung a card from her neck:

Draped
By Request of
Mrs. Carry Nation
of Kansas.

Carry was not satisfied with the sheer netting and told the saloonkeeper that he should dress the nude as he would his sister. His sense of humor prevailed, and he added a Mother Hubbard and a sunbonnet. For many weeks the imbibers at his bar tilted the sunbonnet this way or that, tweaked at the Mother Hubbard, and made merry quips about Carry Nation. She was helped considerably in Chicago by her entourage of reporters who toured the saloons with her and saw to it that she made copy from day to day. There was keen competition among them, and one newspaperwoman kept Carry in a Turkish bath all night so as to get an exclusive story from her. But once away from dry Kansas Carry had to temper her campaign as she traveled through states where liquor was not taboo. To many she was nothing more than a public nuisance. She was apt to ask people in passing if they loved God. Her hosannas were likely to erupt at any moment, and when driving in a buggy she sometimes chose to stand up, raise her hands to heaven, and shout: "Peace on earth, good will to men." In Washington she drew a crowd by tackling men walking past her with cigars in their mouths.

James E. Furlong, who had managed Adelina Patti, took charge of Carry Nation on this tour. She had always rejected theatrical, circus, and museum offers until he moved into the picture and guided her plan of action. She was stunned to find the liquor traffic so powerful in the East, and the police so hostile to her cause. In New York she stayed at the Hotel Victoria and signed the register "Carry Nation, Your Loving Home Defender, Kansas." When she noticed a statue of Diana over a fountain in the lobby, Carry covered her eyes and spoke sharply to the man-

ager: "Cover up that nasty thing or there'll be a little hatchetation around here." Diana was draped in cheesecloth for Mrs.
Nation's benefit.

In New York, as in Chicago, she was encouraged to make
scenes of this sort by the reporters who followed her. She drove
down Fifth Avenue in an open carriage, with a hatchet mounted
on her shoulder like a rifle, but she did not brandish it in New
York, using it only as a symbol. However, in passing saloons,
she shouted: "Rum, Rummies, Murderers, Hell-Holes." The
Nymphs and Satyr mural over the bar at the Hoffman House was
carefully guarded while she was in town. Carry called on the
police commissioner but made little impression there. Her appearance in the Tenderloin caused a traffic jam of carriages, and
in this area she was cheered and jeered with equal gusto. "How
many souls have been murdered in this drunkard factory today?"
she demanded in front of one saloon.

She became more than a nuisance at the Horse Show, marching
up and down the aisles, gibing at women over their décolletage.
She stopped at Reginald C. Vanderbilt's box and asked how many
of the family millions had been used to rescue "the slaves of the
saloon." He looked surprised, but told her quietly to write a
letter about it. Carry was not satisfied. She continued to insult the
women in his box about their clothes, and finally he gave her an
impatient push. Carry was hauled away by the police, shouting
about the "diamond-studded, gold-fobbed rummies." By this time
she had become a restless publicity seeker and would do anything
to make a headline. The police, however, were slow to arrest her,
for she gloried in the number of times she had been in jail. Each
stay behind bars was a star in her crown, and she chose to address
her judges as "Your Dishonor." She passed ten rowdy days at
Coney Island, where she seemed to be in her element, tongue-
lashing bartenders, shouting her way through the open-air beer
gardens, warning the young to go slow in their love-making, and
snatching cigars from the mouths of smokers. "I want all you
hellions to quit puffing that hell fume in God's clean air," she
screamed at them. Her most dignified appearance in New York

was in Carnegie Hall, where she focused an attack on the corset as well as the bottle. Carry was inclined to ring in other social causes, and dress reform had long been a battle cry among the women of advanced views.

But much of her dash and fervor fell flat in the cynical East. The terror of Kansas seemed a crazy old lady to the tough habitués of the Tenderloin. They had watched reformers before, and when Carry did not swing her hatchet, she ceased to be impressive, for she was a poor speaker—ranting, chaotic, ridiculous, and abusive. Her behavior at Coney Island had given her mission the quality of a sideshow, an impression strengthened when she visited California in 1903 and was roped into appearing at the Los Angeles amusement park known as the Chutes. W.C.T.U. officials were appalled that Mrs. Nation should appear under this worldly aegis, with a beer garden and boatloads of joy riders part of the entertainment, but she explained that she considered the amusement park a mission field. She always denied that she had been exhibited as a curiosity in a museum in Chicago.

If side shows seemed a fitting background at times for Carry Nation, she did not neglect the academic side of public life, but made a special point of visiting leading universities across the country, hoping to interest the younger generation in her cause. Yale impressed her as being the worst of all, with liquor, billiard tables, cigarettes, and a smoking room. Even the food was tainted by the demon rum. She cited ham cooked with champagne, apple dumplings with brandy sauce, as well as wine jelly, claret wine punch, and cherry wine sauce. At Harvard she found even the professors puffing away at cigarettes and, as an added offense, "these same professors are the followers of Huxley and Herbert Spencer, who did far more to make the world ignorant than wise." Ann Arbor was a hotbed of dives where "manhood was drugged and destroyed."

Carry was furious when she found a picture of Theodore Roosevelt on the walls of the headquarters of the Anti-Cigarette League. "Don't you know he is a cigar smoker?" she shouted, which Roosevelt was not. She was closer to the truth when she said that his daughter Alice smoked. On two visits to Washington, in 1904 and 1906, Carry caused endless commotion. When President Roosevelt declined to see her she made a scene in the Capitol. "I wanted to do some Hatchetation," she later reported, "but that not being possible I thought I would do some agitation. I took a position in a lobby near the door. I rose to my feet, and with a volume of voice that was distinctly heard all over the halls I cried aloud: 'Treason, anarchy and conspiracy! Discuss these.' "

The office of President was not immune from Carry's abuse. When she said she had no sympathy for President McKinley or his assassin she was mobbed and had to flee into a saloon for protection. She insisted that he would have recovered from his wound had his blood not been poisoned by nicotine. Carry earlier maintained that he rented property of his wife's in Canton, Ohio, to a saloonkeeper. Her several arrests in Washington did not slow Carry's fury for an instant. Roosevelt, whom she called "blood-thirsty, reckless, and a cigarette-smoking rummy," was a particular target of hers, since she also hung on him the label of being a Mason and a member of the Order of Eagles, which she regarded as a potent liquor organization. The genial William Howard Taft also refused to receive Carry when he was in the White House, and she stalked off accusing him of belonging to the legions of the devil, although he, like Roosevelt, was a most abstemious man.

As her fame grew Carry smartened up her costume. She added long white ribbons, a temperance touch but becoming, to her black poke bonnet. A linen duster usually covered the old black alpaca, and over her shoulder she carried a satchel loaded with miniature hatchets, souvenir buttons and photographs. On special occasions a hatchet almost as large as a broadax dangled from her waist. She had finally got rid of David Nation as a husband, although the public in general had forgotten that he existed. Her smashing operations were at their height when the final break came. He had joined her for a time while she was publishing *The Smasher's Mail*, but nothing he did pleased Carry. In the summer of 1901, when he was seventy-three, he returned to Medicine

Lodge and sued her for divorce on grounds of cruelty and desertion. He threw in a few more charges for good measure—that she
had exposed him to ridicule and humiliation, that she had taken
his featherbed and $900 from his bank account. Carry answered
tartly that the featherbed was hers and that she would fight the
case in order to get her share of his pension. "David isn't a bad
fellow, but he is too slow for me," she commented. In the end she
was exonerated on the cruelty charge, but desertion was proved.
The long-suffering David Nation died two years later, and Carry
added her benediction: "Well, I shall meet him on that day when
the secrets of all hearts shall be made manifest." He had never
been a potent force in her life. Dr. Gloyd was the one who had
mattered.

In the spring of 1905 Carry published a temperance magazine,
The Hatchet, in Guthrie, Oklahoma. She traveled from town to
town through the state, pausing to hold meetings in the middle of
a street, in a schoolhouse, a church, a theater, or wherever she
could muster a crowd. In 1907 she was arrested in Hot Springs as
she was touring gambling dens. Finding herself in jail with three
women of the streets, she promptly fell on her knees "at the sight
of these haggard creatures of despair." She made two trips to
Canada and stormed through the Maritime Provinces and Prince
Edward Island, but Canadians received her with less enthusiasm
on her second visit than on the first. A three-month tour of
Britain in 1908, accompanied by her niece, Callie Moore of
Kansas City, was not a great success either. The world was getting tired of Carry Nation and her hatchet, although she had
strong support in England from the temperance forces. They
were politely interested in what she had to say, although the
crowds were disposed to throw rotten eggs at her or guffaw as
she talked. She lectured all over Scotland, where the vile stuff was
brewed, and she was jeered at in Dublin. When she landed back
in New York on a March day in 1909 she observed that the
British were tea fiends, the women were nervous, and England
was cursed with the House of Lords.

That same year Carry went after fashions. The sheath was in

vogue, and she threatened to tear a daring gown off its wearer's back. She could not abide women who wore plumes in their hats or corseted themselves tightly. At this time she settled briefly in a cottage in the Ozarks near the village of Alpena Pass and continued to lecture, but mostly in the Middle West, where she had her most sympathetic audiences. In 1909 she went East again and was arrested in New York and fined for invading the Knickerbocker Hotel bar. She created a disturbance in the barroom of Union Station in Washington and was again arrested and fined. By this time the number of Carry's arrests was beyond count.

Her final smash-up job was in Wichita, where she had first become famous. This time her objective was what she considered a pornographic painting. But both her sight and her memory were failing. She had lived a violent life and was tired. It was 1910, and she had worn out her welcome everywhere. She made one last speaking tour that year and appeared publicly for the last time on January 13, 1911, at Eureka Springs, close to the Missouri border.

"I have done what I could," said Carry in a feeble voice and collapsed as she was leaving the platform. She was taken to Evergreen Hospital at Leavenworth with a nervous seizure, and she died there five months later at the age of sixty-five. The date was June 2, 1911. Carry was buried with her mother at Belton, Missouri. Ultimately a memorial fountain was erected on the spot where she was first arrested in Wichita. In the archives of the Kansas State Historical Society are several of Carry's hatchets, her black cane made from a tree branch, the broad hatchet she used in her famous Topeka raid of 1901, the last mirror she broke, the war club used by her crusaders in the Topeka raid of 1903, and other souvenirs of her smashing career. In 1950 her house in Medicine Lodge was dedicated as a memorial to Carry Nation by the W.C.T.U. and Community Club. A granite shaft has marked her grave in the Belton Cemetery since 1924. It was dedicated by the Carry A. Nation Monument Association and bears the line "She Hath Done What She Could."

Carry Nation's operations paved the way for the powerful

Anti-Saloon League that became a political force and eventually introduced the prohibition era. Melodramatic though her methods were, she influenced lawmakers and stirred the citizenry to action. Liquor laws were tightened and rigorously enforced as a result of her agitation. In Kansas, where her power was greatest, the legislature abandoned a program sponsored by the liquor interests and passed a measure making common nuisances of all places that sold liquor. It became a penal offense to be found where liquor was dispensed, and one person could be arrested for giving another a drink. Carry's work was copied by others, but none matched her fame or fury. Although she irritated the W.C.T.U. from time to time by her extreme effects, its officials valued her zeal and energy and acknowledged her potency in temperance work.

To the public at large Carry Nation was one of the outstanding eccentrics of the nineteenth century; she had found so many different ways to make people laugh as well as to grow angry. The element of farce was always close to the surface in her operations, and the newspapers made the most of this aspect of her work. She took pride in her hatchet technique and liked to rake the blade clear across a row of bottles as if she were using a scythe. She ended up with an enormous collection of hatchets. Admirers sent them, and sometimes they were made of gold or silver. When children gathered around her she pulled shining new weapons from her gunny sack and showed them how to swing the hatchets. She taught them to call the saloons "hell-holes and murder shops," and liquor "hell-broth and devil soup." More than once she led groups of children on wrecking expeditions and brought them back with their clothes splashed with liquor. Policemen were "rum-soaked, whiskey-swilled, satyr-faced rummies." Fashionably dressed women were "mannikins hung with filthy rags." She usually signed her letters "Your loving Home Defender," and she claimed to represent the "distracted, suffering, loving motherhood of the world." She concentrated on what she considered to be the poison spots, like the Red Light district in San Francisco or the Tenderloin in New York. She invaded the American Tobacco Company plants at Durham, exclaiming over the terrible smell in the air. Carry was convinced that rum was used in Bull Durham. Saloons and drinks were named after her, and some of her particular targets adorned their bars with ornamental hatchets or hung signs saying "All Nations Welcome but Carry." One popular jingle written about her that she particularly liked was called *Samantha*:

Hurrah, Samantha, Mrs. Nation is in town!
So wear your brightest bonnet and your alpaca gown.
Oh, I am so jubilated I'm a-hopping up and down,
Hurrah! Hurrah! Samantha, Mrs. Nation is in town.

She sold souvenir hatchets and pewter souvenirs and made a great deal of money in her lifetime, but at the end she had little left but some land in Arkansas and Oklahoma. In spite of the farcical elements of Carry's campaigning, thousands across the country took her seriously. Carry Nation Clubs and Law and Order Leagues were organized. She was invited to address state legislatures, and she was often the subject of sermons by preachers. Women's organizations in general approved of her work and the feeling prevailed in the Middle West that Carry Nation was a martyr to a worthy cause.

Nellie Bly

Nellie Bly, a dauntless girl, had global aspirations as far back as 1889 and made the world her sphere, without benefit of jet propulsion. The dream of Phileas Fogg had beguiled her, and she girdled the globe in seventy-two days, six hours, and eleven minutes, a feat that drew almost as much comment in the Golden Nineties as the astronauts did in the 1960's. In her tweed ulster and ghillie cap she whipped up excitement from Jersey City to Shanghai as she sped from point to point by ship, train, sampan, barouche, and jinricksha. Nellie raced and took short cuts, roasted and froze in the changing climates, until she achieved the climax that her paper, the New York *World*, called "Outdoing Father Time."

"Bravo!" exclaimed the incredulous Jules Verne, whose book had given Nellie her inspiration.

"Très chic!" said the editor of *Le Petit Journal*.

"Prodigious!" added the editor of *Le Figaro*.

"Miss Bly has done for American journalism what Stanley did for it in 1873," said a member of the welcoming committee that greeted Nellie on her return.

But her success was no surprise to her backer, Joseph Pulitzer. Although she had become a world celebrity almost overnight, he had had earlier proof of the seeds of adventure latent in the demure Miss Bly. She had proved that she had nerves of steel before he agreed to her novel request that she race around the world and outdo the record of Phileas Fogg. When he suggested that this was an assignment for a man, she told him firmly that if he turned her down, she would leave on the same day and race his candidate. Her granduncle, Thomas Kenney, had gone round the world in three years. He had planned to write a book about his adventures, but his health failed along the way; now Nellie proposed to fulfill his mission.

Preparations were made with secrecy, for these were fiercely competitive days on Park Row. In three days Nellie had assembled an odd wardrobe—an ulster with shoulder cape made at Ghormley's, a ghillie cap, a plaid cloth dress, and a camel's hair costume that she thought—mistakenly—would serve for the heat. She tucked in three veils, a jacket, a dressing gown, some flannel underwear, and comfortable shoes. A crocodile gripsack held her clothes, and her toothbrush was tucked in the knapsack that she slung over her shoulder. Her most valuable possessions were her twenty-four-hour watch, five hundred dollars in American money, and two hundred pounds in sterling. On her left thumb she wore the ring that she had sported the day she talked Joseph Pulitzer into giving her a job.

Nellie sailed on the *Augusta Victoria* from Jersey City on November 14, 1889, with her mother and a *World* man present to bid her farewell. "I am off but shall I ever get back?" said Nellie, her big gray eyes mournful but her lips determinedly set.

Her chestnut hair, with chignon and bangs, was artfully tucked under her Sherlock Holmes cap.

World correspondents had been instructed to meet Nellie at all her stopping places to speed her on her way with the best local conveyance, whether camel or river boat. Once she was on the high seas the secret was out, and headlines proclaimed her progress from point to point. She swept through Europe like a passing breeze, visiting Jules Verne in his old stone house in France. He stared with Gallic amazement at the small, earnest-minded girl who had grown so serious over a dream. Madame Verne nodded when he expressed doubt that she would succeed —"charming and intrepid though she was."

At home the excitement was intense. A circular chart tracing Nellie's progress was published every day by the *World*. The public followed the game with checkers, pennies, or dice, betting when she would reach a given point. The days, the hours, the minutes were counted, and readers agonized with Nellie as she coped with heat and insects, mashers, beggars, bandits, and filth. Late trains were her particular terror, since her schedule did not allow for a moment's delay. Little pleased her in the world she viewed with such lightning speed. She took a dim view of the passing scene and never failed to find the weak spot as she moved on from country to country. She disliked the railway carriages of Europe, the fog in Italy, the rude stewards, the vagrant storms, the deplorable food. Nellie knew how to rant, and she did.

Meanwhile, the *World* kept drumming up the excitement on the home front. Nellie's dash became a matter of daily prayer, as well as of curses, to the seasoned cynics under the gold dome of Park Row. Behind Mr. Pulitzer's back they said what they thought of girl reporters as they wrote columns of pictorial background to augment Nellie's dispatches and keep the excitement alive on the many days when they did not hear from her. Their readers had daily lessons in geography from whiskered reporters who pored over the gazetteer and spun their counterpoint until Nellie's own high-powered messages came flashing in by cable.

She did full justice to the perils of her trip. When she rode on a donkey's back through the streets of Port Said Nellie caught the glint of sin in every doorway. The heat of the Suez Canal oppressed her, but she wrote graphically of the Arab encampments, with camels and masters huddled around small wood fires. Her ship was two days late in getting to Ceylon, and the *World* made capital out of this delay. But soon her cool gray eyes were focused on the manners of the "Colonials," as well as on the lovely harbor, the brooding mountains, the temples, and the elephants that she saw bathing on her way to Kandy. Before leaving Colombo Nellie remembered the ladies at home in New York and enlarged on the zircons and moonstones that she saw in the jewelry shops.

In Hong Kong she found fresh cause for alarm. Elizabeth Bisland, who had been shipped off in the opposite direction by William Randolph Hearst when he learned that Nellie Bly was whirling around the globe, was making fast time. But such was the stir Nellie was causing by this time that the public scarcely noticed the progress of her rival.

"Go East girls, go East," she exclaimed as she surveyed the sparkling lights on the hillside above the harbor of Hong Kong. Here she took time to shop, abandoning her flannel underwear in favor of tropical muslin. She lunched in the Temple of the Dead and spent Christmas day in Canton. Before leaving she picked up a monkey that sat on her shoulder at subsequent press appearances, for she was now interviewed at every stop. But she was saving her best for the *World*. Before leaving the Orient she announced, with one of her sweeping judgments, that the Japanese had few vices while the Chinese had all the vices in the world.

When she sailed from Yokohama on the *Oceanic* on January 7, 1890, homeward bound, her luck did not fail her. A monsoon gave her ample scope for the high-powered reporting that she preferred, but she feared delay and paced the deck with short, firm steps, concentrating all her will power on the onward sweep of the ship. Time was running short, but everyone was doing his best for her. And the public was getting anxious. Would Nellie make it?

She did. A special train awaited her in San Francisco. When she landed on January 21 the mayor, members of the Press Club, and a huge crowd gathered around her and cheered. But again Nellie had no time to waste, for New York was her destination. The *World* man's train had been stalled in a snowstorm, and he mushed on snowshoes to join Nellie's train at Lathrop, Missouri. Brass bands and joyous shouts greeted her in Albuquerque. When the train stopped to coal, people gathered around to stare at the girl who had raced around the world. The monkey on her shoulder became the authentic symbol of foreign lands. The Chicago Press Club, which had never before received a woman, gave a breakfast for Nellie and could scarcely bear to let her go, but she swallowed her food hastily and kept on the march. It was a triumphal trip, with flags flying along the route, and huzzas reaching from the prairies to New York.

Ten guns boomed from the Battery and Brooklyn to welcome her home. She had traveled 24,899 miles and looked only slightly the worse for wear. Her skin was toasted brown by wind and sun. Her gray eyes were alight with satisfaction, and her firm jaw could now relax in a smile. Nellie's ulster looked worn and her ghillie cap had survived too many showers. But to spruce her up for this occasion would have been to strip the actress of her trappings. The entire front page of the *World* on January 26, 1890, was given up to Nellie Bly's coup. Smashing headlines were followed by an account of her reception as the guns boomed:

Is some one dead?

Only an old era. And the booming yonder at the Battery and Fort Greene tolls its passing away. The stage-coach days are ended, and the new age of lightning travel begun. And amid all the tumult walks the little lady, with just a foot of space between her and that madly joyous mob. She is carrying a little walking-stick in one hand and with the other waves her checkered little fore-and-aft traveling cap, and laughs merrily as her name is hoarsely shouted from innumerable throats. Tense faces stare from the long galleries that bend ominously beneath their awful load of humanity. The tops of passenger coaches lying upon the side tracks are black with men and boys....

But the little girl trips gaily along. The circuit of the globe is behind her. Time is put to blush. She has brushed away distance as if it were down. Oceans and continents she has traversed....

Nellie was treated to a Broadway parade as part of the welcoming ceremonies. There was no thought of ticker tape in 1890, but the crowd was so dense that the horses had to stop from time to time. She waved and bowed; she smiled and sometimes burst into laughter. The police had to clear the way for her to get to the Astor House. For days she moved in a haze of acclamation. Cablegrams and telegrams poured in to the *World*, Joseph Pulitzer was jubilant. William Randolph Hearst still stood by Elizabeth Bisland, who had been left behind in the race but would eventually come through with a good account of herself in one of his magazines. But Nellie was set apart for the rest of her life and heard strange echoes of this welcome even to her dying day.

When she had time to catch her breath she wrote her own story in four detailed chapters, to add to all the episodic dispatches that had been flooding the *World* for ten weeks. She now faced the clamor that roared around her like a storm. Wherever she went she was confronted with her own image—on posters, on sheet music, on cigar bands. She gave testimonials to Pears' Soap, to pills and housecoats. A race horse was named Nellie Bly. A song "Globe Trotting Nellie Bly" was sung on Broadway and across the country. Nellie had become a world celebrity who had left echoes from Park Row to Hong Kong. There were jokes, cartoons, dinner-table conversation to cement her image further in the public consciousness, and games were named after her. A cigar advertisement showed her teetering on the globe. The accompanying jingle ran:

> When Nellie Bly the final Tie
> That bound the earth had knotted
> The World looked on and cried "Well done"
> The Globe was bravely trotted.

Another poster showed her on a tightrope, balancing a parasol, with the world at her feet. It took one of her beaux, James Metcalfe, a magazine writer who had helped to found *Life,* to spoof Nellie's trip. He ran a series of stories on the adventures of "Miss Sadie McGinty, *Life's* Celebrated and Fearless Reporter" in a trip around Manhattan Island. P. T. Barnum took note that a flash of lightning had ripped across Park Row, but Nellie felt that she had a good pulpit of her own at the *World.*

However, having touched the topmost peak, everything she did afterward seemed anticlimactic to the restless, ambitious girl. She went back to what she had been doing before—stunts on the home front, but now she moved in the aura of her own fame. Her name and face were known in every household. She was pointed out in the streets, in theaters, when she walked in the park. Her coup, which remained unmatched until Dorothy Kilgallen sped around the world at a faster pace in 1936, had established Nellie Bly as one of the pioneers.

She came from sturdy stock. Born in a rambling Pennsylvania farmhouse on May 5, 1867, she was twenty-two when she went around the world. Her father, Michael Cochrane, had been a laborer, a mill hand, a postmaster, a justice of the peace, and then an associate judge. As he gained in influence, Pitts Mills, where he lived, became Cochrane's Mills in his honor. He was a studious man, and he encouraged his daughter Elizabeth to read. She was the third child of his second marriage and everyone knew her as Pinky, for her mother invariably dressed her in pink gingham. She had three brothers, two half-brothers, and a sister. Elizabeth was delicate and was quickly brought home from the boarding school in Indiana that she attended in her thirteenth year.

The Cochranes moved eventually to Apollo, a mining town, but soon afterward the judge died and Mrs. Cochrane took the children to live in Pittsburgh. For a short time Nellie worked as a governess, but as she fed on the romantic serials of the day, she burned with ambition to get out into the larger world. After the Civil War women were groping for some better understanding of their status, and Elizabeth was indignant over the scathing tone of an editorial in the Pittsburgh *Dispatch* entitled "What Girls Are

Good For." Apparently nothing but to have children, cook, sew, and nurse. She thought this outrageous and wrote a sizzling answer. George Madden, who had written the editorial, was struck by the logic and good writing in this anonymous letter. He inserted an advertisement, asking its author to get in touch with him. Elizabeth soon walked into his office, a shy girl, with a wide, firm mouth and sad gray eyes that turned cold and calculating as she talked with quiet force. The meek and melancholy air that stayed with Nellie to the time of her death concealed the terrific driving force that was part of her nature. She quickly sold him the idea of doing personal experience stories, flashing the slums, the prisons, the sweatshops of Pittsburgh as bait, but first they agreed that she should write a piece on divorce. It was sharp and controversial, and brought so much response that she was accepted as a member of the staff. Her pen name, Nellie Bly, was taken from Stephen Foster's song. He was a native of Pittsburgh and everyone seemed to be singing his songs at this time.

Nellie adapted herself smoothly to journalism. She had three central ideas—to focus on the ills of the social body; to get her facts from first-hand experience; to clothe them in pointed prose. The times were such that she had plenty to work on, and she showed a sure touch for the slightest suggestion of injustice or inequality in public institutions. Margaret Fuller had been doing something of the sort for Horace Greeley's *Tribune*. She had visited Blackwell's Island and Sing Sing, writing philosophical essays on the treatment of the prisoners; on the plight of the city prostitute. She had raised class issues in the 1840's. Nellie Bly was no Margaret Fuller. Her exclamatory prose was far removed from the felicitous style that had charmed *Dial* subscribers, but it drove to the heart of an issue and held the reader's attention. All around her new causes were fomenting, and she was in tune with the revolutionary spirit. She was not a theorist or even an idealist, and it was all too clear to those who knew her best that her enterprise was dedicated to the glory of Nellie Bly. But she touched some chord and created enough stir to leave a wake of reform behind her.

Nellie developed an infallible instinct for the topic guaranteed to engage public interest. She explored the factories and work-shops of Pittsburgh and stood at a machine for fourteen hours a day in a bottling factory. Vermin and rats scurried around her, and she earned five dollars a week. Her fellow workers, in their innocence of her identity, talked freely to Nellie of the sodden conditions under which they labored. But she had not been in action long before the city fathers and the big businessmen began to protest. Who was this wild woman who was blowing up such storms? The advertisers viewed her operations with open distaste, but the preachers swore by Nellie Bly and her revelations. Her editor liked her and saw the value of her work, but the pressure on him was great and he steered her into the quieter channels of social news, where she could comment on books, music, and the theater. But not for long. Nellie rejected this humdrum routine and headed west to expose conditions in a penitentiary. On her return she wrote another inflammatory factory exposé. Her col-leagues were now beginning to regard her as the town terror and Madden, studying her trim little figure, her quietly insistent manner and mournful eyes, wondered what strange furies drove her to such extremes.

Again he retired her to the academic sidelines, but Nellie con-sidered it her lot to tilt at the big interests, to identify herself with the fighting legions. And since her editor was obviously trying to clip her wings she set off with her mother for six months in Mexico. Although she was not on the payroll, her editors agreed to buy any articles that they liked. Americans were just becoming aware of the riotous beauties of the Mexican land-scape, but behind the bright colors, the picturesque dress, the lush vegetation Nellie sought the seeds of corruption. She lashed out at the men who stared at her in the streets, their treatment of women, the ignorance that underlay the glowing scene around her. President Diaz was opening up the country by railroad communication, and Nellie decided to do a thorough tour, to visit the silver mines, to explore remote regions of the country. She and her mother went jogging over rough roads on strenuous pack trips. They stayed at small inns and haciendas, and Nellie picked up some Spanish as she traveled.

In Mexico City she was invited to bull fights, to fiestas and parties of various kinds, but when word came back from Pittsburgh that her dispatches were none too friendly, the air became chilly around her. When she returned home she continued to write of the land south of the border and still had plenty of material left to use when she reached New York, for Nellie now headed east to try for Park Row. She told one of her editors that she wanted to work for a New York newspaper, to reform the world, to fall in love, and to marry a millionaire. In course of time she managed it all, except for the small matter of reforming the world. She had been stirred by Joseph Pulitzer's talk of sending up a balloon at St. Louis. Nellie began to think in terms of space.

She arrived in New York on a hot July day in 1887, wearing a flowered hat that she had bought in Mexico City. But the walls of Jericho did not crumble at the first blast of her trumpet. She went straight to Park Row and made the first of many visits to the *World* offices. Each time she was turned away with the brief suggestion that she write a letter. But Nellie was not a girl to waste her time, and while she waited for further developments she batted out stories on Mexico for a small syndicate. Her funds were meager but her nerve was unshaken. After having her purse with her last hundred dollars stolen, she pushed her way past the gatekeeper into an office where Joseph Pulitzer was conferring with Colonel John A. Cockerill, his managing editor. Pulitzer peered at her shortsightedly through his pince-nez. The carefully tailored and dignified Colonel Cockerill greeted her politely and listened to what Nellie had to say. Neither man knew how she had ferreted her way in to see them, but she soon caught their attention. She began by telling about her stolen purse, and then she whipped out a list of suggestions for personal experience stories. The colonel studied her list, talked to Pulitzer, and ticked off those that interested him. The first involved a stay on Blackwell's Island, an asylum run by the city. The era of the stunt girl had dawned.

Nellie trod on air, no longer envious of the men she had seen coming out of the *World* and the *Tribune* and swinging into saloons around Park Row. Her chance had come, and not for a moment did she doubt her own capacity. To live among the insane she must play her part to the hilt, and she took extravagant measures to bolster up her imposture. She practiced mad scenes before the dingy mirror in her room, grimacing, laughing, and shrieking. From frenzy she lapsed into the glazed stare of one in a trance. Because Nellie never did anything by halves she read ghost stories, and novels about the demented. Finally she stayed in a temporary home for females to earn committal to Blackwell's Island. Here she threw herself on the floor, behaved in cataleptic fashion, and varied her acting with some wistful Ophelia moments. The matron summoned police, and she was taken to Blackwell's Island, with four doctors pronouncing her a hysteric. On the island she kept up the masquerade, shifting from apathy to frenzied twitching and babbling nonsense. Only one doctor became skeptical as the days went on. The New York *Evening Telegram* described the lovely and cultivated girl who had landed on Blackwell's Island in a mad state, but the *World* kept quiet, sustaining Nellie in her deception.

Nothing that went on around her escaped her keen eye, and when finally freed her articles were so sensational that there were instant repercussions. She enlarged on the brutal treatment of the patients, the callous nurses, the inedible food, the ice-cold baths from which patients were flung wringing wet into bed, the flirtations between doctors and nurses, the unsanitary conditions and disregard for human decencies. She said that the patients were dosed with chloral and morphine, and she was denied water until her throat was so parched that she could scarcely speak.

New Yorkers talked for days of Nellie Bly's revelations. An investigation was ordered, and she testified before the grand jury. Later she accompanied its members on a tour of the island. Everyone had had warning of what was coming, and things had been spruced up. The patients Nellie had quoted could not be found. The nurses contradicted her on every point. But although little was found to substantiate her charges, the grand jury was on her side and believed her story. They sustained her findings, and the city voted $3,000,000 for the improvement of Blackwell's Island.

With this coup behind her she turned her attention to the jails. She checked in at the Gedney House and framed a theft with a friend so as to be committed to jail. Once behind bars she scooped up facts and soon *World* readers were following her exposé of filthy conditions, of leering turnkeys and ribald calls from drunken men, of insensate indifference to human needs. As a result of Nellie's findings matrons were assigned to women prisoners. She now moved smoothly from one area to another, studying employment agencies that exploited immigrant girls, and matrimonial agencies that were swindling concerns. A quick turn in the chorus line persuaded Nellie that the Broadway show girls were the victims of inhuman practices, too. She answered a call for a hundred girls for a pantomime given at the Academy of Music. Even here she found ground for complaint. The dressing rooms were crowded. The girls earned only five dollars a week. Her tights did not fit. Her ballet slippers were sizes too large for Nellie's tiny feet.

Reformers found her a good ally as she investigated the conditions surrounding the servant, the shopgirl, the factory girl, the chorus girl. The "female operator," as the working girl was known, was coming into prominence. She was viewed as a wretched creature unable to find a husband. Dr. Charles H. Parkhurst, heading the Society for the Prevention of Crime, was exploring dens of vice in his showy campaign to clean up the city. He turned to Nellie Bly as one who could get his message on the front page. Since white slavers were supposed to haunt the factories, Nellie arrived at a box factory in gingham, carrying her lunch in a brown paper bag. She made $2.50 a week for piecework and found abuses at every turn.

By this time Nellie had become something of a terror, and sinners were apt to look hard at applicants wearing uncommonly rustic bonnets, to make sure that the girl reporter's cool gray eyes were not fixed on them with attention. She was as ubiquitous and unexpected as Candid Camera in the 1960's. But she did much good. Factory girls worked a twelve-hour day and often made less than fifty cents a week. By bringing this constantly to the attention of the public she created sympathy for them, and threw some light on the wretched conditions under which they worked. She was fearless in going into tenements to help the sick and to get aid for ailing children. Time and again she emerged unscathed from epidemics and continued to answer the calls that reached the *World* asking for her help. Nellie had become the champion of the hungry, the sick, the abused, and the under-privileged. She invaded homes for the aged and pointed up what could be done to improve them. At the same time she was strongly moralistic. In many respects she was ahead of her time, and she constantly urged her fellow workers in shops and fac-tories to go to Cooper Institute for free education. Eventually she had a long list of girls who said they owed their start to her advice. As she stood behind a glove counter and picked up facts for a story, she also did a little preaching on the side, urging the girls to stand up for themselves and demand their rights. One of her most successful stunts was the period she spent as a Salvation Army lass. The ten-column story that followed brought a tre-mendous response.

Everything that Nellie wrote was in the first person, and she made an emotional play that has not been duplicated in her field. Much of it might seem like drivel in today's newspaper, yet it fitted the contemporary frame, and no one could question her right to front-page attention. She thought up nearly all her own stories, although her paper backed her in her crusades. No one ever knew what Nellie's own opinions were, for she had stock sentiments that she trotted out to suit any occasion that might arise. Her colleagues in the city room did not warm to her, but her comings and goings were of constant interest, and they were never surprised to see her walking in with some fantastic disguise. When she was strictly herself she had the air of a prim little Puritan, with immaculate kid gloves and neatly coiffed dark hair. Her editors valued her highly, and so did Joseph Pulitzer. She visited him on his yacht and sat with him in the soundproof room from which he directed the destiny of his paper on Park Row. He was always interested in Nellie's original ideas, and the *World* was heavily committed to the technique of the exposé. Soon the men were being assigned to major crusades and exposés.

Nellie had many serious interviews and made a point of seeking out the wives of presidents, both in and out of office. Mrs. John Tyler, the beautiful Julia Gardiner of Long Island, recalled how her husband had written "Sweet Lady, Awake" for her. She told Nellie that she had worn a white tarletan gown and a crimson Grecian cap on the night he proposed. Mrs. Ulysses S. Grant, wife of a great soldier and a controversial president, said that self-forgetfulness was "death to fear." She found Mrs. James Knox Polk contented in her old age, with distant memories of the days before the Civil War. Mrs. Rutherford B. Hayes and Mrs. James A. Garfield were as interested in Nellie as she was in them. Mrs. Grover Cleveland received her at Oak View, the President's summer home, and expressed interest in what she was doing for the working girl. Mrs. Andrew Johnson, and Mrs. Mary Arthur McElroy, the sister of President Arthur, were subjects also for Nellie's sometimes naïve and always persistent flow of questions. She carefully assessed another lady who aspired to the White House—not as a wife, but as President. Belva Ann Lockwood, nominated by the National Equal Rights party both in 1884 and 1888, was successor to Victoria Woodhull and forerunner of Margaret Chase Smith. Nellie found her severe, gray-haired, and the opposite of the fascinating Mrs. Woodhull. Mrs. Lockwood told Nellie that her great interest was the establishment of a court of international arbitration for settling all differences between the United States and other countries. Another type of woman agitator was Emma Goldman, the Russian anarchist whom Nellie Bly visited on Blackwell's Island in 1893. Emma told her frankly: "I have been an anarchist all my life. I am, because I am an egotist."

It was inevitable that Nellie should interview Buffalo Bill behind the scenes at his Wild West show. He recognized a fellow showman in demure little Nellie. But Nellie was in full cry when she turned her attention to the evils of Tammany Hall. She followed the roisterers and corrupters to Saratoga, and a contemporary cartoon showed her leading the Tammany tiger on a chain. She was as formidable on the political front as she was in exposing jails. One of her most discussed campaigns was directed against Edward R. Phelps, a fixer and lobbyist at Albany. She followed him there and inveigled him into collusion by asking his help in fighting a patent medicine bill. Nellie posed as the wife of a man with a small patent medicine factory, concerned because the object of the bill was to protect the public from false medicines. He told her how much he would need to put through the deal, and he named the legislators whom he thought he could bribe to vote against it. She met him the following day in a hotel lobby, and in the end she went off with a list of the men involved. A *World* reporter stayed in the background, watching over Nellie and observing the man's movements. Nellie was to meet Phelps the following day with the cash he demanded, but by that time she was on her way to New York to make fresh headlines. A state investigation followed, and she took the stand to testify against Phelps. He was found guilty, but in the meantime she had to move about with a bodyguard.

Nellie called him the Lobby King of Albany and launched a rollicking verse on his operations, in the Gilbert and Sullivan vein:

> For I'm a Pirate King!
> I'm in the lobby ring!
> Oh, what an uproarious
> Jolly and glorious
> Biz for a pirate king.

Her next exploit involved a bold masher in Central Park, who drove a dashing pair of bays at a smart clip through the park, ogled girls, and usually made off with a victim to what Nellie took to be a life of prostitution. She arrayed herself in flowered cotton and wore a wide straw hat with roses; a shawl covered her shoulders and she looked as if she had just arrived from the country. She settled herself on a park bench facing the drive and waited for the man with bronze whiskers to drive up. Her coy air of invitation worked at once, and he invited her to get into his carriage. They went north to a roadhouse at 116th Street, and he promised that he would help her to get on the stage. Nellie lured him on to his own undoing. He talked freely and told her that he watched for girls fresh from the country and showed them how to earn a living. At the roadhouse he offered Nellie a drink. In the end she told him that she was not a friendless girl from the country, and she proved so discouraging that he drove her back to the park in a fury. But he had no idea that she was Nellie Bly until the *World* appeared with three sizzling columns on his operations. It developed that he was the foreman of a livery stable who, on his day off, drove through the park, dressed and pomaded to the hilt. After Nellie had done with him he was seen no more in Central Park nor in his livery stable.

There were lighter moments in her career. She drove through fields of hop in Oneida County, seeing what the farmers were up to, and this time it was all innocent fun as Nellie danced the Money Musk in a barn, with flickering lanterns lighting up the scene, and three fiddlers providing music. She could shift from the worldly to the rustic tempo at a moment's notice, but she was more often serious than gay.

Mrs. Cochrane, a delicate, fastidious woman who kept house for Nellie after her daughter became so successful, was often her chaperone at the theater and restaurants. Jim Metcalfe was her favorite escort in 1888, before she went round the world, and they would picnic on Riverside Drive or stroll through the Metropolitan Museum. Metcalfe was witty and sardonic, and he liked to make fun of Nellie's high-powered operations, but even he had to doff his hat to her after her race around the world. Life seemed dull for her after that, however. She had her own Sunday column in the *World,* embellished with wreaths and flowers, in which she was free to say what she liked. In introducing it she wrote: "This is all my own. Herein every Sunday I may say all I please and what I please." Her interest in stunts was fading by this time. Other newspaper girls had come along, willing to throw themselves in the way of street cars, to be arrested and taken to hospitals, to go down in diving bells and up in balloons, to pose as Salvation Army lasses or factory girls. But her sympathy was always with the workers. She wrote sympathetically of Coxey's Army when it stormed Washington, and she went to Chicago at the time of the Pullman strike and sent back enthusiastic reports of the men who had turned the tables on their self-avowed benefactor. Again she went west to write of the drought-ridden areas in Nebraska and South Dakota where thousands were destitute after two dry summers and severe winters. She organized a relief committee in New York to send food and medical aid to the sufferers.

Nellie was on this assignment when she met the millionaire she had always said she would marry. He was Robert L. Seaman, a hardware manufacturer, seventy-two years old. They had their first encounter on the train traveling west, and he was struck by Nellie's charitable impulses as she went to work on her story. He was already quite familiar with her by-line in the *World*. They were married a few days after their return in the Church of the Epiphany. The year was 1895 and Nellie was twenty-eight. The *World*, losing one of the most sensational reporters in its history, commented on this much-discussed wedding:

> The readers of the Sunday World will surely be interested to know that Nellie Bly is married. She is now Mrs. Robert Seaman. Her marriage, like most of the other important events in Nellie Bly's life, was out of the ordinary. She met her husband on the train, on the way to Chicago, only a few days before she became a bride.
>
> Miss Bly will become the mistress of a metropolitan residence, a magnificent country seat, a whole stableful of horses, and nearly everything the good fairy of the story books always pictures. Few young women have had more worldly experience than Miss Bly and few are more capable of enjoying the pleasures of a millionaire's existence.

Nellie was immediately established in a four-story brownstone mansion at 15 West Thirty-seventh Street. The Seamans had a farm of three hundred acres in the Catskills and other farms in New York State, as well as real estate holdings in New York. Nellie's husband had courtly manners and strong convictions. He was quite as firm-willed as his enterprising wife, and they had not been married a year before he turned over to her the Ironclad Company that he owned in Brooklyn. It employed a thousand workers and turned out a great variety of hardware—from milk cans and coal scuttles to barrels and garbage containers. Until 1904 the Seamans ran their flourishing business together, entertained on Murray Hill, and traveled at will. No longer did Nellie race from point to point with knapsack and notebook. She made leisurely trips in luxurious liners and took time to study the art galleries and treasures of Europe. Americans abroad took note of the famous Nellie Bly dining in the leading restaurants of Paris and buying clothes in the most fashionable establishments. Among her friends was Hetty Green, who had little use for human contacts but who found in Nellie a responsive spark, an understanding of the intense drive that made both women such strong individualists. Nellie was now as gorgeously arrayed as Hetty was dingy in her rags and tatters. She enjoyed the days of her prosperity to the full until Seaman died in 1904. The years that followed were a nightmare of business confusion, disputes, bankruptcy, and litigation that ate up nearly all her fortune.

Nellie had been an astute and wary reporter, but she was ill-equipped for the business world. At first she had success, but she became too ambitious. She was at her office from seven to six each day, and she made over her husband's business, introducing new methods. She put up new buildings, and in five years the business had expanded to where the American Steel Barrel Company was the largest factory of its kind in the country and was doing a million dollars' worth of business each year. In 1912 she was listed as one of the leading women industrialists in the country, but by this time disasters were beginning to mount. One of the largest of her buildings burned down. She was sued for breach of contract by an employee, and it then came to light that the company had been swindled right and left. Nellie insisted that her name had been forged for large amounts. A $25,000 yacht had been charged to her account, and her mother was held responsible for $12,000 worth of boilers and cans.

The company had lost more than two million dollars, and there was nothing for Nellie to do but go bankrupt. She believed that the receivers were in collusion with faithless workers to deprive her of her holdings, and she fought them with a battery of high-priced lawyers. Her charges of forgery were described as hallucinations, and she was accused of trying to defraud her own company. Finally an indictment for perjury was drawn up against her. She refused to produce the company books when the court ruled in 1914 that she must do so. Like Hetty Green, she became a professional litigant. One moment she was tight-fisted; the next, generous to an excessive degree. But she could never quite believe that her fortune had melted away so unreasonably.

Bitter and chagrined, Nellie set off for Europe. Her business had not only failed but a cloud of doubt and suspicion now surrounded her operations. While she was still abroad, and brooding constantly over her business disasters, the First World War broke out. She was in Austria at the time and soon became romantically interested in Oscar Bondy, a wealthy Viennese. When she returned to the United States in 1919, at the end of the war, the Brooklyn *Eagle* noted that the famous Nellie Bly was "charmingly garbed in silks and furs, still as vivacious as the indefatigable, fearless investigator of years ago. Nellie Bly still overpowers one with her striking personality."

On her return she was cleared of the indictment that had stood against her for five years, and she considered this moral vindication. But soon she and her mother were battling each other in the courts for ownership of the American Steel Barrel Company. Nellie had transferred the stock to Bondy in Vienna to save it from her creditors, but in the meantime it had been confiscated by the United States Alien Custodian, since he was an enemy alien. When Nellie's mother tried to recover it as her own stock Nellie became co-defendant. In 1920 the court ruled that while the transfer of the stock had not been fraudulent, Bondy should maintain control of the company until Mrs. Cochrane's death, and then Nellie could settle the question of ownership. But there was little left in any event, and Nellie's life spiraled off into impoverished obscurity.

Finally Arthur Brisbane brought her back to Park Row, to work on the New York *Journal*. But the newspaper world had changed, and so had Nellie Bly. A new generation of newspaper girls had arisen and stunts no longer prevailed. They went in for clean, hard reporting, without emotional overtones or editorial comment. Nellie's style was anachronistic. Colleagues meeting her on a story scarcely knew who she was. She had a private room at the *Journal*, and she walked through the city room with her face hidden behind a heavy veil studded with chenille dots. She was no longer the sprightly little figure that had raced around the world, for she had put on weight and moved with slow dignity. At no time in her life had she ever been friendly with other reporters; she had always preferred to play a solo hand and aim for the larger audience. But now she stood aloof even from the men and women in her own office. She was little more than a legend. If this was bitter for her, no one knew it. In any event, she was tired and ill, and her main preoccupation was with her abandoned children. Although she had never had any children of her own, she had helped a great many in the course of her lifetime, and one of her best friends in her last years was Edwin Gould, founder of the Gould Foundation for children.

But on January 30, 1920, Nellie Bly again made a bid for the headlines with her last stunt. She witnessed the execution of Gordon Hamby, a spectacular young murderer who died in Sing Sing. She had made friends with him as he waited for death, and he left her his Ouija board with a note: "A slight remembrance (all I have at this time) for your infinite kindness and friendship." Hamby was one of the murderers of the 1920's who, like Gerald Chapman, was built up in the papers as a "gentleman and a scholar." They were not in the tradition of Jack Diamond, Dutch Schultz, and the other speakeasy killers because they could parse and spell, and even write poetry. As Hamby went to the chair he smoked a cigarette that Nellie had given him. She shut her eyes when the current was turned on. She was the first woman in twenty-nine years to witness an execution in New York State, and her story was written in her old florid style:

> Horrible! Horrible! Horrible!
> Hamby is dead. The law has been carried out—presumably the law is satisfied. . . . Through my mind flitted the thought that one time this young boy going to the death chair had been welcomed by some fond mother. He had been a baby, lo, loved and cherished. And this is the end. . . .

The women reporters scarcely noticed that Nellie had scored another tremendous beat, and, if they did, it no longer seemed to matter, for the day for such tricks was over. Her pretext for viewing the execution was to campaign against capital punishment.

Two years later Nellie Bly was dead. The *World*, which had once devoted pages to her first-person stories, ran an obscure half-column on an inside page on the most spectacular star the paper had ever had. The *Journal* noted that she was considered the best reporter in America. She had died of pneumonia in a hospital at the age of fifty-six, and funeral services were held for her at the Church of the Transfiguration, better known as the Little Church Around the Corner. But here and there, throughout the city, were aging men and women with sharp memories of the exciting days on Park Row, when Pulitzer and Hearst were in deadly combat, and Nellie Bly—never aggressive, always a trifle demure—had moved mountains with her indomitable will.

Isadora Duncan

============

"*You are part of the trees, the sky, you are the dominating* goddess of Nature," Gabriel d'Annunzio told Isadora Duncan as they walked together in a forest. The Niobe whose tears flowed for twelve years after her two children were drowned in the Seine, whose own life would end as dramatically as it had been lived—with a scarlet scarf caught in the wheel of a racing car wound around her throat—was used to the homage of famous men. Her creative dancing, her magic influence over audiences, her ballet schools, her lovers, and her revolutionary politics made her one of the most discussed artists of her era, and in the long run left an impression of stormy eccentricity. Rodin admired her, Duse was her friend, Stravinsky went into raptures over her dancing. She won her way in Paris, London, Berlin, Vienna,

Budapest, Moscow, Athens, and New York. She knew the raptures of great ovations and the chill contempt of those who thought that Isadora Duncan posed but did not dance.

Her personal life shared interest with her art, for the two were indistinguishable. To some she was a genius; to others a political defector; to herself a scourge; to her friends a trial; to her lovers a torment. There were no half measures in her life, but there was always raw passion, and a genius for causing trouble, to the point where even her family abandoned her. She lived a vagabond life when she was not wrapped in luxury. She had no sense of time, of money, of obligation, and contracts and engagements were forgotten when she was caught in the web of her own emotions. She made no secret of the fact that she was a revolutionist, and the violence of her emotions brought her often to the brink of tragedy. From the loveliness of her youth she became fat, lazy, and intemperate as the years went on, so that George Balanchine, the choreographer, viewed her with horror when he saw her in Russia in the early 1920's. "I thought she was awful," he wrote. "I don't understand it when people say she was a great dancer. To me it was absolutely unbelievable—a drunken, fat woman who for hours was rolling around like a pig."

Yet at the turn of the century she was a symbol of grace—with her auburn hair, her slightly tilted nose, her blue-gray eyes so often dense with feeling, her instinct for rhythmic motion. It was her aim to blend a poem, a melody, a dance, so that the watcher would not listen to the music, see the dance, or hear the poem, but would absorb the thought that all were expressing. Isadora's flowing tunic and bare feet, the dark blue curtains and stripped stage, started a new fashion in the dance. She moved out of the darkness with the impact of a primitive force, progressing in trancelike attitudes, or bounding in joyous bursts of motion. Serge Koussevitzky said of her: "I consider Isadora Duncan epoch-making in the sphere of the dance—for she is the first artist who did not dance to the music, but incarnated music in her dance."

For using classical music in the projection of her art, Isadora came under fire, but both Michael Fokine and Leonide Massine later used the symphonic ballet. She scorned the classical ballet at a time when it was having a great revival. Pink tights and ballet slippers filled her with contempt, but she liked Pavlova and considered her a great dancer. Opinions differ on the ultimate effect Isadora Duncan had on the dance world, but for years she led a movement and had many copyists. She trained her pupils strenuously but gave the children more freedom than the formal ballet schools allowed. Her aims were different. Her constant quest was for the unconscious, instinctive effect.

Isadora always said that she absorbed her first impression of movement from the rhythms of the waves, for she was born close to the ocean and always afterward sought it in moments of sorrow. At the height of her agony over the death of her children she wandered along the Adriatic shore, longing for death, drawn by the deep sweep of the water. "I have noticed that all the great events of my life have taken place by the sea," she wrote, and she died within sight of it. With equal fervor she hated the mountains.

Her Hellenic interests first made her famous, as she danced on Mount Olympus and with her brother Raymond sought to build a temple to the dance in Greece, but long before that she had made a profound impression on the poets, musicians, sculptors, and artists of Paris. She stirred them with her pagan spirit, and they felt that she had something dynamic and different to give to the dance. In her heyday they valued her for what she was—a creator, a woman who dared to live and love as she wished, and they watched her ultimate demoralization with sadness. Isadora's ballet schools perpetuated her name, even after she had little to do with them.

Blasco-Ibáñez called her the "female Casanova of America" and Lola Kinel, who worked briefly as her secretary and later wrote a book about her, thought her "the greatest courtesan of our times, in the rich grand old sense of this word." Isadora's loves were as various as her moods—a millionaire businessman, a poet, a designer, a variety of musicians, actors, and writers, as well as wastrels of various kinds. "Isadora could no more live without human love than she could without food or music," wrote her close friend and biographer, Mary Desti. "They were as necessary to her as the breath of life, and without them she sank into melancholia, from which nothing could rouse her."

Isadora, who believed in signs and portents of all kinds, insisted that she was born under the star of Aphrodite. Another of her theories was that she derived her artistic impulses from the fact that her mother lived solely on champagne and oysters while she was bearing her. Mary Dora (Gray) Duncan was an unusual woman whose "beautiful and restless spirit made us artists," said Isadora. Her bohemian way of life set the pattern for Isadora and the other children, Augustin, Mary Elizabeth, and Raymond. Mrs. Duncan was musical, impulsive, and irresponsible. Her husband, Joseph Charles Duncan, was a charmer with much the same insouciant approach to life. They were divorced soon after Dora Angela, always known as Isadora, was born in San Francisco on May 27, 1878. The children ate at odd hours, slept when they wished, and listened to their mother play classical music until all hours of the night. In the daytime she gave music lessons to support them and at night played with some of the passion that Isadora later gave to dancing. It was a shiftless life, and they moved from one lodging to another, usually leaving debts behind them. But Mrs. Duncan's children always believed that she had greatly enriched their lives. Although they might sleep on the floor in a room without furniture, and go hungry for days, she always had time to read the great poets to them, or to play from the masters, so that they all developed in original ways, if not in the normal pattern of childhood.

Isadora attended a school briefly when she was five, and at six she was showing other children how to wave their arms gracefully in the gestures of dancing. As the little-theater movement developed in the United States Mrs. Duncan traveled about with her children. Isadora danced. Augustin recited poems. Elizabeth and Raymond staged comedies. At times they performed in the homes of prosperous San Franciscans, usually where Mrs. Duncan had been giving music lessons to the children. They were like Sanger's Circus, a blithe troupe, impecunious, scrounging meat from the butcher, staving off landlords, snatching a free meal wherever they could get it. Their mother was so insistent on the unimportance of material possessions that Isadora was indifferent all her life to clothes and jewels. But she took books from the Oakland library; she danced as she breathed, and was happy in a restless, seeking way.

In later years Isadora tended to magnifiy the hardships of her childhood days. Her father, who had moved west during the Gold Rush, had a variety of business interests, as well as being a poet and art dealer. He sold real estate, was a journalist for a time and wound up in banking. In 1898 he died in a shipwreck. Isadora had never had a chance to know him, but after he deserted them they lived for a time in a big house he had provided, and there they gave music and dancing lessons before the life of vagabondage began. When they decided to move east their first important stop was at Chicago, which they reached on a hot summer day with twenty-five dollars among them and some antique jewelry that had belonged to their grandmother. Soon they were sleeping on park benches or on bare floors. They pawned the jewelry and Isadora, with her heavy red hair piled high on top of her head, passed for sixteen, although she was still a child. They moved on to New York, where she wheedled an interview with Augustin Daly. In no way impressed by his power in the theater, Isadora told him that she had "discovered the dance." He smiled and put her in the fairy group of *A Midsummer Night's Dream*, but she stubbornly insisted on dancing in her own way. The audience applauded, but Daly was angry and told her that he was not running a music hall. She had refused to wear the fairy wings, and she paid no attention to the motions of her fellow dancers. Daly sent her out with a road company, but Isadora felt lost and obscure. Her ego was already strong. Ada Rehan was the star, and she never addressed one word to her fellow players.

The Duncans finally rented a studio in Carnegie Hall, and Isadora hung the blue curtains that were to be as distinctive of her work as the Greek tunic. Her décor would always be of the simplest, with lights, shadows, and nothing to distract the eye from the dancer. Again they slept on mattresses on the floor and lived the bohemian life, close to the Metropolitan Opera House which was flourishing with the full glory of the 1890's. Isadora watched the great opera stars come and go and she begged Daly for a singing part. He tried her in *Geisha* and quickly told her that she could not sing. Isadora resigned and never saw him again, nor did she have happy memories of her first plunge into the theatrical world. But he was responsible for her going to London in the summer of 1897, and taking dancing lessons with Ketti Lanner.

To make ends meet the Duncans rented their studio in the daytime to teachers, while they stayed in the park or roamed around the city. Isadora became friendly with Ethelbert Nevin, a young composer who had a studio in Carnegie Hall, and she danced *Ophelia* for him in her own distinctive way. Her curious style was discussed among artists, and she made so many connections that before long she was engaged to dance at private entertainments in the homes of Mrs. O. H. P. Belmont, Mrs. Daniel Chester French, Mrs. Stuyvesant Fish, Mrs. Whitelaw Reid, and for Mrs. Astor at Newport. But her diaphanous veilings were not approved; her style seemed eccentric, with sudden runs and bounds, followed by slow, interpretive moments. It was avant-garde for the 1890's, and Isadora felt the chill in the air as she experimented with free flowing movement. However, her interpretation of the *Rubaiyat*, read by Justin Huntly McCarthy at the Lyceum Theater in 1899, caused a mild sensation.

The Duncans moved from Carnegie Hall to the Windsor Hotel, and they went through the great fire there in 1899, losing the family pictures and the few possessions they had brought from California. Isadora led her pupils calmly from the hotel as the fire raged with great loss of life. They settled next in the Buckingham Hotel where Elizabeth, the most disciplined and businesslike member of the family, started a dancing school. But their prospects in New York seemed poor, and Mrs. Duncan decided to try London. Augustin married just before they sailed and stayed behind with his bride, ultimately becoming a well-known actor. Isadora raised money for their trip by dancing, but they had only enough for a cattle boat and ever afterward Raymond was a vegetarian, sickened by the sight of the animals bruising one another in the hold. After landing they settled in lodgings close to the Marble Arch, and had a delirious time seeing London. They rode the buses, lived on penny buns, and occasionally slept on benches in Green Park. When they were thrown out of their lodgings Isadora walked majestically into one of the most luxurious hotels in the city, demanding quarters and saying that they had just arrived on the night train and their luggage would follow. For one night at least they slept in downy beds, ordered fine food, and relaxed, the Sanger troupe at rest. At dawn they walked out, unobserved by the porter.

They were practically down and out when Isadora noticed in a newspaper that one of her patronesses in America had taken a house in Grosvenor Square. She went to her at once, asked for money in advance, and arranged for a performance. After supplying the family with tinned food she went to Liberty's and bought yards of veiling to wear when she danced Nevin's *Narcissus* and *Ophelia*, followed by Mendelssohn's *Spring Song*. Her recital was a success, and her mother promptly took a house in Kensington Square. Mrs. Patrick Campbell soon opened doors for Isadora. She introduced her to Mrs. George Wyndham, who invited a picked group of artists and writers to watch the young American dance in her drawing room. She met the Prince of Wales at the home of Mrs. Pierre Lorillard Ronalds, and her hostess told her that she had the beauty of a Gainsborough painting. Sir Charles Hallé, director of the New Gallery, had her dance to a distinguished audience around a fountain in the central courtyard. She joined F. R. Benson's company but showed little talent for the stage. However, her circle of friends widened, and the young beauty from San Francisco expounded her theories on the dance to Andrew Lang, Sir Edwin Arnold, Max Beerbohm, and other celebrities. John Singer Sargent praised her work. She danced at Mrs. Holman Hunt's, and she spent much time at the British Museum studying Grecian effects. Alma-Tadema encouraged her, and Gutzon Borglum helped her, both in London and New York. The London *Times* commented that she was "Botticelli like," with her golden sandals, her long dark hair crowned with roses, and ropes of roses around her waist.

Raymond Duncan, already an individualist, with his wide black hat, flowing tie, and sandals, crossed to Paris, where Isadora soon joined him. The Left Bank was a natural setting for her, but in the midst of much revelry she shut herself up and worked with all the intensity of her high-powered nature. It was at this time that she developed her theory that the solar plexus was the seat of power in dancing. She would stand immobile for hours, with her hands clasped between her breasts, as she sought to find the core of the dance. In her absorption she became almost cataleptic, but she finally found what she called the "centrifugal force reflecting the spirit's vision." The classical school taught that the central spring of movement lay at the base of the spine. Isadora's theory was revolutionary in its way, and she made it the central principle of her school of dancing. From that point on she put in endless hours of drudgery trying to perfect her technique in the "divine expression of the human spirit through the medium of the body's movement." Instinctive though it was, Isadora liked to cloak her art in words. Raymond was doing sketches from the Greek vases in the Louvre, and she accompanied him, to study the attitudes and movement of the figures. Both became enthusiastic about the Hellenic tradition, encouraged by Alma-Tadema.

Isadora had caught the Delsartean influence, but Paris chose to accept her as a genuine innovator. The interpretive principle was strong in all her work. She attracted a great deal of attention as she expounded her theories at the café tables, and she was always surrounded by groups of students and artists. She danced an idyll of Theocritus for Rodin that André Beaunier had translated for her. Rodin became one of her admirers and later sketched her. Loie Fuller, the American girl who had developed the serpentine dance and had her own theater, soon heard about Isadora and decided that she had something new and fresh to offer. Loie invited her to go with her to Berlin. Things went well there, and they proceeded to Leipzig and Vienna. Isadora was a sensation in Budapest, and Alexander Gross offered her a contract to dance in the Urania Theater. Every time she did her interpretation of *The Blue Danube* the response was ecstatic, but here she had her first authentic love affair, and it was shattering to her work for the time being. Isadora fell madly in love with Oscar Boregi, Hungary's leading actor, who was then playing *Romeo*, the name she always used for him. Without stopping to count the cost she broke her engagement at the Urania and ran off with him to a peasant's hut. After that it became a lifelong habit with Isadora to cut her professional engagements if they interfered with love. She lost Boregi in the end, when his role changed from Romeo to Mark Antony. From 1900 to the end of her life she struggled between the discipline of the dedicated artist and the free existence of the bacchante. For years she managed to keep her balance and her fame grew, but toward the end she had become so unreliable that no one wished to engage her. She and Loie Fuller, with her shimmering effects of moths and flames, made a strange combination, for Isadora's style was strong and individual, and she never thought in terms of the ensemble.

Mary Sturges Desti, a young singer, came into Isadora's life in 1901 when Mrs. Desti arrived with a divorce decree and a three-year-old son who grew up to be well known in the theatrical world as Preston Sturges, the producer, who died in 1959. The Duncans and the Destis shared quarters on the Left Bank, but Mary soon returned home and when she saw Isadora again in 1904 the dancer was living in Berlin and had founded a ballet school at Grünewald. Mary Desti was with her when she went to Bayreuth and became friendly with Richard Wagner's family. Frau Cosima Wagner showed great interest in Isadora's art, and King Ferdinand of Bulgaria attended a party at which she danced. In Florence she frolicked to the music of Monteverdi and, full of wine, danced joyously through the streets. Her appearance in Kroll's Opera House in Berlin with the Philharmonic

Orchestra took the city by storm. The Germans, who one day would despise her, were at her feet. She was "die göttliche, heilige Isadora."

But Raymond's sights were on Greece, and she followed him there, since her mother and Elizabeth had returned to the United States. She and her brother always had much in common and this was the start of the Hellenic period in their lives. In the Acropolis they both found "all joy and inspiration." In fact, they threw themselves so violently into the Attic mood that the Greeks were more amused than impressed. Raymond now wore a toga and flowing robes, and he and Isadora, also uniquely dressed, became strange wayfarers along the dusty roads around Athens. They studied frescoes, vases, and Tanagra figures by the hour. They visited the Acropolis in moonlight and at dawn. Isadora danced as the spirit moved her—along the roads, amid the ruins, and sometimes in the cafés. A magazine writer recalled seeing her standing on the hill of Kopanos overlooking the Acropolis, with the blue Hymettus mountains in the background. Out of it all, she wrote, "has come my dancing, neither Greek nor antique, but the spontaneous expression of my soul lifted up by beauty." She was called the "Maid of Athens" and 40,000 Greeks saw her dance in the Theater of Bacchus.

Finally, she and Raymond chose the spot where they would build a temple for the dance and found a school. They selected a Greek chorus from urchins assembled for an auditioning, and they trained them to sing the choruses. Isadora concentrated on watching the essence of the Greek drama emerge in dance form, and this period had a profound effect on her entire career. She danced in the Theater of Dionysius with the Greek chorus assisting. By degrees Kopanos, the Duncans' Greek temple, took some sort of form. Although they hoped to get state backing, none was forthcoming. Raymond had been stubborn about employing architects. He insisted that the workmen and stone carriers must build the temple according to his specifications, and the flaws in the half-baked project soon were apparent.

Isadora was invited by King George to dance at a royal performance, but she saw at once that she made no impression and that the "ballet would always be the dance par excellence for Royal personages." It was a disillusioning evening for her. She did not sleep that night, and at dawn she went to the Acropolis by herself, and danced in the Theater of Dionysius. It was a dance of despair, and she described it thus:

> I felt it was for the last time. Suddenly it seemed to me as if all our dreams burst like a glorious bubble, and we were not, nor ever could be, other than moderns. . . . The beautiful illusion of one year spent in Hellas seemed suddenly to break. The strains of Byzantine Greek music grew fainter and fainter, and through it all the great chords of the Death of Isolda floated upon my ears.

This was like many moments in Isadora's life—a sudden swing from ecstasy to defeat. She wrapped herself in the Greek flag as she left for Vienna, and the boys' chorus sang the national anthem along with the people. Her dream of reviving the classical dance and the Greek chorus in the twentieth century had come to nothing, but she took the boys with her to Vienna and had them intone *The Suppliants* of Aeschylus while she danced. The Austrians were responsive to Isadora but cold to the Greek chorus. The boys became so spoiled and troublesome that she was glad to send them back to their native country.

Meanwhile, Cosima Wagner had Isadora dance in a production of *Tannhäuser* at Bayreuth. Her Grecian effects were magnified since her stay in Athens. She wore sandals, and her hair was coiled with ribbons in a classic effect. But she was not a success on this occasion. The audience thought her draperies too revealing. They disliked her static effects and criticized her lack of form. She was surrounded by the traditional ballet dancers, and the effect was discordant. Stung by the criticism, Isadora remarked that the dancers' pink tights were vulgar and their steps inartistic. However, her successes in Berlin, Vienna, and Budapest, her experience in Greece, and the sponsorship of Frau Wagner had added to her fame and helped to build up her fortune. She danced now to the music of Wagner and Beethoven, of Gluck, Chopin, and Mendelssohn. As she toured Europe many thought her dancing eccentric and awkward, but the rapture she felt in her work conveyed itself across the footlights, as she danced more by intuition than by form. Her personality and her flair for getting in the headlines helped to build up her reputation, for better or for worse.

In Bayreuth Heinrich Thode read her each chapter of his *St. Francis of Assisi* as he wrote it. But in 1904 a strong new force came into Isadora's life when she met Edward Gordon Craig, the son of Ellen Terry and E. W. Godwin. They went straight to his studio on top of a high building in Berlin. Rose leaves were strewn over the black waxed floor. Craig was penniless at the time and had no furniture. "As flame meets flame, we burned in one bright fire," she wrote, describing her great love. "Here at last was my mate; my love; myself, for we were not two but one, two halves of the same soul. It was my fate to inspire the great love of this genius and it was my fate to endeavor to reconcile the continuing of my own career with his love." This resolved itself into a mighty struggle, and for a time Isadora did not care if she danced or not. She became indifferent to her engagements and felt that the world was well lost for Gordon Craig. He had already caused a stir in Britain with his inspired stage designs. His work had appealed to poets and artists, but the commercial interests ignored him. Isadora brought him fresh inspiration.

She helped to bring Craig and Eleanora Duse together, and he became the great Italian's choreographer and also Stanislavski's. Isadora viewed Duse as some "divine image of Petrarch or Dante." They became close friends, and Duse helped her many times, though Isadora considered Eleanora arrogant, scornful of people, living in a world apart, wrapped up in her art, a woman with little sympathy for "poor humanity." During this period Isadora bore Deirdre, Gordon Craig's child, in a village on the shores of the North Sea, close to the Hague. Her school in Berlin flourished. She had forty pupils, occupying small beds with white muslin curtains bowed with blue ribbon, and tiny figures representing Donatello's dancing children. She called it the Isadora Duncan School for Talented Children. They were severely disciplined and were kept on a vegetarian diet. Hour after hour she trained them, but in the end it was her sister Elizabeth who carried the full responsibility for the school, under the sponsorship of a committee of women from Scandinavia, Denmark, and Germany. Artists and poets visited the school to watch the children weaving and twining, parting and uniting, in endless rounds and processions. Isadora saw them as figures on a Pompeiian frieze, or as the youthful graces of Donatello.

By this time she had given up all hope of a school in Greece. Raymond reported that their experiment was dying. Their temple remained a ruin on the hill, and later the Greek revolutionaries used it as a fortress. But fresh interest entered her life when she visited Russia in 1905 and 1907, and made a deep impression on the people so noted for their classical ballet. Serge Diaghileff, the Russian impresario who would shake up the dance world a few years later with his epochal ballet, watched her with attention. He wrote that she gave an "irreparable jolt to the classic ballet of Imperial Russia." Stanislavski hurried down to the footlights to applaud when he first saw her dance. Pavlova took her up, too, although they represented two extremes in grace and technique. Bakst sketched her and Fokine, choreographer of the traditional ballet in St. Petersburg, observed her with interest. Many thought that her unorthodox use of great musical compositions influenced his work and specifically in *Les Sylphides*, danced to Chopin's music. Isadora had come on the scene at a time when a brilliant era in classical dancing was opening up, with Mordkin, Nijinsky, Massine, Karsavina, and Pavlova on the brink of electrifying the world with their talent. She danced in Vienna with Nijinsky and was keenly aware of his genius. But she belonged to the era of Maud Allan, of Loie Fuller and Ida Rubenstein, as well as to that of the new Russian stars. Copyists of her methods sprang up in various places, for the originality of her work had made an impression, and when she was beleaguered in later years Ruth St. Denis said of her: "To reject her genius is unthinkable."

After her first trip Isadora's interest switched from Greece as a focus for her work. She returned to Russia with her dancing children in 1907 to discuss founding a school in St. Petersburg, but the Imperial Ballet was so firmly established that she saw she could make no headway there. Her own free-wheeling children were allowed to watch the inexorable routine of the Ballet School, and Isadora thought that their Russian counterparts studied them as "canary birds in a cage might view the circling swallows in the air." She took them next to London, where they danced in the Duke of York Theatre. Ellen Terry, Deirdre's grandmother, accompanied them all to the Zoo, and Queen Alexandra came to the theater to watch them perform. But Isadora, as usual, was in financial trouble. Unable to make ends meet she signed a contract with Charles Frohman for an American tour. It proved to be a total failure, for her own country was cold to Isadora. "America does not understand your art," said the chagrined Frohman.

But Isadora set up her own studio in the Beaux Arts building, hung her blue curtains, and gave dance recitals for poets and artists, always her friends. As in Paris, the practitioners of the arts adored Isadora and her work. The New York *Sun* viewed her as a "pagan spirit, stepping naturally from a bit of broken marble as if that were the most obvious thing in the world to do." She found one substantial friend in Walter Damrosch, who had been impressed with her work when he saw her do an interpretation of Beethoven's Seventh Symphony with a poor orchestra in the Criterion Theatre. He immediately saw the possibilities of her art with proper musical effects, and Isadora had the most satisfying of all her tours when she crossed the country with Damrosch and an orchestra of eighty musicians. She even danced to the *Liebestod*, and the critics wrote admiringly of her work. "There was a marvellous sympathy between Damrosch and me, and to each one of his gestures I instantly felt the answering vibration," she later wrote. For once she was not harassed by financial or professional problems but was guided by a master hand, a man who always drew crowds. This was Isadora's only satisfactory experience in the United States, for she was always appreciated abroad more than at home.

When President Theodore Roosevelt saw her he thought her innocent as a child "dancing through the garden in the morning sunshine and picking the beautiful flowers of her fantasy." Some of his cabinet members were less approving of Isadora's original style. However, she returned to Europe with added prestige and saw her little daughter for the first time in six months. She had finished with Gordon Craig, for their fierce jealousies had rent them apart and interfered with their work. Nevertheless, each continued to admire the other, and Isadora crusaded as hard for his vision of the theater as for her own conception of the dance. In many ways she was able to help him professionally.

A number of talented men circled around her in 1909, but the one who counted, and who stood by her for years, was Paris Eugene Singer, son of Isaac Singer, founder of the sewing machine fortune. After seeing her dance in Paris he went back stage and, as in the case of Gordon Craig, Isadora fell madly in love with him. Singer was more than six feet tall, blond, bearded, and authoritative in manner. He was both worldly and artistic, equally at home in bohemian or conservative social circles. His sister Winnaretta was married to Prince de Polignac. Singer brought luxury and devotion into Isadora's disordered life. No longer did she have to worry about hotel bills, or where her next meal was to come from, or how she would meet her obligations. In her autobiography she called him "Lohengrin," and their love affair was one of the more famous of the era. Isadora was soon involved in revels of one kind or another, her most discussed being a house party that started in Paris, gathered force in Venice, and culminated weeks later on a houseboat on the Nile. Now fantastically opulent, she spent long summer days on Singer's yacht or at his villa at Beaulieu. Her epicurean tastes for once were satisfied. Isadora loved good food and good wine, and now she had both. It was her custom, even in the lean years, to hunt up the best restaurants and order meals that she could not afford. But since she was already a student of Marx she would sigh, even in a moment of dalliance, over the men in the engine room of Singer's yacht who sweated at their work while she enjoyed the sun and the wind. However, her happiness was complete when she saw her dancing girls bounding and leaping under the orange trees on the Riviera, with flowers and fruit in their hands; or when she was able to take Deirdre to Venice and let her romp on the sand. Singer's Paris apartment was on the Place des Vosges, and now a new Isadora Duncan appeared in the French capital. She frequented the finest restaurants, wearing sophisticated clothes and looking groomed and worldly. The first pleated Fortuny dress was designed for her in 1910. When Damrosch invited her back to the United States for another tour the public was soon aware that Isadora was *enceinte*. Her sister Elizabeth looked after the school in her absence, and on her return she sailed up the Nile on the *Isis* with Singer, while she waited for the birth of her child. He was born in Beaulieu and was named Patrick. When she reappeared in Paris there were fresh festivities —a fete in the park at Versailles, a Wagnerian concert.

Singer had a stroke at this time and retired to the chateau he had built for himself in Devonshire. Isadora joined him there with the thought that she might found a school in England, but she disliked the foggy climate. The rain depressed her, and she was glad to return to Paris. However, in the years from 1910 to 1913 she changed from a child of nature to an opinionated woman, ambitious, determined to have her school and, in the words of Koussevitsky, "to have the world dancing in her wake." With a yacht, fourteen cars at her command, and Paul Poiret to dress her, she became arrogant and quarrelsome. Her dreams were many but her plans all blew apart as the vagaries of her private life drove her to impulsive action. "Let me be Pagan," she wrote, and pagan she was. "I had discovered that Love might be a pastime as well as a tragedy. I gave myself to it with pagan innocence."

She now lived in a house in Neuilly where Paul Poiret had hung black velvet curtains in her studio and gold mirrors on the walls, to reflect Isadora's dancing. Here she gave dinner parties and fetes, turning her home into a tropical garden or a Spanish palace as the spirit moved her. Celebrities flocked around her, and her parties became notorious. Singer, who had come back, left her again one evening, in a distressed mood, when he found her making love to one of her guests. She went downstairs at once and danced the death of Iseult, for in moments of sorrow, as well as of joy, Isadora's first instinct was to dance. But to the end of her life Singer was kind to her, helping her when she fell into penury, and coming to her rescue in times of crisis. Before long she needed this solace, for the great tragedy of her life occurred in the spring of 1913.

Her children were a particular delight to her—when she could find time for them. Deirdre was a graceful child who improvised dances of her own. Patrick liked to spin around to weird music. They were fair-haired, beautiful children, and she proudly showed them off to her friends. On an April day that spring Singer asked Isadora to come in to Paris to meet him and to bring the children with her. He had not seen them in four months. They had a merry luncheon at an Italian restaurant, Singer jesting with the children and Isadora talking about having a theater of her own. With Annie Sims, their Scottish nurse, they returned to Neuilly after Singer had left them. Then Isadora sent them off for a drive to Versailles. It was a wet and misty day. The children and their nurse had gone only a few yards from the Rue Chauveau, where their mother lived, when their driver had to pull up suddenly to avoid hitting a taxicab. He got out to crank up his car again but failed to adjust the speed lever. In trying to get back into the car he was tossed off the footboard by the jerk when the wheels hit the pavement as the car crossed the Boulevard Bourdon and slipped down the grassy bank and into the Seine. It was swept along in a parallel course to the bank and disappeared from view.

Workmen seated in a café across the street saw it all happen. They went into action fast. One dived into the river; others called police and firemen. Divers came from the Ile St. Louis. It took some time to find the car, but a large motor boat finally established contact. A long period elapsed before it was pulled to the surface with ropes and anchors. The children were found clinging to their dead nurse. Deirdre, aged six, was dead. Patrick, who was three, had turned his head to his nurse's bosom and there was still a flicker of life, but all efforts to revive him at the American Hospital failed.

Isadora was resting in her studio when Singer burst in and told her that the children were dead. Mary Desti chanced to arrive a moment later with lilacs in her arms. She knew nothing of what had happened until she found a great crowd gathered at the gate. Singer was comforting Isadora, but she turned eagerly to Mary and cried: "Tell me it isn't true. My children are not dead."

Their bodies were brought to the studio, and hundreds of students from the Beaux Arts collected all the white flowers they could find in Paris and adorned the trees and bushes of Isadora's garden with them. She was calm and composed on the day of their funeral. "No tears, Mary, no tears," she said. "They never had a sorrow, and we must not be sorrowful today. I want to be brave enough to make death beautiful, to help all the other mothers of the world who have lost their babies." Later Isadora went majestically through a death dance for her children. Many were shocked, but she explained that this was her way of showing her sorrow. Cecile Sorel, Mounet-Sully, and other celebrities attended the service at the Cemetery of Père-Lachaise. All Paris mourned with Isadora. Singer stayed for a time to comfort and sustain her, but her grief was so overwhelming, her mourning so constant, that at last he felt he must leave her alone once more.

Gordon Craig tried to console her with a series of letters at this time. "Dear—dear—You are bearing all the grief which would have been theirs—then dry your eyes for them," he wrote to her on April 23, 1913. "Be sure the Gods are looking at you now and I am sure you are bearing yourself nobly. Dear and great Isadora, now is your time—to say I love you would not cover the whole. I take your fingers your hands in mine and I pray a great prayer."

Isadora changed greatly after the death of her children. She became more reckless than ever, and life seemed to blow apart for her. She traveled across Europe, restless, melancholy, seeking diversion in Turkey, in Switzerland, in Albania, where she worked briefly for destitute children. Gordon Craig wrote to her again on May 15, 1913, when she was in Corfu and he in Paris. This was a revealing letter, with undertones of their old love affair:

> My life as yours has been *strange* . . . you are *strange*—but *not to me*. And my darling I know how you can suffer and not show more than a smile. I know your weakness which is that of a little, dear little fool, for I, a big fool, have looked at you. I know your strength too for I who can taste strength have seen all yours. Never was there one so weak or so strong as you and all for Hecuba. My heart has often broken to see your weakness. My heart has often shaken with terror to see your strength. For my heart and your heart are one heart . . . as I am with you, being you, what more is there to be said? Let us not be sorry for anything —or where should we begin?

Finally, as the restless quest went on, Duse invited Isadora to join her at Viareggio, where the actress had a rose-colored villa close to a vineyard. "Isadora, don't seek happiness again," the tragedienne advised her when she saw her friend embarking on a futile love affair. "You have on your brow the mark of the great unhappy ones of the earth. Do not tempt Fate again."

Isadora walked by the sea. She wanted to drown herself, and at one point she cut off a lock of her hair that had turned white from grief and flung it into the water. For years afterward the sight of a blonde child would start her tears flowing, and she never spoke of Deirdre and Patrick. Worried over her state of despair, Singer brought her back to Paris and she stayed at the Crillon until he bought the Hôtel Bellevue, a huge mansion with a terrace overlooking Paris, and room enough to house hundreds of Isadora's dancing children. She gathered up her pupils to make a fresh start, dressing them in multicolored capes and leading them through the woods, where they "danced like a flock of beautiful birds." Rodin sketched them as they danced, and Antoine Bourdell made three hundred sketches of Isadora. A festival at the Trocadéro was one of her triumphs, and her students were hailed as the "future dancers of the Ninth Symphony of Beethoven."

Isadora was planning a festival theater, with Singer's backing, when the war broke out, putting an end to all cultivation of the arts for the time being. He turned over the great mansion in Paris, and also his place in Devonshire, to be used as war hospitals. "My Temple of Art," wrote Isadora, "was turned into a Calvary of Martyrdom and, in the end, into a charnel house of bloody wounds and death." Mary Desti, who by this time had a perfume shop on the Rue de la Paix, decorated by Poiret and haunted by Cecile Sorel, Ganna Walska, and other stars, gave up her business and devoted herself to war work. Isadora bore another baby, who died almost as soon as it was born. Her reputation was now worldwide. The drowning of her children had added a touch of tragedy to her artistic fame.

With the war raging in France and Belgium, she moved her students from Germany and England to the United States, and opened a studio at Fourth Avenue and Twenty-third Street in New York. The familiar blue curtains were hung, but Isadora now danced without joy. Poets, artists, and dancers flocked in, and Otto Kahn leased the Century Theatre for her for a season, but this was not a success. The night she opened there Isadora bought up every Easter lily in Manhattan to decorate the theater. Her Easter program cost her $2,000 and she had only $3,000 at the time, so she squandered the remaining thousand on a champagne supper. She staged Attic plays and Biblical episodes but her dances in these settings had less appeal for the public than her own dances with a stark décor. She always had the best response when she danced alone. Few turned out to see the medley offered. By this time Isadora had become unreasonable in her demands, and she quarreled with everyone around her, ranting against the rich and biting the hand that fed her. When she sailed for Europe she left a trail of debts and much ill-will behind her.

She landed in Naples on the day that Italy entered the war.

That same year—1916—she danced in Paris for the first time since the death of her children. She seemed to be the old Isadora, and her audience went wild over her interpretation of the *Marseillaise*. The war was raging and patriotism was at a high peak. But there was no place for her art in a country engaged in fighting for its life, and she decided to tour South America. In Brazil she was madly applauded; in the Argentine she was jeered at and tormented. On her return to New York, Singer came to her rescue again and engaged the Metropolitan Opera House, where she repeated her *Marseillaise* dance to a standing audience and a blaze of applause. It was 1916 and the war spirit was mounting in the United States, too. Singer talked of buying Madison Square Garden for her at this time. She had a studio on top of the Garden, but when she gave a Wagnerian concert she roused antagonistic feeling, for the anti-German sentiment was strong. Singer was disturbed, too, by her fiery interpretation of Tchaikovsky's *March Slav* and her ranting against the capitalist class, to which he clearly belonged.

Her artistic friends rallied around her as she came under fire, but she was still deeply depressed and was drinking heavily. Singer sent her to Cuba with his secretary, hoping that her health would improve, but she went dancing through the streets of Havana from one bar to another. San Francisco gave her a cool reception when she returned there in 1917 for her first visit since leaving California in 1895. She tried both in New York and in San Francisco to promote the idea of a municipal dance school, but there was no response. Singer had done his best to help her, but when he saw her dancing the Apache tango with Maurice in Sherry's at a party he was giving for her, he was swept with rage. Isadora, as usual, was lost to the propriety of her surroundings but was brought to sudden consciousness when Singer wrenched her from the well-known dancer's arms. He then seized the table-cloth and swept china, glass, and flowers to the floor in one great pile. The sound of breaking glass, of his angry words, caused uproar in the staid dining room, and this incident became one of the mounting number of scandals in which Isadora was involved. It had repercussions for Singer, too. Within a year his wife had divorced him. Later he married again.

There was a parting of the ways between Singer and Isadora after the scene at Sherry's, although he never wholly abandoned her. For once his self-control had deserted him. He was doubly furious because he had just given her a magnificent diamond necklace which she wore that night. She quickly pawned it when her bills mounted and Singer no longer footed them. An emerald bought for her from the son of a maharajah shared the same fate. Bills had to be paid, and jewels in themselves meant nothing to Isadora. Gordon Selfridge paid her passage back to Europe but her star pupils stayed behind and became well known as the Isadorables. The most noted were Anna, Lysel, Theresa, Erica, and Irma. None of them became great dancers, but they were successful as a troupe. Only Irma, who took the name Duncan, later rejoined Isadora, accompanied her to Russia and was a loyal friend.

When the war ended she was back in Paris and she watched the Victory Parade stream through the Arc de Triomphe. Bellevue, where she had trained forty-five pupils, had fallen into a state of decay and was sold to the French Government. She settled in a house on the Rue de la Pompe and soon fell in love with Walter M. Rummel, the concert pianist and composer who was a grandson of Samuel F. B. Morse. After touring France with her he left her for one of her young pupils while they were all together in Athens. Such was her bitterness that she considered leaping from Parthenon's Rock. She had returned in the hope of restoring Kopanos and pursuing her dream of the Attic theater. Edward Steichen was with her entourage at this time, taking pictures at the Acropolis. When Venizelos resigned as premier in 1920 she returned to Paris, with all hope gone of founding a school either in Greece or in France. Five years earlier she had championed Venizelos when he upheld the Allied cause against the pro-German king. At that time she had danced from square to square until she reached his house, brandishing his portrait and leading an enthusiastic crowd.

When Leonid Krassin, heading a Trade Commission in London from Russia, saw her dance the *March Slav* accompanied by the London Symphony Orchestra, he went back stage to invite her to visit Russia. They talked of founding a school of the dance along lines laid down by Isadora. She was assured that she could carry out her ideas on a broad scale and that she would have a thousand pupils. But disillusionment followed. The Isadora Duncan State School opened on December 3, 1921, in the Balchova Palace, a barnlike place in which the students froze. Hundreds flocked in, but only fifty of the most promising were accepted. Isadora's idea was to abolish not only the conventional ballet but the peasant dances traditional to Russia—an ambitious program, even for a supreme egotist. But she had not counted on the strong opposition of the Moscow Ballet, with its school and governmental subsidy.

Asked to dance in the Bolshoi Theatre on the fourth anniversary of the revolution, she composed a special dance for the Internationale. Draped in red, she mimicked the overthrow of the old order and the coming of the new. Irma Duncan, who had been a favorite pupil since 1905, now left the Isadorables and joined her. But Isadora was soon in all kinds of trouble, both personal and political. She had fallen madly in love with Sergei Essenine, a tall young poet with deep-set blue eyes and a mop of flaxen curls. It mattered not that he was an epileptic, subject to occasional fits of madness; he was also a boisterous hedonist after her own heart. He was the peasant poet laureate of the new republic and was something of a national pet. But when Isadora tied her fortunes to his she was involved in an endless brawl as they traveled across Europe, with Sergei wrecking hotel rooms, smashing furniture, dashing nude into crowds, running up bills, and creating such a succession of scenes that few hotels would take them in.

Isadora's only marriage was to this wild young man, in May,

1922, and it took place chiefly because they were going to the United States where he would be denied admission unless he could prove marriage to an American citizen. The poet was twenty-seven. She was forty-four. They flew to Berlin through a snowstorm and settled briefly at the Adlon Hotel. Isadora visited her sister Elizabeth, who had followed a steady course down the years and was again running their dance school at Potsdam.

Isadora had slimmed down and had recovered some of the beauty that she had lost through years of self-indulgence. She bought fine clothes for her poet husband, who reminded her of Robert Burns, and soon the rough-hewn Sergei was strutting about, perfumed, carefully tailored, and madly elated. He pounced on the best of Parisian food and drank champagne all night. In his cups he brawled, fought, and shouted. Since Isadora knew little Russian and Sergei even less English, they communicated in a pidgin language of their own. There was trouble at once about visas, since no one wanted Isadora. She was persona non grata because of her enthusiastic espousal of the Bolshevik cause. Actually she was the first visitor from the Soviet to get into France after the war, and Cecile Sorel helped her in this. England did not want her, and when she and her poet reached the United States they were held at Ellis Island.

But she would not keep quiet on the subject. She and Sergei had no sooner settled at the Waldorf-Astoria than she began to talk volubly of the new paradise that she had recently left. She gave a successful performance at Carnegie Hall in October, 1922, but the tour that followed was disastrous. When she danced in Boston she felt that her audience was "cold and grey," and at the end of her performance she waved her red silk scarf around her head and cried: "This is red. So am I! It is the color of life and vigor. You were once wild here. Don't let them tame you!" Then, as Sol Hurok, who was managing her tour, recalled, Isadora pointed to replicas of Greek statues and cried: "These are not Greek gods—they are false. And you are as false as those plaster statues. You don't know what beauty is!" At this point she was reported to have torn down her tunic and bared one of her breasts, exclaiming: "This—this is beauty."

Students cheered her, but their elders left the hall in droves. The headlines that followed were sensational. Isadora was pictured as having pulled off her draperies, leaving herself half nude. Mayor Curley banned her from getting a license for further appearances in Boston. She talked defiantly at the Copley-Plaza Hotel, in the presence of Essenine, who had added insult to injury by tossing a red flag from the window of Symphony Hall and crying out "Long live Bolshevism." "They say I mismanaged my garments," Isadora commented. "A mere disarrangement of a garment means nothing. Why should I care what part of my body I reveal. . . . Is not all body and soul an instrument through which the artist expresses his inner message of beauty?"

The question remained unanswered, and Isadora denied her nudity. By the time she reached Chicago she insisted that she could not have torn off her dress because it was held by elastic at the shoulders, waist, and hips. There were cries for her deportation, and Billy Sunday called her "that Bolshevik hussy." Hurok frantically urged her to stop making speeches, but she paid no attention to his warnings. In Indianapolis policemen were stationed on the stage to prevent trouble. Many of her engagements were canceled, but she appeared in St. Louis, Kansas City, Memphis, Detroit, Cleveland, Baltimore, Philadelphia, and wound up her tour with a performance at the Academy of Music in Brooklyn on Christmas night. Instead of an encore she voiced all the views that she "had been compelled" to keep to herself. She was not quite sober on this occasion, and the evening was a debacle. Again she bared her bosom to the public. This was the era of prohibition, and Isadora invariably had a bottle of champagne or whiskey back stage to help her get started and to keep her going.

Sergei had gone completely wild with all the luxury that surrounded him. He got roaring drunk in public and whenever possible defended the Bolsheviki. He was particularly insulting at a

Russian Jewish Poets evening, and on this occasion ripped off his wife's gown. Isadora was controversial enough in her own right, but with Sergei she had become a national scandal. Hurok, finding that he could not exercise any control, later commented:

> I know that Isadora loved life as perhaps no human being had ever loved it; that she was the embodiment of life, rich, generous, zestful life, to those who knew and loved her. Because of her, women were freed at one stroke from corsets and their conventions. The bodies of little children were freed. She brought sunlight and fresh air into the lives and the thinking of all of us; she cut the bonds of spirit as well as flesh.

Isadora gave her last performance at Carnegie Hall in January, 1923, and she never returned to the United States after that. The tour had been a disaster from start to finish. Singer bought passage back to France for her and Essenine, and on landing she announced: "I am not an anarchist or a Bolshevik. My husband and I are revolutionists. All geniuses worthy of the name are."

Essenine was thoroughly convinced of his own genius. He picked up a picture of Gordon Craig from a table one day and remarked: "I also am a genius. Essenine genius. Craig nothing." Gordon Craig by this time was firmly established as a brilliant producer and stage designer. The poet of the revolution meanwhile was embarrassing Isadora seriously in Paris. He heaved a dressing table and couch through a closed window in the Crillon, tore the sheets, smashed the bed springs, broke the mirrors, and beat up a porter until he was carted off to jail and then to a hospital. Isadora, whom he had already threatened with a pistol in New York, fled and joined Mrs. Desti at the Grand Hotel. Mary wrote feelingly later of the wild Russian nights of drinking, brawling, and debauchery that Isadora survived. They moved on to Venice where Lola Kinel, a Polish girl who spoke Russian, was their secretary briefly. Sergei read his poetry to her, and she translated it as best she could for Isadora, while he craftily watched his wife's face for signs of appreciation. He flew into rages if she did not respond at once. Lola found Isadora's Russian to be "twisted, naive and broken, but very charming." She thought her dancing pure magic and she compared her in the Chopin prelude, when she merely walked from one end of the stage to the other, to the Brahms waltz, in which she was like a "Goddess of Joy strewing flowers around her."

Sergei sang Russian folk songs with Lola in a gondola while Isadora listened lazily. He had ego equal to his wife's and told her on more than one occasion: "You are just a dancer. People may come and admire you . . . but after you are dead, no one will remember. Within a few years all your great fame will be gone . . . poems like mine live forever." This was trying for Isadora's vanity, and she promptly told him that her gods were love and beauty. Sometimes Sergei hid in the bushes to get away from his ardent wife, and in Venice he made off with her trunks containing her letters and clothes. One by one she sold the valuable pieces of furniture that Singer had bought for her, in order to keep them in funds. The last time that Isadora saw Sergei was in Moscow, when he found her going through the trunks he had stolen. They were filled with her gowns, lingerie, perfumes, and toilet articles that he intended to scatter among his Russian friends. He went into a frenzy when he saw Isadora bending over the trunks. She left him then and sued for divorce. "God bless him but he's no good for a husband," she wrote to Irma Duncan, the former member of her troupe who now ran her school in Moscow. He promptly became involved with a granddaughter of Tolstoi, but in the following year he hanged himself in the room at the Hotel d'Angleterre in Leningrad where he had originally stayed with Isadora, first cutting a vein in his wrist and writing her name in blood. Sergei had a state funeral, and the proceeds from his works, which were popular, were offered to Isadora, but she said that his family should have them.

With Sergei completely out of her life she settled down to her school and to touring Russia to help finance it. In November, 1923, she attended the first Octobrina Christening in the Bolshoi Theatre, and without thinking of the Communist Party's repudiation of God she danced to the music of Schubert's *Ave Maria*.

When Lenin died two months later she stood in line for hours in the snow with the peasants waiting to file past his bier. She composed dances in memory of the revolutionist and did them for the first time at Kharkov as she started out on a tour of the Ukraine. She danced for eighteen evenings in Kiev; not even in Paris had she ever danced so many times in succession. Children followed her through the streets crying: "Duncan, Duncan, Beautiful Lady, give us bread." Isadora scattered coins when she had any to spare.

She was heading for a performance in Leningrad when her car was wrecked and she was buried under luggage in a ditch. After recovering from her injuries she returned to Moscow but decided to continue her tour of the Ukraine, taking the children with her this time. She would dance alone first; then Irma would lead in the dancing girls. Since the public preferred to have Isadora alone she soon sent the girls back to school with Irma. With a pianist and a manager she traveled to Orenburg, Samarkand, Samara, Tashkent, Ekaterinburg, and Vyatka in the summer of 1924, but she was soon in a desperate plight and kept bombarding Irma, Elizabeth, and other members of her family for funds. She found the stark life unbearable. The towns she visited were small, ruined, and forlorn. She could not stand dancing with white lights and without her blue curtains. The children alone were touching in their life and enthusiasm, and she wrote of them to Irma on July 10, 1924:

> My art was the flower of an epoch but that epoch is dead and Europe is the past. These red tunic kids are the future, so it is fine to work for them. Plough the ground and sow the seed and prepare for the next generation that will express the new world. What else is there to do. . . . You are my only disciple and with you I see the future. It is *there* and we will dance the Ninth Symphony yet.

When she wrote this letter Isadora was penniless, wandering about the streets, hungry, resting on park benches. No one seemed to have money except the "new bourgeoisie," whom she detested. The communists and workmen for whom she danced had no money to buy tickets. "Hell of a life anyway," Isadora wrote. She returned to Moscow and gave one last performance at the Bolshoi Theatre. But she was no better off when she reached Berlin. With her usual insouciance Isadora took rooms at the luxurious Eden Hotel, without a penny to pay her bill. "I am quite stranded," she wrote to Irma, "the audiences enthusiastic and the critics most insulting for some reason. . . . I am nearly on the verge of suicide. . . . The newspapers here naturally are fearfully hostile and treat me as if I had only come paid to make Bolshevik propaganda which considering the truth is a very poor joke. Elizabeth says I never danced so well before and raves about my art."

Before long, however, Elizabeth had closed the doors of her school at Potsdam to Isadora and would have nothing to do with her. Wretched as she had been in Russia, things were still worse now, aggravated by the fact that she had bronchitis and an ulcerated tooth. The hotel manager would no longer allow her to order food, since she had no money. An American friend brought her a slice of roast beef every day, but he was impoverished, too. Isadora yearned to be back in Russia and wrote to Irma:

> Here is no spirit—everything congested into patriotism—& fatherland . . . it is hell!!! I spend my time wondering which sort of poison does not hurt the most—I don't want to take any of the fearful kind. Europe is quite impossible. I am homesick for the soldiers singing—and the children singing and the marching. This old world is dead as a door nail. The children here look like ruffians compared to the Russians . . . at present here all is dead. . . . Germany is the limit . . . simply fearful.

Isadora sent frantic messages to all her remaining relatives, but no one responded and she grew more desperate. Too many times she had harried them in the same way with threats of suicide and appeals for money. Her Russian links had made her unwelcome all over Europe. "Every country has refused me a visa on account of my 'political connections,'" she wrote to Irma. "Where are my 'political connections' I'd like to know. I am utterly stranded and lost here—in a very hostile city—I haven't a single friend. Why in the name of humanity don't you answer my telegrams and letters? Your dying Isadora."

She had never been worse off, and she was haunted by memories of brilliant days and nights in Berlin, the city that now rejected her. Both her art and her body were failing her, and she was burned up with a longing for drink that she could not afford to buy. She had squandered fortunes on hotels and orchestras, on food and drink, on helping the needy, for when Isadora had money she tossed it around with abandon. Now even the patient Elizabeth could do no more for her, because she had brought them all such sorrow and trouble.

Somehow she managed to get back to Paris in the autumn of 1925. Her house there was put up for auction, but it was saved by public subscription when her friends learned how broken down she was. A committee was appointed to handle the proceeds, however, lest Isadora cast them away in her spendthrift fashion. Her artist friends gathered around her again, and at every chance she shared in Communist demonstrations. She took part in the Sacco-Vanzetti protests and held a burning taper in front of the American Embassy on the night that the condemned men were executed. "Go home, Isadora," said the gendarmes goodnaturedly, knowing her well. She was at Le Bourget when Charles A. Lindbergh landed, and later she wrote verse about his flight. When Mary Desti joined her in Paris in the spring of 1927 to help her write her autobiography she found Isadora blowzy and puffy, with bottles strewn around her. She had not danced in three years when she gave one last recital at the Théâtre Mogador on a July day that year. She danced to the *Ave Maria*, and Mary regarded this as her "glorious adieu to Paris, to the stage, to the dance." They had been friends for twenty-seven years, and Mary had seen her in some of her most triumphant, as well as in her most terrible moments. She was to be present at her death.

At the end Isadora was back in Nice. Raymond now had a flourishing business in hand-woven carpets, blankets, and fabrics, painted or stenciled by his disciples. He had two shops, and homes both in Paris and Nice. He drove back and forth in a battered Ford, and was a familiar figure in flowing robes and toga. He and his followers lived on rice and lentils, slept on wooden benches, and scourged the flesh. Raymond had become famous in his own way, and he finally took pity on Isadora and drove her to the Riviera. After signing a contract for her autobiography she had some money, and her spirits revived. She drove back and forth with Raymond between Paris and Nice, and resumed her old rounds of the restaurants and night clubs. Whenever she could she scrounged a meal or a bottle of wine. Occasionally she showed up at the parties given by Peggy Guggenheim, American art connoisseur and noted hostess. Food and wine had become her final preoccupation. Isadora cared no more for clothes than she ever had and was happiest in splashy flowered dresses, an Indian hat, and her sandals.

Her spirits picked up as her writing progressed. Robert Winthrop Chanler, the artist, gave a luncheon for her at Antibes, attended by a score of American artists. It was reported in the papers that Isadora would marry him, but this was denied as a joke. Drawing an allusion from *Parsifal* she called Nice "Kundry's Garden," and she often bathed at the Negresco Hotel, where Singer stayed, as well as at his villa. Allan Ross Macdougall, the writer, acted as her companion and secretary and she sometimes dined with Frank Harris in his flat at Cimiez. She gave three summer programs in Nice—two with Cocteau, who accompanied her dancing with his spoken verse. A masseur pounded her into shape before each appearance, but she postured rather than danced in her final performances. She spent hours gazing out at the Mediterranean with the tears streaming down her cheeks. In one of her sad moods she walked into the sea in an attempt to drown herself and was rescued by one of her fellow guests at a party she had just left. One moment she would be planning a school of aesthetics on the Riviera; the next she would be lauding Russia and saying that she had reached the highest realization of her being there. Singer was only a few miles away at his villa, but he had lost much of his fortune when the Florida boom collapsed, and he felt that there was no more he could do to check Isadora's ruin. He had helped her innumerable times, and on his last visit she had said to him: "I am beginning to be a great nuisance; nothing can be done with me, and I can no more change my habits than a leopard his spots." At this time she told Mary Desti that Singer was the only man she had ever truly loved.

However, she was in high spirits on September 14, 1927, and was thinking of buying a Bugatti car with money that Singer had given her. The mechanic at the garage was Benoit Falchetto, a handsome young flying ace, and she asked him to bring the car around in the evening for a trial spin. She went to the hairdresser that day and her hair shone with some of its old radiance. With Mary Desti she lunched at a famous restaurant on the Promenade des Anglais and later danced the tango wildly to gramophone records in her studio. Singer called to see her in the afternoon. It was the last time she ever talked to him, and they discussed the car and its driver. As evening approached she and Mary went out to have cocktails at a bar, and then decided to stay for dinner. Isadora danced across the street to leave a note on her studio door for the young driver: "Suis en face Chez Henry."

When he came she flung her Chinese-red shawl around her neck and shoulders, for the evening had the coolness of the Riviera after dusk. Mary Desti had painted great yellow birds and blue Chinese asters on the heavy crepe of Isadora's shawl, which was two yards long. It was a spectacular scarf, and she usually hung it on the balcony of her studio when she was not wearing it. The driver offered her his leather coat to keep her warm, but as she stepped into the car she swung the scarf closer around her, shook her head and cried: "Adieu, mes amis. Je vais à la gloire" as she settled in her seat. These were the last words she ever spoke.

As she swept the scarf around her neck the heavy fringe hung down and caught in the rear wheel of the low, two-seated racing car. "Isadora, ton châle, ton châle," Mary Desti cried as the wheels started to revolve. The car stopped almost at once and the driver shouted, "J'ai tué la Madonne. J'ai tué la Madonne." The first revolution of the wheel had broken Isadora's neck. Mary could not believe that she was dead. She ran into the restaurant and snatched a knife to cut the shawl. Cars slowed down, and Isadora was rushed to a hospital and then taken back to her studio, where her body lay on one of the eighteen couches, wearing a red dress and her dancing veils, arranged by Mary. Her purple mantle was thrown across her feet. The room was filled with flowers, and hundreds of candles burned, suffusing the studio with the blue light that Isadora had always used for her dancing. Mary laid one red rose on Isadora's breast, and there were three sprays of lilies of France—from Augustin, from Elizabeth, and from Raymond. The news of Isadora's death had been flashed around the world, and flowers came from Preston Sturges, Edward Steichen, Arnold Genthe, Eva le Gallienne, Mercedes de Acosta, and other American friends who had not deserted her.

Singer made all the funeral arrangements, and Isadora's body was taken to Paris, to lie in state at Raymond's studio. Once again the purple cape that she had worn when dancing Chopin's *Funeral March* and Liszt's *Les Funérailles* was spread across her coffin, and to this was soon added a spray of red lilies with the inscription "From the heart of Russia, which mourns Isadora." Her blue velvet dancing carpets covered the floor, and her old blue curtains gave the studio a twilight haze. All through Saturday and Sunday friends, flowers, and messages arrived. The city was full of American soldiers, for American Legion Day was being celebrated with a great parade. The Stars and Stripes floated everywhere, and Raymond saw to it that an American flag, drawn from beneath his voluminous robes, draped his sister's coffin at the end.

Three Legionnaires saluted as the cortege passed the Trocadéro, where a quarter of a century earlier Isadora had been fired with her passion for Greek drama when she saw Mounet-Sully play *Oedipus Rex*. A decade later she had danced Gluck's *Orphée* there, to the same actor's reading of the choruses. She had danced with her pupils in the Trocadéro to the music of Tchaikovsky, Wagner, Schubert, and Scriabine. As they passed the Théâtre des Champs Élysées, Mary Desti reflected on the bas-reliefs by Bourdelle, which were inspired by Isadora and were her lasting memorial in Paris. Here she had flouted authority by giving a Wagnerian program after the war, and by shouting "Vive la Russie" after dancing the *March Slav* at the time of the Bolshevik revolution.

More than ten thousand persons had gathered for Isadora's funeral. The alleys around the Père-Lachaise Crematorium were jammed, and cordons of police kept order. A quartette played Bach's *Aria for the G String*, one of Isadora's favorite compositions. Ralph Lawton, who had often accompanied her in Paris and Brussels, played Liszt's *Les Funérailles*, but even at her funeral the eccentric touch prevailed. Raymond unexpectedly marched down the aisle in his flowing robes, had the doors opened, and shouted in French to the crowd outside: "We started out from San Francisco many years ago. We were four and now we are three. . . ." Inside the chapel Mary Desti, sobbing loudly, exclaimed: "They were *one* and now they are *none*." The poet Fernande Divoire gave a funeral oration, and Garcia Marsellac sang *Ave Maria* as Isadora's tortured body was consigned to the flames. Her mother had been cremated there, and also her children.

Yvette Guilbert spoke for the artists of Paris when she wrote her farewell to Isadora: "We thank you for having quenched the thirsts of us, the thirsty, the *Artistes!* Genius of flesh and of blood, human superhuman, may Olympus greet you!" Some months before her death the *New Yorker* commented:

> Eurythmic movements now appear in the curriculum of girls schools. Vestal virgins frieze about the altar fire of St. Mark's-in-the-Bouwerie on Sabbath afternoons. . . . Greek dance camps flourish in the Catskills. . . . She was the first artist to appear uncinctured, barefooted and free . . . she came like a figure from the Elgin marbles. She has danced before Kings and peasants. She has danced from the Pacific

to London, from Petrograd to the Black Sea, from Athens to Paris and Berlin.

Isadora was only forty-nine when she died, but her entire life had been packed with drama, triumph and, more often, despair. She had been a destructive force to herself and to others, but she had influenced the dance tradition of her generation, and her personality was as deeply impressed on the public as her art.

Aimee Semple McPherson

<hr>

Aimee Semple McPherson was the saint pictured as having
turned sinner, the Angel of Angelus Temple who stirred up
thousands around the world in the course of her ministry. Her
Four Square Gospel was one of cheer and sunshine. It was
brightness, roses, and song. Her spell was cast by the vitality of
her nature, and the practical benefits of the Temple work. There
was never another evangelist like Aimee, or one who caused such
stir, got more headlines, or had so mighty a fall from grace. Her
kidnaping story kept her on the front pages for eight months, and
the twists and turns of this fantastic episode became part of the
history of the 1920's. She was the natural child of the era of the
speakeasy, the night club, flaming youth, and corrupt politics.
Aimee challenged sin with the brassy music of her Temple,

with theatrical effects tied to the old-time gospel message, with the strength and imagination of her own power complex. In addition, she did a great many practical things for a great many people, and Angelus Temple was a beehive of activity. Its presiding goddess was never mercenary in the way that her mother, Minnie Kennedy, was reported to be. Although Aimee ran through a large fortune, she squandered her money for the public good as readily as for herself. She survived a long succession of scandals, law suits, and personal attacks, and when the shouting died she could still don her white robes, raise her arms to heaven, and sway a multitude. There was something primitive and simple in her nature, so that she never caught the drift of her plight or profited by her mistakes. Aimee was ruled by instinct, and the flattery of her disciples sustained her for many years. Even after the kidnaping mystery of 1926 had pulled down her house of cards, she continued to trail clouds of glory after her. Her strength of purpose, hardihood, and faith in her own invulnerability were not wholly shattered until the last years of her life.

She was never out of the headlines for long. When things were quiet she turned up another avenue, seeking converts in Boston and Shanghai night clubs, or in Texas Guinan's famous club in New York. In her later years she made up and dressed like a film star. Her law suits brought her into conflict with members of her own family, and she survived several marriages. At the end she was in and out of hospitals and sanitariums, but she was picturesque even as her powers failed. In a gleaming white satin gown with black fringed stole and a cross of brilliants quivering on her bosom, she conducted a crusade on Broadway in 1933, and *Variety* called her "sexy but Episcopalian," an angel with an oblique Mona Lisa smile.

Aimee had traveled a long way in worldly knowledge since she ran wild as a child and was rocked to sleep with Bible stories and hymns on a farm near Ingersoll, Ontario. She was born there on October 9, 1890, in answer to her mother's prayer for a woman preacher in the family, or so she often told her audiences. Mrs. Kennedy had been a Salvation Army lass, a strong, good-looking girl who had shaken her tambourine on many street corners. Much of Aimee's evangelistic fervor came from this source. Her father, too, was a deeply religious man, who studied the Bible as he ran his farm. Mrs. Kennedy, much his junior, dominated the household, and she continued to mastermind her daughter's operations until her last years. Aimee was a healthy, self-assertive girl full of high spirits, a show-off and even a tomboy. She swam and rode with ease and spirit. Then came the day of revelation when she was converted at a Holy Roller Pentecostal revival conducted by a handsome young preacher named Robert Semple. When only a few weeks old she had been dedicated to the Lord's service by her mother in a Salvation Army barracks.

"Repent!" shouted Semple to the farmers and their families gathered in a bare hall. They shouted and twitched. Aimee threw herself heart and soul into the excitement and then, as she leaned from her bedroom window one night, she had a vision that she liked to recall in her preaching days: "It was like a shaft of light shooting through the darkness—like the rending of the temple from the top to the bottom—like the brushing of all the cobwebs from the mind, as though from the cellar I had been lifted to the housetop under the shining of the open Heavens." The spell lasted for three days, while Aimee wrestled with a sense of sin until she could no longer bear it, and then, as she was driving home from school: "It seemed that the heavens were brass and would fall upon me and I would be lost if I did not immediately repent of my unbelief and Christ's rejection." She raised her hands to heaven and cried: "God, be merciful to me, a sinner." And then, as Aimee told it: "The light streamed over my soul. . . . My fear was gone and in its place there was a blessed rest and sense of security. . . . I consecrated my life to Christ then and there. I have never done anything half heartedly. . . ."

A young girl's religious exaltation was not unusual after one of the Pentecostal revivals, but in Aimee's case a whole new world of evangelism had opened up. When she reached home she swept the ragtime music off her piano. She read the Bible at every opportunity, even concealing it inside her algebra book, and she attended prayer meetings in a nearby cottage. Slowly the conviction grew in her that it was her mission to save souls. But how? The answer came when young Semple returned and visited the Kennedy farm. He watched Aimee's fresh young face as she told him of her conversion. An eager spirit seemed to flame through her, and before long he asked her to marry him and go with him to China to do missionary work.

"I said 'Yes' to God and I said 'Yes' to Robert," Aimee later recalled. They were married on the farm in a room decorated with jonquils, hydrangeas, and golden glow. Their wedding feast was held in the orchard, under the apple trees. Robert had a pastorate in Stratford, Ontario, but soon after marrying Aimee he set out for China, going first to Ireland, where his parents lived. Wherever he went he preached, and his bride added warmth to his meetings as she testified, played the piano, and led the hymns. Semple had only begun his missionary work in China when he developed fever and ague and died in Hong Kong a month before their daughter, Roberta Star, was born.

Aimee returned home, to find that her parents had moved to the United States. Soon after that her father died of a stroke and her mother went back to the Salvation Army in New York. Meanwhile Aimee married her second husband—a grocery clerk named Harold S. McPherson. She brought him into the fold as an evangelist and persuaded him to try a tent meeting campaign when life seemed too flat to her after all the revivalist excitement. They moved about in Ontario, preaching to farmers, but McPherson had no heart for what he was doing and could not understand why his wife should not be content to stay at home like other women. When they separated in 1916 he sent her a message: "I have tried to walk your way and have failed. Won't you come now and walk my way? I am sure we would be happy."

But Aimee was dissatisfied on the farm. They made several attempts at reconciliation before McPherson finally divorced her in 1921 for desertion. He had nothing but bitter memories of his evangelist wife and in 1926, when Aimee was showing up as a somewhat tarnished angel, he recalled her "wild cat" habits in the home, and the way in which she had walked out on him after a camp meeting, without leaving him carfare to get home. They had a son, so that Aimee, at the age of twenty-six, was left with two children to support.

Her life now took a wide range. After traveling through Ontario, conducting tent revivals, she moved down the Eastern seaboard from Maine to Florida. Her methods at first were of the simplest and smacked of circus ballyhoo. She painted bright mottoes on the canvas sides of a tent and carried it around in her shabby automobile. She slept on a soldier's canvas cot in a small tent beside the larger one in which she preached, but when her mother joined her in Key West things looked up. Mrs. Kennedy was a practical businesswoman, with Salvation Army training. She understood what was needed, and soon they were touring in comfort with a caravan, water-tight tents, and advance agents to make bookings. Aimee was always her own best promoter. Her style was theatrical, but not in the Holy Roller tradition. She dwelt on song and sunshine, and projected a glowing brand of Christianity. Hell-fire and brimstone gave way to affirmative living.

One of her tricks was to stand immobile at a street corner, with closed eyes and her arms lifted in prayer. When a crowd had collected she would pick up her chair and run to a hall, a church or a tent with the challenge "Follow me." She soon had her audience captive and money rolled in, but her mother took tight hold of her finances. Aimee thought that the methods then used to spread the gospel were lifeless and archaic, and she decided to add her own personal magnetism to the picture. Later, when thousands stormed her Temple in Los Angeles she cried: "We sing because we are happy in the Lord. . . . Our Gospel is the Foursquare Gospel, and the very warp and woof of it is evangelism. . . . Thousands of people come to the Temple every night, and other countless thousands listen over the radio, because the old-fashioned gospel is practicable and applicable to everyday life."

As she traveled, Aimee sowed "Gospel Seed"—her booklets and tracts. Often she slept in her car and sometimes she preached from it. "Wherever the running board moved, there was an altar, and many a time sinners stepping from the crowd kneeled there, confessing their sins. . . ." she wrote. At times she used a megaphone to startle passersby with a loud warning: "Do you know that you are on your way to perdition?" After touring the Florida resorts she landed in St. Petersburg during Mardi Gras and promptly created her own float and joined the parade. She poised a small white tent in her car, with a baby organ and some singers on top of a mound of greenery. Palmetto, ferns, and moss were woven over the wheels, and she painted signs on the white sheets: "Jesus Saves!" "Repent and Be Converted." "I'm on the way to the Tent Revival. R.U.?" The crowds stared at the evangelist with interest. She was sturdily built, with masses of brown hair piled high on her head. Her eyes were large and expressive, and she had an encompassing smile. She was not the chic Aimee of later years but looked heavy and dowdy in her cumbersome clothes. Many of the revelers trailed her to her meeting.

Aimee reached Los Angeles during the flu epidemic of 1918, and after Roberta recovered from a severe illness, she decided to take a bungalow and establish a home there for the children. They had never stayed long enough anywhere to go to school. Two days later she held a revival. This was the one that, in Aimee's words, sounded around the world, for it set the wagon wheels revolving. They met first in a hall, then in a church, and finally in the Philharmonic Auditorium, with thousands pouring in to hear the eloquent new evangelist. Between her first campaign in Los Angeles and the building of her Temple, she made four transcontinental tours and held revivals in Canada, New Zealand, and Australia, her fame growing with every month. She used auditoriums, schools, churches, or a huge tent, and in San Francisco even the Coliseum could scarcely hold the crowds that flocked to hear Mrs. McPherson preach. She had established herself firmly as an exponent of the Four Square Gospel and a faith healer. Because she was novel and dramatic, she drew enormous crowds and reaped a harvest of publicity even before scandal broke around her. The first story to appear about her in the West was an item in a Los Angeles paper from San Diego: "Sky Pilot Will Fly. Woman Evangelist to Preach from Airplane and Scatter Tracts." A decade later she was considering flying over Russia to drop tracts for the conversion of the Communists.

In the early years of Aimee's evangelism, faith healing was an important part of her mission. Even in the conservative Episcopal Church the laying on of hands had a revival in the 1920's. With her own private approach Aimee built up a reputation for success in this field, but she later abandoned it. Although she never made extravagant claims of cures, she was accused of paying some to bear witness to her methods. In Southern California there were many physically handicapped people, so that it was a natural field for this type of evangelism. In the summer of 1921 eight thousand crowded in to her opening meeting at San Jose, and the papers gave lurid reports of shell-shocked war veterans who regained their sight and paralytics who flung away their crutches. Canes, braces, and other aids were piled up on the platform around Aimee. This was repeated in one place after another, but her faith healing was forgotten in her later years of temple euphoria. Chastened by attacks made by fellow ministers about her methods, she soon decided that her reputation should not depend on this type of ministration. After a series of mammoth outdoor meetings she announced to reporters at the Palace Hotel in San Francisco in the spring of 1922: "I say very definitely, right now, that I do not wish the lame, the halt, the blind and the crippled to crowd my meetings. I hope they will stay away. . . . That is the portion of my work to which I am least attracted. . . ."

She pointed out that she had been forced into faith healing by public demand. Almost from the beginning she ran into opposition from other denominations. Her emotional methods were scorned by the ministerial associations, and although she was ordained a pastor in the First Baptist Church of San Jose, her own denomination showed concern over her work being publicized as a Baptist movement. But by degrees she developed her own

Four Square Gospel and made plans for Angelus Temple, an inspiration that came to her, she always said, when she noticed the vacant lots adjoining Echo Park. Aimee immediately sketched the outlines of a temple on the signboard that advertised the property for sale. She had $5,000 when she began, but funds rolled in as she toured to raise money, and on January 1, 1923, Angelus Temple was officially opened.

With this event a new era in evangelism had dawned. The huge white building with five entrances, topped by painted shields and draped flags, was of stucco, with wrought-iron balconies. Its seating capacity was 5300, and its eight stained-glass windows were thirty feet high. It was Aimee's creation, from its cornice and arch, its parapet and dome, to its crystal doors and radio towers. To some it seemed a hideous edifice. To Aimee and her followers it was one step to paradise. Soon she was preaching to the largest congregation in the world. By the end of 1925 collections amounted to more than a million dollars and the property holdings represented another half million. It had taken Aimee less than a decade to climb from penniless obscurity to riches and reputation. Women evangelists were few, although she had some copyists in the 1920's, but none could offer the glamour, the strength, the sunshine that surrounded Sister Aimee, or the theatrical effects that she developed.

The Temple lights never went out. Its doors were never closed. Men prayed all night and women all day in two-hour shifts in the Watch Tower. The services were only a part of the great community center that Aimee organized. It had twenty-four departments and a Bible School with a thousand students. Its commissary shelves were loaded with food, blankets, and clothing for the needy. The Four Square City Sisters provided nurses and distributed food, clothing, and furniture. Volunteer workers in Temple uniform went out to scrub floors and bathe babies. The Temple Brotherhood ran an employment agency and seventeen committees. They toured the mills and factories, hospitals and jails, and found employment for prisoners when they were freed. Parents dedicated their babies in the Cradle Room, and toys and baskets of comforts awaited distribution. A day and night telephone service was maintained to meet appeals for help, or to answer questions; jobs were found for the unemployed; day and night schools were run for business people. The Temple developed its own staff of radio talent, and the music department was a vital part of its organization. It had three bands, three choirs, two orchestras, six quartets, glee clubs, and scores of soloists and musicians. The Salvation Army touch was present in glorified form, a blend of gospel, brassy music, and practical help.

Special electric trains ran to the Temple, and the waste area around Echo Park bloomed with flowers, houses, and new boulevards. Mrs. Kennedy took charge of all business matters. She had her daughter's physical charm but none of her warmth or persuasive power. Aimee was doled out twenty-five dollars a week by her mother as the Temple returns became ever more impressive, but like a traveling monarch, she rarely handled cash. Her bright gospel technique had great appeal for the unhappy, and it often pulled them out of the doldrums. Anyone could find something useful to do at the Temple. It was unconscious therapy, with the High Priestess playing her role more by instinct than by deliberation. She brought thousands into the fold with her altar calls. In Denver 2800 people rose and moved forward in a solid body. By degrees she became a public image, and branches of her church opened in England, Australia, and across the United States. She was deluged with gifts and moved about in waves of adulation.

As time went on feuds raged around her for her mother was imperious, harsh, and unrelenting. Aimee, too, could beat up a fierce storm when she was annoyed. There were murmurs of discontent and flashes of anger in the midst of all the cheer, vitality, and exhortatory words. But Aimee moved on her way untroubled, the Ministering Angel on whom the spotlight played with colors, as she stood in her white robes, a great sheaf of red roses in her arms. Everything about the Four Square Gospel was theatrical. She illustrated her sermons with tableaux and pantomimes from a fully equipped stage. The radio station became a sensational sideline as an assortment of derelicts told their stories over the air. They were converts to her gospel—men and women who had been gamblers, alcoholics, drug addicts, and white slavers. In the end it was Aimee's chief radio operator who brought her perhaps her greatest fame and deepest ignominy. Just before this scandal broke she went to Europe and visited the Holy Land.

When she filled Albert Hall in London the *Daily Mail* called her meeting one of the "merriest religious revivals the world has ever known," and the British press made much of her short skirts, her flesh-colored stockings and elaborate coiffure. It was her custom to pile her hair in heavy rolls on top of her head. Sometimes it was Titian-red, sometimes blonde, but it was always her own, as she insisted on demonstrating in court during one of her hearings. She brought it tumbling down and had it up again in three minutes flat, to the edification of the spectators. Aimee now wore costly shoes, imported lingerie, and Paris gowns, although she quickly assumed a decorous appearance for services of any kind. But with lipstick, tinted hair, and a dash of rouge there was a strong suggestion of the music hall about her when she returned from this trip and was suddenly tangled up in one of the strangest episodes in all evangelistic history.

After her strenuous Sunday services she usually rested on Mondays and Tuesdays. This gave her time to edit her paper and relax. She rode or swam and usually took her secretary Emma Schaffer with her, so that she could dictate her sermons. On May 19, 1926, a flash went around the world that Aimee Semple McPherson had walked into the ocean and disappeared. It was feared that she had drowned. She had gone with Miss Schaffer, who did not swim, to Ocean Park, a beach near Los Angeles and, as Aimee later told it, "On this particular Tuesday, as I drove to Ocean Park, any sense of impending disaster was the farthest thought from my mind."

For the next eight months her name was never out of the headlines. As the story was reconstructed later, she went to the beach wearing a white and yellow sports dress, then changed into a green bathing suit and brown bathing cap at the small hotel where she had rooms reserved in summer. For a time she rested in her robe under a sun umbrella on the beach, going over the notes for her next sermon. After her first dip she came out of the water and told Emma to telephone to her mother that she would not keep the appointment she had for four o'clock at the Temple. At the same time she asked her secretary to bring her some orange juice while she took another dip. When Emma returned with the juice and some candy she saw Aimee swimming far out, or so she later testified. Then the secretary picked up the Bible and Aimee's notes to look up references. When she glanced out to sea again the evangelist was no longer in sight.

The lifeguards were alerted at once, and the shoreline was patroled. "Drowned!" was Mrs. Kennedy's first comment when Miss Schaffer telephoned her that lifeguards were looking for her daughter but could find no trace of her. The water that day was still as glass. The temperature was 68 degrees. There were many people around, but none could say that they had seen Mrs. Mc-Pherson walk into the sea and disappear. Crowds gathered at the Temple to weep and pray. Her mother conducted a service that evening and showed pictures of the Holy Land on a screen. At the end she said without further explanation: "Sister is gone. We know she is with Jesus. Pray for her."

Excitement at the Temple was intense. Bulletins were posted hourly on a blackboard outside so that the crowd that gathered could get the latest news. Inside there were prayers and tears, and many kneeled at the altar rail to stare at the platform where Aimee's radiant figure usually stood. Mrs. Kennedy failed to show any sign of stress. She was determined that things should follow their usual course, and she kept denying that there were financial troubles at the Temple. When Roberta wept she told her: "Just remember always, Roberta, your mother's body is in the sea—but her spirit is with the Lord, shouting victory."

The searchers along the ocean front never rested. Rowboats went out with divers, airplanes circled close to the water, men grappled from motor launches, police and reporters swarmed over the beach. Temple workers converged in hundreds and ran about, scouting for Mrs. McPherson. One man shouted that he had seen her rise from the waves in her white robes, beckon to him, and then sink back again. Some believed that Aimee would arise and speak to them. The emotionalism in which she had always traded came to the surface in a tidal wave. Reporters frantically ran down one tip after another as false rumors spread in all directions. Mrs. Kennedy, who took a fatalistic view of things from the start, offered $500 for the recovery of her daughter's body and voiced worry over the fact that money was still owing at the Temple. The church routine went on as usual although the radio station went off the air. Temple workers recalled that Aimee had said on her return from Europe: "I am weary, weary. I think only Christ could have been as tired as I."

The following night the patrol continued along the beach and floodlights cast strange reflections on the water. Inevitably the suggestion of violence arose, for Aimee was planning to expose the Venice dance halls. She had many enemies and critics, and someone remembered that she was handed a letter that seemed to upset her as she walked into the Ocean View Hotel. Another woman fancied she had heard a scream from the water. Still another witness recalled that Mrs. McPherson had asked when the lifeguards came on duty at their various stations. Rolf Kennedy McPherson, her son by her second husband, was on a ranch near Sacramento for his health when his mother disappeared. He was then thirteen. The following Sunday Roberta appeared on the Temple platform in her white robes and said: "I am sure Mother is looking down from Heaven and sees this sight." The audience rose in a body, raised their hands, and prayed with the utmost intensity. The Temple was filled to overflowing at each of the three services that day, and Mrs. Kennedy preached and told the congregation that church property was in her name as well as in Aimee's. On May 25, six days after her daughter's disappearance, she announced that there was "absolutely no hope on our part that Sister is alive on land or sea."

Mrs. Kennedy had just received a letter signed "Revengers,"

demanding $500,000 in currency and suggesting that a Temple worker bring the money to the lobby of the Palace Hotel in San Francisco. The letter was not turned over to the police, but news of it leaked out. A second kidnap letter was addressed to Mrs. Kennedy on June 18. This was a typewritten document containing a lock of her daughter's hair. It came to be known as the "Avengers" letter. She withheld this one also from the authorities and was never able to explain how she permitted a memorial service to be held for Aimee immediately after she had received it. The authorship of the kidnap notes was never conclusively established, although efforts were made by the investigators to prove that they were fakes and part of a hoax.

On the day that she supposedly gave up hope Mrs. Kennedy visited Ocean Beach for the first time, looked over the scene, wept discreetly, and posed with her daughter's Bible open at the last passage she had read. She thanked the beach patrol for their work. Two men lost their lives in the hunt for Aimee. A concessionaire set up a life-size wax figure of her robed in white and stretching out a hand in blessing, but the police quickly ended this side show as a mob gathered around. For a long time pictures of Aimee rising like a wraith from the ocean were sold along the waterfront.

Meanwhile reports began to drift in that the missing evangelist had been seen here and there—usually with a man in a blue Chrysler. At this point, on May 26, the name of Kenneth G. Ormiston flashed into the headlines. He was a handsome, mature man with a pronounced limp who had installed radio equipment at Angelus Temple in 1924 and had worked there as chief engineer until January, 1926. He had also been radio editor and had operated the station of the Los Angeles *Times*. There had been some gossip about long conversations between Mrs. McPherson and Ormiston at the Temple, and the story spread that he had been with her on her trip to Europe and the Holy Land. Now he was absent from Los Angeles. In fact, his wife, Ruth Peters Ormiston, on January 22 had turned in a missing persons report on him, with the added note that a prominent woman was responsible for his disappearance. After warning Mrs. Kennedy that she would name her daughter in a divorce suit, Mrs. Ormiston went back to Australia within a matter of weeks to join her own family there. The feeling grew that Aimee might be anywhere but at the bottom of the sea.

At this point District Attorney Asa Keyes stepped in and said that he would question Emma Schaffer and Ormiston. The radio man's car had been traced traveling south, with a woman in it wearing goggles. This pair were also reported to have been seen at a hotel in San Francisco, at another in San Luis Obispo, about a hundred miles south of Salinas, and also at Sacramento, where they had registered as Mr. and Mrs. Frank Gibson. When his name showed up in the papers Ormiston went to the Los Angeles police on May 27 and offered to help in the investigation. He told the press that a "noble and sincere woman had been grossly insulted" by having her name linked with his. He spoke of the jealousy of his wife and said that he had been moving about doing radio work and using aliases, in particular the name James Wallace, to avoid the suit that she was threatening.

Mrs. Kennedy backed up Ormiston's story. Aimee, she said, was "nobody's sweetheart. . . . Aimee was the World's Sister who led a spotless and blameless life." She raised the reward for her daughter's recovery to $25,000, but already the Sacramento *Union* and other papers were crying hoax, a publicity stunt. The Los Angeles *Times* and the Los Angeles *Examiner* went into deadly combat on the evolving story, and needled the prosecution into action. On Memorial Day, services for Aimee were held at the Temple and white roses were dropped into the sea at the spot where she was presumed to have disappeared. Her worshipers knelt by the sea while Mrs. Kennedy's voice reached them by loud-speaker. On June 3 she and Roberta strewed white carnations on the waves. The reward was withdrawn and Mrs. Kennedy, at least, took the stand that Aimee was no more. When she had been missing for a month a great memorial service was held for her on June 20 at the Temple, with 17,000 worshipers mourning her, and millions more following it all by radio. The evangelist's chair was banked with flowers. White satin badges were distributed, and Emma Schaffer, in black from head to foot, sat looking blank and sorrowful. She had already begun to baffle the authorities. Fiercely loyal to her employer, she told the same story time after time without a varying detail. All attempts to trip her failed.

Three days later, on June 23, Aimee was talking to her mother on the telephone from Douglas, Arizona. She had turned up, gaunt-eyed, hysterical, with a fantastic story of having been kidnaped and kept a prisoner in a shack in Mexico, and of escaping and fleeing across the desert to Agua Prieta, just south of the border. She had welts on her wrists, cactus thorns in her ankles, but no sunburn, no thirst, no emaciation, no dehydration. The world learned quickly that Aimee Semple McPherson was alive. As the first excitement died down, the story was put together, but the pieces did not fit. The police grew suspicious and the papers pushed hard. The public became skeptical, as conflicting headlines streamed across America and around the world.

Aimee was first seen by the custodian of a slaughterhouse a mile and a half from the border at Agua Prieta. When his dogs wakened him with their barking at midnight, he went out and found a woman at the gate begging to use his telephone to call the police. He went in to dress, and when he returned she had moved on to the village. Ramon R. Gonzales, an Agua Prieta barber and bartender, saw her next. It was 1 A.M., and he had just closed his bar when he found her lying unconscious outside. When she revived it was clear at once who she was. She was driven across the border to Douglas, where she told her story to the police and was then taken to the local hospital.

The excitement in Douglas was intense as long distance calls poured in from all quarters. By 7:30 A.M. Aimee was talking to her mother, and the word was spreading in Los Angeles that she was safe. She told the abduction story over and over again. According to her version, when she came out of the water after her second swim she saw a man and a woman standing on the shore. The woman was crying, and since Aimee thought they were in trouble she spoke to them. They said their baby was dying and that her prayers alone could save it. The child supposedly was in their car, and she went with them. They would not give her time to go back and put on her clothes, but the woman flung a coat around her shoulders. A second man sat in the car but there was no sign of a child. Suddenly she was pulled inside and a blanket was thrown over her head. She was given something to smell, which made her faint. When she awakened she was in a darkened room, lying on a cheap iron bed. She began to scream but was quickly gagged. One of the men said that they had planned her capture for some time. They took two locks of her hair to send to her mother as identification with a kidnaping note. The woman lent her cotton dresses and shoes. Then after some days they moved her to a second shack, more miserable than the first. Finally they left her on a cot, tied hand and foot. This was the story, as Aimee volunteered it.

She told of rolling off the bed and of using a tin can with jagged edges to cut the strap binding her wrists. Then she unfastened the wraps on her ankles, climbed through a window, and started on her desert trek. She grew eloquent about the horror, the heat, the tremendous effort involved. There were cougars, coyotes, dogs, and snakes along the way. The borrowed shoes were too large for her and gave her blisters. Used to dramatizing a story, Aimee made the most of this recital, dwelling on "those anguished hours," bumping over the sand, watching for an approaching automobile with lights, torn between hope that it would hold rescuers and not the "iron woman from the shack." She pictured herself as a "drooping, forlorn, cotton-clad figure, trudging falteringly into the welling gloom."

From what she had heard Aimee was persuaded that her abduction was planned by a crime syndicate for ransom; $500,000 was the sum involved. Her keepers tortured her, she said, burning her fingers with a lighted cigar. A woman named Rose stayed with her constantly, and when the men urged her to write to her mother she refused. It was then that they cut the locks of hair to send along for identification, said Aimee, and they told her they would cut off one of her fingers, which happened to have a recognizable scar, and send it also to her mother if she did not co-operate. She denied that she had seen Ormiston, and when asked if she intended to marry again Aimee said: "My life will always be for Jesus."

Her mother and children joined her in a demonstrative reunion at the hospital in Douglas, with cameras at hand. It was noticed that Mrs. Kennedy and her daughter had a whispered conversation before settling down to an interview. The discrepancies in her story were soon evident to all. Why no tears in her clothes, no dust or perspiration from her fourteen-hour flight across the Sonora wastelands? Why was she not thirsty or dehydrated? Aimee went back to the desert to go over the ground with the investigating authorities. She thanked the men who had helped her and matched her footprints with those close to the slaughter-house, but she could find nothing familiar in the landscape that she had supposedly traversed forty-eight hours earlier. Aimee led the quest for the two shacks, one of which she described as being an adobe hut with a wooden floor. How did so wretched a shack have running water? she was asked. She volunteered to demon-strate that she could walk twenty miles in the desert without feeling thirst, but the watchful reporters observed that she walked only a few yards now and again from her car, and that she took surreptitious sips of water from a canteen. It rained heavily the day after she left Douglas and all footprints were wiped out.

Woodrow Wilson, William Howard Taft, and the King of the Belgians caused slightly less stir on their visits to Los Angeles than Mrs. Aimee Semple McPherson did on her return home after the great kidnaping episode. Crowds swarmed around her private car as it was shunted into place at Angelus Temple. Her train had traveled with reporters, cameras, flags, and Aimee pre-siding in state.

"Aimee! Aimee! Hallelujah!" came a roar from the waiting crowd as she stepped on to the platform.

"They love her so," said Mrs. Kennedy, as roses rained down

from a circling airplane. The band of the Fire Department, which was much attached to the evangelist for favors the Temple had done them, played the doxology. "This wonderful demonstration! I want to thank everyone—the police officers and the firemen and God, from whom all blessings flow!" said Aimee, beaming and looking a Puritan in her all-gray costume.

She drove to Angelus Temple in an automobile buried in flowers, and another crowd awaited her at her home. She had been away for thirty-nine days, and she looked thin and worn. But when she made her first appearance at the Temple she was made up like an actress, and she carried lilies of the valley instead of the usual red roses. Roberta and Rolf were at either side of her. The audience of six thousand stood and roared a welcome, stamping their feet and shouting hallelujahs. The doxology thundered through the auditorium, and Aimee threw herself on her knees to pray. She seemed about to faint but pulled herself up under her canopy of flowers and proceeded to preach on "The Conquering Host," telling her audience that it would have to be a short sermon for she needed more beefsteaks to give her strength.

"We are alive from the dead! The work is going on. Praise the Lord."

Each sentence met with a roar of applause. Aimee compared herself with Job and Daniel, who were "betrayed by false witnesses." The whole business, she insisted, was a plot hatched by the devil, not to extort dollars but to wreck Angelus Temple. Aimee then gave her version of what had happened to her, moving about on the platform as if it were a stage and dramatizing each incident. With an attempt at humor she mimicked the police officer who had smelled her breath for liquor when she was brought in from the desert. She drew her skirt over her head to create the effect of a sunbonnet and said that this was how she had shielded her face from the sun—a trick she had learned on the Canadian farm where she grew up. Aimee ended with a flourish: "I was a Queen in my kingdom, and I am not boasting. Why, then, should I run away and hide? There was absolutely nothing that I wanted my followers would not give me gladly."

When she had finished she asked those who believed her to raise their hands, and nearly everyone did. She repeated this performance, and the Rev. Robert Shuler, the rector of Trinity Church, who constantly attacked her, said that she was "born knowing all there is to know about mob psychology." This, indeed, was Aimee's particular genius, but for once it did not carry her far. District Attorney Asa Keyes, egged on by the press, pushed the investigation. Aimee went to the Ocean View Hotel and re-enacted the scene there, but now the whispers grew to a roar. The details she gave differed in many respects from the story she had told in Douglas. The spot where she had placed the car used by the kidnapers turned out to be a no-parking zone. The papers were now hot on her trail, and every discrepancy was promptly played up.

Although Aimee kept repeating "My character has always been spotless, my life has always been the church," the talk would not die down, and soon she was threatening libel suits against the papers. She and her mother left suddenly for Douglas, ostensibly to hunt once more for the shacks. Aimee demonstrated how she had climbed out a window, and she went through another routine of acting out the incident for the cameras, but on her return two grand juries were investigating the matter. The "Avengers" letter to Mrs. Kennedy, demanding the ransom, became a fresh issue. Had it been suppressed, and had Minnie known at the time the memorial service was held that her daughter was alive? And the wrist watch that Aimee was wearing in the pictures taken of her in the hospital—had she gone in swimming wearing it?

By this time Ormiston had disappeared again, and Aimee was being asked if she had been at the International Club, a saloon in Agua Prieta, with a woman and two men, five days before her reappearance.

"Isn't it ridiculous that anyone should say they saw me coming out of a roadhouse?" she responded, laughing heartily.

Finally Aimee, her mother, Emma Schaffer, the children, and various Temple workers were summoned before the county grand jury. The evangelist ducked process servers at first but finally swept into court with her Temple guard of honor—seven women all dressed in the Angelus costume, white gowns with starched collars and long blue capes lined with gray. They were selected because they resembled Aimee and wore their hair piled high on top of their heads, as she did. Her disciples in the crowd outside cried hallelujah as this entourage entered the courthouse.

Aimee refused to take the oath of secrecy, and once again she told her story, while her guard of honor prayed outside the jury room. She testified that she never handled finances, and that when she wished for money it was given to her as if she were a child. She denied all discord with her mother before the kidnaping, for rumors had been spreading that they were at deadly odds over Temple finances. She also denied that love, publicity, sickness, fatigue, or amnesia were involved. But she made the most of the fact that she had formidable enemies because she had fought the "dope ring, gambling, liquor, tobacco and dancing."

The jurors were pleased with Mrs. McPherson's frank and responsive manner in answering questions. Her mother was crisp, businesslike, and canny in her answers, and made a good impression. Miss Schaffer, the solemn, loyal secretary, stuck firmly to her original story. Handwriting experts who studied the letter from the "Avengers" thought it too literate, well-spelled, and precise to have been written by such characters as Aimee described. The man who said he had seen Mrs. McPherson in front of the Club International in Agua Prieta recalled her auburn hair and her expressive eyes.

With this ordeal behind her, Aimee went back to the Temple and told her followers all that had taken place in the grand jury room, since she had not taken the oath of secrecy. She based her sermon on the notes she had made as she sat on the beach, and she promised her kidnapers forgiveness and immunity if they would step forward. The grand jury took no action, and her followers continued to stand by Aimee, in spite of all the rumors, the red herrings across the trail, the frantic tips pursued by competing reporters. But again the Rev. Robert Shuler preached lustily against Sister Aimee, calling the hearing a legal whitewash.

The furor was dying down, and she had gone back to baptizing her people and spreading balm when a cottage in Carmel became the focal point of renewed interest. Headlines suggested that during her disappearance Aimee had stayed there with Ormiston, but this had still to be proved conclusively in court, and it never was. The shack had a high stone wall around its stucco front, which faced the ocean, and the blue Chrysler car that had been seen here and there with a man who limped and a woman who wore goggles, stood outside it during the period of the evangelist's disappearance. The man with the limp, calling himself George McIntire, had rented it for three months at $150 a month, telling the owner that his wife was ill and needed quiet and privacy. The owner, Henry C. Benedict, came close to identifying the woman he had seen in the garden as Aimee Semple McPherson. He remembered her chiefly by her thick ankles, which was a sore point then and later with Aimee. Although otherwise graceful, she had massive legs.

With all these fresh revelations and the dovetailing of details, the grand jury that had voted to drop the case, announced one week later that the inquiry would be reopened to consider the Carmel evidence. Aimee appealed to Ormiston through the grand jury to come back and make known his whereabouts and actions during the crucial period from May 19 to May 28. Benedict showed little doubt about the identity of either of them as he testified. He recalled how abruptly they had departed on May 29, leaving behind them a portable radio receiving set, groceries, hairpins, a small new Bible, some inspirational books, and two kitchen aprons. The address left for mail by the unidentified couple was the Pennsylvania Hotel in New York.

The boy who had delivered groceries remembered that the lady had masses of piled-up hair and seemed to resemble Mrs. McPherson. A neighbor, feeding her baby at four o'clock in the morning after Aimee had disappeared, testified that she had seen the pair in the kitchen after their arrival. She noticed the "very beautiful hair" piled on top of the woman's head. For the next ten days the curtains were drawn, but she saw them in the yard and thought she could identify them. A green bathing suit hung on the line the first day they were there. Another neighbor noticed that the woman wore black satin slippers in the garden, which struck him as being odd. McIntire drove in and out of town every day, but his companion stayed at the cottage. When she went out she wore goggles and a tight-fitting turban pulled down over her eyes. The San Francisco papers were delivered at the cottage, and the grocery slips with the unidentified woman's writing were introduced as important evidence, but one of the women jurors was thought to have flushed them away when she took them to the bathroom. Fourteen witnesses altogether identified Ormiston, but the evidence in Aimee's case was inconclusive, since the woman at the cottage had stayed out of sight and had gone to some effort to disguise herself.

Aimee raged as one incriminating circumstance after another came to light. She continued to preach, her wings sharply clipped, her sermon titles provocative, such as "Fingerprints" and "I Am Doing a Great Work and Cannot Come Down to Carmel." She appealed to her congregation: "Dear Folk, it seems to me that if you ever intended to stand by Sister McPherson, now in her time of trial and persecution is the time. . . . They may bury my body but they will never bury my soul." She called for a showdown of her traducers, and when she was accused of hiding, she appeared at the district attorney's office and accepted service of subpoenas. The story that evolved at the second hearing was more precise. It suggested that Mrs. McPherson might have left Ocean Park between 3 and 4 o'clock on May 18 and at 4 o'clock the next morning have been in the cottage at Carmel, a hundred miles south of San Francisco and 325 miles from Ocean Park. On May 29, when Ormiston's name first appeared in the papers in connection with Mrs. McPherson's disappearance, the mysterious pair hurriedly gave up the cottage and drove off.

Ormiston now came forward and admitted practically everything except that Mrs. McPherson was the woman who was with him. His companion, he said, was a mysterious Miss X, and the final grotesque touch was added when Mrs. Lorraine Wiseman-Sielaff, a voluble witness who closely resembled Aimee, appeared on the scene and insisted that she was the sister of Miss X, who was ill and had asked her to join her at the Carmel cottage. Mrs. Wiseman produced an affidavit signed "Miss X" which said that she was the woman with Ormiston at the Benedict cottage, and that her sister Lorraine had visited them from time to time. Both Mrs. McPherson and Mrs. Wiseman had masses of coppery hair. They were about the same age, weight, and height, but Mrs. Wiseman had slim ankles and so did not pass muster with Benedict when the moment came for identification.

The sudden appearance of this curious witness in Mrs. McPherson's defense gave the case a wry twist. The reporters found her first in the office of Aimee's chief counsel, and she announced that she was in Los Angeles to exonerate the evangelist in the Carmel episode. But police investigation soon showed that Mrs. Wiseman, who had a history of mental instability, could not possibly have been anywhere near Carmel during the period that Mrs. McPherson was missing. She had been accused of passing bad checks, and after being bailed out of jail she became a star witness for the prosecution. Her handbag held documents that seemed to link her to Mrs. McPherson. Photographs showed the two women in identical pose and dress, standing together with their hair coiffed in exactly the same way. Mrs. Wiseman quickly broke down and told a strange story of being hired by Aimee to impersonate her. She insisted that the evangelist had coached her in her handwriting to offset the grocery slip evidence, and had perpetrated a hoax with the aid of her mother.

Aimee professed to be sorry for Mrs. Wiseman, but District Attorney Keyes issued felony complaints against Mrs. Kennedy, Mrs. Wiseman, Ormiston, and the evangelist. Four months had passed since she had disappeared, and he now announced that a "tainted atmosphere of a gigantic hoax surrounded the brazen activities of Mrs. McPherson and her friends to build up a false alibi for her." Aimee was in deep trouble this time. With charges of conspiracy, perjury, and a hoax thick in the air, with her reputation greatly tarnished around the world, she turned to her people. Her prayers were as fervent, her words as eloquent as always, but she felt the growing tide of skepticism that washed around her, even among her followers. After being ill and submitting herself to the laying on of hands at the Temple, she appeared again in her pulpit, the high priestess in distress, but expecting support.

Again she stood with her children by her side, and a great spray of flowers in her arms. The lights blazed down on her, and the congregation shouted "Hallelujah, Praise the Lord. Sweet Jesus. Amen." This time she spoke up for her mother as she reviewed the charges all over again. "My dear, little sweet, lovable mother, who has been brought into this diabolic plot," said Aimee. "I don't care what they do to me—but oh, my mother." She wound up with style, defying her enemies: "Turn loose your packs, bring in your bloodhounds. Go back over the seventeen years of my life I have devoted to preaching the gospel and see if you can find a flaw anywhere."

Aimee stood under the flag, the spotlight playing on her figure, the house lights dimmed while the national anthem was played. Then she asked for money—large sums for a time of crisis. She warned her disciples not to appear at the Hall of Justice where she was to have her hearing. Aimee arrived there looking subdued in a severely tailored black silk dress and black straw hat. Mrs. Wiseman wore a swagger cape, and her hat was rakishly tilted. Neither woman used lipstick on this occasion, and the resemblance between them was striking. The parade of witnesses was a strange one. Stories had been changed overnight, while the press muttered about manufactured evidence. But the two stars played their role to a finish, with Aimee casting looks that were sometimes angry and sometimes pitying in the direction of the flamboyant Mrs. Wiseman. The evangelist was in luck. None of the prosecution witnesses could now identify her as the woman they had seen at Carmel, and Mrs. Wiseman's history, past and present, did little to commend her to her listeners. In January, 1927, the case that had raged for eight months was dismissed, and was never wholly solved.

Within two weeks Mrs. Wiseman was operating a concession at Long Beach. She was billed as "The Hoax Woman," lecturing on "The Truth About the McPherson Case." Protests from Temple followers brought a quick end to this venture. Mrs. McPherson, insisting that "no woman of the streets had ever been given less consideration" than she, set off on a tour, leaving behind her the mounting dissension at the Temple, the whispers of corruption among officials who had handled the case, and the echoes of secret visits paid by witnesses to Mrs. Kennedy.

Before leaving Los Angeles Aimee staged a pageant, "The March of the Martyr," at the Temple, tracing the history of religious persecution, and followed it with "The Great Coronation Day," using a crown of thorns, and a crown of jewels, to prove her point. She spoke in all the large cities across the country and now charged admission for those who wished to hear "The Story of My Life." But when only seventy-five tickets were sold in Kansas City, she switched back to the collection system, saying that she did not wish to commercialize herself in any way on the tour.

Aimee did not seem at all the martyr when she appeared in the Glad Tidings Tabernacle in New York. Shouts of approval swept in a tidal wave around her as she told the story of her life, with elisions that covered a multitude of missteps. Every adult in the auditorium knew that Mrs. McPherson was publicly disowning Kenneth Ormiston, and she gave thanks to heaven that New Yorkers seemed to believe her—or so it appeared to Aimee, always in a state of euphoria. Men flung out their arms and women sobbed at her meetings, but the press corps was critical and unbelieving. The discovery of a trunk in a New York hotel filled with expensive gowns and lingerie which allegedly was left in Ormiston's name was another straw in the wind. Had this been Aimee's trousseau for a projected long trip with Ormiston at the time of her disappearance? Had she worn some of these garments on her trip to the Holy Land? She answered the questions boldly in the Glad Tidings Tabernacle: "The devil thought he could frame me with a little blue trunk filled with circus clothes, but the Almighty confused the language so that nobody could tell the same story twice," said Aimee to the sound of cheers.

It was scarcely an evangelist's trousseau that was pulled out of the trunk. The spangles, bows, and gossamer effects were more suggestive of the chorus line, and the various items were listed in newspapers across the country. There were beaded gowns and peach silk nightgowns, a hair band with pink ostrich feathers and a silver sash, a gold headband and rhinestone hair ornaments, a hoop skirt with flowers, and black satin slippers with steel buckles, a variety of negligees from a purple gown embroidered with gold thread to a bright cerise model lined with iridescent silk. The gowns ranged from a pink panne velvet dress with a salmon rose to an imported gold-beaded evening gown, and the lingerie from a "flesh silk brassière" to a salmon chemise and pink pajamas. The sixty-six items pulled from the famous blue trunk were sent to a bank vault for safekeeping after being seized, but the dark blue serge traveling dress, a blouse with the mark of a Carmel dry cleaner, a gray silk dress, and the black satin slippers were carefully scrutinized by the authorities. The slippers were well worn, and it was recalled as a curious coincidence that the woman in the cottage at Carmel had been seen in the garden wearing black satin slippers. Moreover, a photograph of Mrs. McPherson leaving for her trip to the Holy Land showed her wearing a blue serge dress with cape remarkably like the one found in the mysterious trunk.

All things considered, Mrs. McPherson did not meet with universal acclaim when she started on her tour to try to undo the damage resulting from eight months of merciless publicity and a series of charges that would have extinguished a public figure less buoyant than Aimee. She was denounced from the pulpits in Boston, and nowhere did she encounter the old-time warmth and response. After visiting twenty-two cities she returned to Los Angeles in April, 1927, to find Temple affairs in chaos without her guiding hand. Her mother was now her major enemy, and she cracked the whip over Aimee. She had been spreading the impression that her daughter was completely out of Temple affairs. They no longer shared the house beside the Temple, Aimee moving with her children to a cottage at Ocean Park that Nat Goodwin, the actor, had owned. But many of her old followers were still behind her, and were hostile to her mother. They rallied around Sister Aimee, but she went off touring again and when next she returned she refused to pose with her mother and announced firmly that she had come back "to take the helm." Aimee charged that Mrs. Kennedy had tried to crush and break her and to close every pulpit in the country to her.

Convinced that her mother had tried to wrest the Temple from her during her absence, Aimee finally ousted her, with a financial settlement. But peace did not settle on Aimee or on the Temple after that. Everything she did now came under fire. The undertone of scandal lay so close to the surface that her publicity was tinged with ridicule and skepticism. She was accused of using circus methods to stay in the limelight. She considered making a film but the plan fell through. She defied the Temple taboo on entering a theater or other worldly place of amusement. She bobbed her hair and paid forty dollars each for beauty treatments. This was not in the tradition of evangelism, and Aimee soon seemed to be more of an actress than a preacher.

When she toured Europe in 1928 the London *Daily Mail*, recalling that the Countess Cathcart had been held at Ellis Island for "moral turpitude," suggested that the Home Secretary should inquire into Mrs. McPherson's visit to Britain. Reporters took her to Soho, Limehouse, and to night clubs. In Paris she toured Montmartre. Still the faithful again received her with enthusiasm on her return to Los Angeles. She embarked on disastrous real estate ventures and by 1929 was deep in lawsuits. In the following year she led a crusade to the Holy Land, with more than a hundred pilgrims, whom she left suddenly, explaining later that she had gone to Ireland to see her daughter Roberta, who was recuperating from a fall she had had on shipboard.

Aimee was now a fashionable figure, her hair bright gold, her clothes the epitome of the abbreviated styles of the 1920's. On landing she was fined for not declaring all her purchases, and she had no sooner reached Los Angeles than she was in the headlines again. Mrs. Kennedy was in a hospital with a battered nose, and she charged that Sister Aimee had knocked her down and threatened to have her killed. Aimee admitted having had a mild argument with her mother, but insisted that she was hurt when she flung herself on the floor in a tantrum. On another occasion Mrs. Kennedy reportedly was locked in a closet to keep her quiet. But it was difficult to silence this angry woman.

She soon announced that she would sue Aimee and would produce secret documents that would clear up the mystery of her disappearance. Minnie maintained that the congregation had never accepted her daughter's own version of what had happened, and she threatened to tell the true story in a book. If anyone held the key to the mystery Mrs. Kennedy did, and Aimee had some unhappy moments over her mother's threats. For good measure she chose to announce that her daughter had had her face lifted while she was in Europe. This act of vanity was regarded as sinful by the Temple followers. Aimee indignantly denied the charge, but the uproar that followed led her to have two selected disciples examine her face for incriminating scars. They said that they could not find a trace of surgery. Meanwhile, Aimee's face-lifting had become a front-page issue, and the name of the plastic surgeon, the price he had charged, and all the accompanying details, soon became public knowledge.

When she made her next appearance there was no doubt that she looked much younger. Her skin was unlined. She had thinned down, but she was tired and ill. The glow had gone out of her; it became increasingly difficult for her to assume her old buoyant manner, and from time to time she had to rest, for her heart was affected. She spent a great deal of time at Malibu Beach, where Emma Schaffer, still her loyal friend, protected her from invasion and stalled off the press. Finally she slipped off to Panama, intending to keep out of sight for the time being, but when she toured the night clubs she was back under fire. Much was made of the fact that one café proprietor distributed postcards advertising a "Hallelujah Cocktail." The evangelist had become fair game for suggestive comment. By this time Aimee ran into trouble wherever she appeared. Her prestige was gone, although interest in her was still strong, and she continued to rate publicity of one kind or another.

When she preached at the Temple in November, 1930, she was noticeably ill and tired. She posed as a saint, wearing a long gown, with a cross glittering on her breast. The spotlight flashed on a purple curtain behind her, and six girls showered rose petals down on her from an arc above the pulpit. "Welcome Home Our Sister," read the banner over her head. But there were moments when Aimee felt overwhelmed by her troubles and expressed the wish that she might die.

In 1931 she went to the Orient with Roberta. Before the voyage was over her daughter fell in love with William Bradley Smyth, the ship's purser, and married him in Singapore. Roberta later married Harry Salter, the band leader. When they reached Hong Kong Aimee went to Robert Semple's grave and placed a wreath on it, with the inscription. "To whom I owe all that I am that is sincere and thoughtful." This was also the year in which she married her third husband, David L. Hutton, a jovial baritone at the Temple. They flew to Yuma, Arizona, on September 12, 1931, and were married on the steps of the airplane. But again Aimee had made a mistake. Hutton divorced her two years later, insisting that she had pulled a hoax on him in Paris by pretending that she was going to have a baby. Romantic problems beset all members of the family at this time. Mrs. Kennedy had eloped with Guy E. Hudson, whom she later divorced. After that she faded from view but outlived her storm-tossed daughter, dying in 1948. A report that Aimee would marry Homer Rodeheaver, who had been singing master for Billy Sunday, was quickly denied.

In the autumn of 1933 she toured the night clubs of New York with reporters and was paid $5,000 a week to preach in a New

York theater. To the tune of "Tipperary" her audience sang "It's a Good Thing to be a Christian" and then shouted the Ted Lewis refrain "Is Everybody Happy?" She was called the "Star Saleswoman of God" when she appeared on the stage in the wake of the Chester Hale dancing girls. All this was a long way from her early evangelism in Ontario. In the following year, 1934, she resigned as active pastor of Angelus Temple, although retaining her title as leader of the congregation of 15,000 members. She was succeeded by Mrs. Rheba Crawford Splivalo, known as the Angel of Broadway. Rheba, who had been a Salvation Army worker, filed a million dollar slander suit against Aimee two years later, charging that the evangelist had called her a Jezebel. Court appearances and law suits now became a regular pattern in Aimee's life. She sued *Look* magazine for libel. Everything she turned to seemed to collapse. In 1935 a $250,000 campaign promoted by Guido Orlando, the film producer, to present Aimee Semple McPherson as an American Joan of Arc saving the country from atheism and communism, was abandoned for lack of financial support. She was to have gone on a fifty-week speaking tour with a tableau of fifty girls dressed in white. Aimee demanded a minimum of $2,500 for the role that never came to anything.

But her magnificent health was failing her now, and she had frequent collapses, staying for brief periods in hospitals and sanitariums. She was keenly alive to the note of skepticism that underlay even the sparse applause that reached her ears. While visiting Mexico in 1942 she had a tropical fever, and soon after her return she fainted in the Temple pulpit. This was ascribed to an electric shock when she touched a microphone. An announcement was made immediately afterward that she was suffering from a nervous breakdown brought on by overwork. It was clear to all that Sister Aimee had outstayed her welcome. The 1920's had passed; the mood of the 1930's was subdued; and the 1940's found Mrs. McPherson in a sharp decline.

She was only fifty-four years old when she was found dead on September 27, 1944, in a hotel in Oakland, California, where she had delivered a lecture the night before. The verdict was an overdose of sleeping tablets, and it was called an accident. Some of her past glory was revived at the end. Thousands flocked past her bier in Angelus Temple, and fifteen hundred ministers representing the Four Square Gospel were among them. All had been ordained by Mrs. McPherson. Her coffin was placed in a marble vault, mounted with two life-sized angels.

After her death her son Rolf took hold, and the church, with its neo-Romanesque exterior and its twentieth-century interior, continued to flourish. Its members adhered to the fourfold teaching expounded by Aimee Semple McPherson of Christ as savior, healer, baptizer, and coming King. The Bible was supplemented with a book of her teachings, and she was remembered in the 226 churches she had founded. Her birthday, October 9, continued to be celebrated at the Temple as Founders Day. Aimee had been a bright comet, dashed to earth but leaving sparks behind her. She had given happiness to many, but had found little herself.

Notes

Madame Jumel

Jumel papers in New York Historical Society; divorce papers, Eliza Burr *v.* Aaron Burr, July 8, 1836, Circuit Court in Chancery; Jumel and Desorby Letter Books; Stephen Jumel to Eliza Jumel, June 3, 1815, and December 5, 1826; George Washington Bowen, Transcript of Record in will contest, Supreme Court of the United States, No. 312; William Henry Shelton, "New Clues in the Enigma of Mme. Jumel's Life," New York *Times*, May 13, 1926; New York *Times*, July 18, 1854, March 5, 1916, May 13, 1926, May 23, 1964; Gamaliel Bradford, "Damaged Souls: Aaron Burr," *Harper's Monthly Magazine*, December, 1922; Gamaliel Bradford, "Glimpses of Great People," *The Forum*, April, 1925; Meade Minnegerode, "Stephen Jumel, Merchant," *Saturday Evening Post*, May 31, 1924; *The Nation*, August 8, 1925; *Outlook*, September 19, 1917; Gertrude Atherton, *The Con-*

queror, New York: Macmillan, 1902; Margaret M. Coghlan, *Memories of Mrs. M. M. Coghlan*, New York: T. H. Morrell, 1864; Mary C. Crawford, *Romantic Days in the Early Republic*, New York: Little, Brown & Company, 1912; Mrs. John King van Rensselaer, in collaboration with Frederic van der Water, *Social Ladder*, New York: Henry Holt & Company, 1924; *Magazine of American History*, edited by Mrs. Martha J. Lamb, vol. XXI, Historical Copyright Company, 1889; Matthew L. Davis, *Memoirs of Aaron Burr*, New York: Harper & Brothers, 1837; William Cary Duncan, *The Amazing Madame Jumel*, New York: Frederick A. Stokes Company, 1935; Leonard Falkner, *Painted Lady*, New York: E. & P. Dutton Company, 1962; Meade Minnegerode, *Lives and Times: Four Informal American Biographies*, New York: G. P. Putnam's Sons, 1924; James Parton, *The Life and Times of Aaron Burr*, New York: Mason Brothers, 1859; William Henry Shelton, *The Jumel Mansion*, Boston: Houghton Mifflin Company, 1916; Samuel H. Wandell, *Aaron Burr in Literature*, London: K. Paul, Trench Trubner & Company, 1936.

Hetty Green

Hetty Green, "Why Women Are Not Money Makers," *Harpers Bazaar*, March 10, 1900; Peter Wyckoff, "Queen Midas: Hetty Robinson Green," *The New England Quarterly*, June, 1950; "Hetty Green —Millionairess of Bellows Falls," *The Rural Vermonter*, winter issue, 1962; "Burden of Money," *Outlook*, February 28, 1917; Dale Shaw, "The Witch of Wall Street," *Argosy Magazine*, February, 1959; "Hetty Green's Philosophy," *Literary Digest*, August 5, 1916; Helen Worden, "America's Richest Woman," *Colliers*, February 9, 1947; Portrait, *Putnam's*, April, 1908; Herbert Michelson, "Women You Can't Forget," Boston *Sunday Globe*, May 4, 1958; "In the Camera's Eye," *Cosmopolitan*, June, 1910; Leigh Mitchell Hodges, "Hetty Green, the Richest Woman in America," *Ladies' Home Journal*, June, 1900; "Hetty's Daughter Dies," *Life*, February 19, 1951; New Bedford *Standard-Times*, June 6, 1894, May 18, 1895, July 14, 1896, May 22, 1912, July 3, 1916, January 8, 1929, March 3, 1929, April 13, 1930, February 28, 1938, February 4, 1940, May 3, 1940, November 25, 1945, June 13, 1948, February 11, 1951, May 4, 1953, April 5, 1954; Boston *Herald*, July 14, 1896, March 19, 1902, May 22, 1912, June 9, 1936; New York *Tribune*, May 27, 1886, July 17, 1888, February 24, 1909; New York *Herald*, February 24, 1909; New York *World*, December 27, 1887, February 24, 1909; New York *Times*, August 16, 1892, August 22, 1893, March 20, 1902, February 24, 1909, July 23, 1909,

May 11, 1915, July 4, 1916; New York *Journal*, February 17, 1891; Dallas *News*, November 1, 1910; Philadelphia *North American*, September 6, 1909; Chicago *Sunday News*, July 14, 1891; John T. Flynn, *Men of Wealth*, New York: Simon and Schuster, 1941; Arthur H. Lewis, *The Day They Shook the Plum Tree*, New York: Harcourt, Brace & World, 1963; Boyden Sparkes and Samuel Taylor Moore, *Hetty Green*, New York: Doubleday, Doran & Company, 1930; Black, Ladbrooke, *Some Queer People*, London: Sampson Low, Marston & Company; William Morrell Emery, *The Howland Heirs*, New Bedford: E. Anthony & Sons, 1919; William Morrell Emery, *Gideon Howland's Kith and Kin*, New Bedford: Mercury Publishing Company, 1916.

Mrs. Frank Leslie

Ephraim George Squier correspondence in New York Historical Society: Squier to his parents, Mr. and Mrs. Joel Squier, September 10, 1857, May 10 and 28, 1858, December 31, 1858, September 21, 1859, April 10 and 19, 1860, April 26, 1861, October 12, 1861, February 4, 1862, June 10, 1862, December 13, 1863, March 8 and 13, 1867, January 12, 1869, June 17, 1871, March 1, 1871; Squier to Douglas Campbell, April 25, 1873, June 5, 1873; Douglas Campbell to Squier, June 3, 1873; Squier to Miriam Follin Squier, June 5, 1875; Mrs. Squier to Squier, April 12, 1864; Squier to Frank Squier, June 8 and 16, July 15, August 1, September 9 and 27, 1870; Squier to Charles Squier, December 10, 1859; Henry B. Anthony to Squier, October 17, and November 7, 1857, January 25, 1861, March 13, 1861; Squier papers, Library of Congress; Mrs. Frank Leslie letters in De Courcey Fales Collection, Manuscript Division, New York Public Library; Manuscript of "Two Weeks in a British Bastille," by Ephraim George Squier, New York Historical Society; Squier to Frank Leslie, March 11, 1861; Miriam Florence Squier, *Santa Rosa of Lima*, *Harper's New Monthly Magazine*, December, 1866; Ephraim George Squier, *Peru: Incidents of Travel and Exploration in the Land of the Incas*, New York: Harper & Brothers, 1877; Fulton Oursler, "Frank Leslie," *The American Mercury*, May 1930; Joaquin Miller, "Mrs. Frank Leslie," *Golden Era*, May, 1887; Olive Logan, "Life at Long Branch," *Harper's New Monthly Magazine*, September 1876; Mrs. Frank Leslie, "Women in Business Life," *Ladies' Home Journal*, May, 1890; Mrs. Frank Leslie, "Are Our Girls Too Independent," *Ladies' Home Journal*, March, 1892; Mrs. Frank Leslie, "Which Is Woman's Happiest Hour?" *Ladies' Home Journal*, August, 1890; "Women in Journalism," *The*

Fourth Estate, April 5, 1894; "Reminiscences of a Woman's Work in Journalism," delivered at the International League of Press Clubs, January 14, 1892; Mrs. Frank Leslie, "Scenes in Sun-Lands," *Frank Leslie's Monthly*, March, 1862, August, October, and November, 1878; Mrs. Frank Leslie, "Cuban Bygones," *Frank Leslie's Popular Monthly*, December, 1898; *Frank Leslie's Illustrated Newspaper*, March 7, 1857; Mrs. E. G. Squier, "The Ladies of Lima," *Frank Leslie's Chimney Corner*, June 3, 1865; R. B. Kimball, "Frank Leslie," *Frank Leslie's Popular Monthly*, March 3, 1880; "General Gossip of Authors and Writers," *Current Literature*, February, 1889; "Mrs. Frank Leslie," *The City Item*, April 14, 1883, October 6, 1883, May 22, 1886; "From Puddle to Palace," *Town Topics*, March 27, 1886; "Our Transcontinental Caravan," *Frank Leslie's Popular Monthly*, May, 1892; *Territorial Enterprise*, Virginia City, Nevada, Extra on "Frank Leslie and Wife," 1878; Rose Emmet Young, "The Record of the Leslie Woman Suffrage Commission, 1917–1929," New York: Published by the Commission, 1929; New York *Times*, July 14, 1874, February 9, 1875, September 11, 13, and 30, 1877, January 30, 1878, September 10, 1887, April 18, 1888, February 24, 1889, October 5 and 21, 1891, September 18, 1893, April 25, 1893, June 6 and 11, 1893, November 30, 1897, March 14, 1899, October 2, 1900, December 24, 1901, September 28, 1914, December 8, 13, and 14, 1914, January 18, 1915, February 10, 1915, September 16, 1915, November 18, 1915, December 24, 1915, January 29, 1916, February 5, 1916, January 6, 1917; New York *Daily Tribune*, October 26, 1857, July 14, 1874, November 25, 1879, January 11, 1880, June 5, 1881, October 5, 1891, May 20, 1895, August 12, 1897, October 2, 1900, September 21, 1914; New York *World*, January 11, 1880, *The Daily Graphic*, March 17, 1888; Chicago *Daily Inter-Ocean*, October 15, 1890; New York *Evening Post*, April 10, 1877; New York *Sun*, June 27 and 28, 1868, September 14, 15, and 16, 1887; New York *Herald*, March 20, 22, and 29, 1854; June 23, 1855; October 24, 1857; January 18, 1861, April 1, 1867, June 28, 1868, August 18, 1874, February 9, 1875, October 5, 1891, April 6, 1892, May 1 and 12, 1892, August 22, 1892, June 6, 1893, April 7, 1895, January 18, 1915, June 16, 1917; *Daily National Intelligencer*, March 4, 1861; Washington *Evening Star*, March 5, 1961; Providence *Journal*, October 23, 1857, February 12 to 17, 1857, Detroit *Free Press*, November 3, 1890; Albany *Morning Times*, February 4 and 7, 1857, June 25, 1857; Mrs. E. G. Squier (tr.), *The Demi-Monde* by Dumas, Philadelphia, J. B. Lippincott, 1858; Mrs. E. G. Squier (tr.), *Travels in Central America* by Arthur Morelet, New York: Leypoldt, Holt and

Williams, 1871; Mrs. Frank Leslie, *Are Men Gay Deceivers?* Chicago: F. T. Neely Company, 1893; Mrs. Frank Leslie, *Rents in Our Robes*, Chicago: Belford, Clarke & Company, 1888; *A Social Mirage*, New York: F. Tennyson Neely, 1899; *A Brief History of the Frank Leslie Publishing House*, New York: Frank Leslie Publishing House, 1887; Mrs. Frank Leslie, *California: A Pleasure Trip from Gotham to the Golden Gate*, New York: G. W. Carleton Company, 1927; Frank H. Norton (ed.), *Historical Register of the United States Centennial Exposition, 1876*, New York: Frank Leslie's Publishing Company, 1887; Willard Grosvenor Bleyer, *Main Currents in the History of American Journalism*, Boston: Houghton Mifflin Company, 1927; Isaac Goldberg, *Queen of Hearts*, New York: John Day Company, 1936; Frank Luther Mott, *A History of American Magazines*, Cambridge: Harvard University Press, 1938–57; Madeleine B. Stern, *Purple Passage*, Norman, Oklahoma: University of Oklahoma Press, 1953; Henry Dickinson Stone, *Personal Recollections of the Drama*, Albany: C. Van Venthuysen, 1873; Ella Wheeler Wilcox, *The Worlds and I*, New York: George H. Doran, 1918; Catharine Read Williams, *Annals of the Aristocracy*, Providence: B. T. Albro, 1845.

Margaret and Kate Fox

Adelbert Cronise, "The Beginnings of Modern Spiritualism in and near Rochester," *Rochester Historical Society Fund Series*, vol. V; William Crookes, "Notes of an Enquiry into the Phenomena called Spiritual," *Journal of Science*, January, 1874; Trevor H. Hall, *The Spiritualists*, London: Gerald Duckworth & Company, 1962; Frank Podmore, *Modern Spiritualism*, New York: Charles Scribner's Sons, 1902, 2 vols.; Nathaniel Pitcher Tallmadge, *The Healing of the Nations*, New York: Society for the Diffusion of Spiritual Knowledge, 1855; Sarah E. L. Taylor (ed.), *Fox-Taylor Record*, Boston: Bruce Humphries, 1936; W. G. Langworthy Taylor, *Katie Fox and the Fox-Taylor Record*, New York: G. P. Putnams Sons, 1933; A. Leah Underhill, *The Missing Link in Modern Spiritualism*, New York: Thomas R. Knox & Company, 1885; A. Leah Fox Underhill, *Rochester Knockings*, Buffalo: G. H. Derby, 1851; London *Times*, April 21, 1913, September 14, 1927; Boston *Traveler*, June 25, 26, and 27, 1857; Buffalo *Commercial Advertiser*, February 17 and March 14, 1851; New York *World*, October 21 and 22, 1888; New York *Weekly Tribune*, December 8, 1849; New York *Daily Tribune*, June 8, 1850, November 6, 1855, October 10, 1886, June 3, 1892, March 10, 1893;

New York *Herald*, April 17, 1851, August 16, 1858, May 27, 1888, September 10, 24, and 25, 1888, October 11 and 22, 1888, March 9, 1893, October 7, 1893; Gilbert Seldes, *The Stammering Century*, New York: The John Day Company, 1928; Arch Merrill, *The Towpath*, reprinted from the Rochester *Democrat and Chronicle*, Rochester, N. Y., 1945; Rev. Orlo J. Price, "The Significance of the Early Religious History of Rochester," *The Rochester Historical Society Publication Fund Series*, vol. III; Rev. Augustus Hopkins Strong, "Reminiscences of Early Rochester," *The Rochester Historical Society Publication Fund Series*, vol. IV; Charles F. Pond, "History of the Third War," *The Rochester Historical Society Fund Series*, vol. 1; E. E. Lewis, *A Report of the Mysterious Noises Heard in the House of John D. Fox at Hydesville, Wayne County*; William F. Peck, *Semi-Centennial History of Rochester*, 1884; Rev. John C. Bywater, *The Mystery Solved*, Rochester, New York: The Advent Harbinger Office, 1852; Isaac Post, *Voices from the Spirit World*, Rochester, New York: Charles H. McDonell, 1852; *The Rappers*, New York: H. Long & Brother, 1854; Arthur C. Parker, "The Funny-Bone of Early Rochester," *Centennial History of Rochester, N. Y.*, vol. II; Emma Hardinge Britten, *Modern American Spiritualism*, New York: published by the author, 1870; E. W. Capron and Henry D. Barron, *Explanation and History of the Mysterious Communion with Spirits*, Auburn, New York, 1850; Carl Carmer, *Listen for a Lonesome Drum*, New York: Farrar and Rinehart, 1936; Reuben Briggs Davenport, *The Death Blow to Spiritualism*, New York: G. W. Dillingham, 1888; Dellon M. Dewey, *History of the Strange Sounds of Rappings*, Rochester, New York: D. M. Dewey, 1850; John W. Edmonds and G. T. Dexter, *Spiritualism*, vol. 1. New York: Partridge and Brittain, 1853–55; William Elder, *Biography of Elisha Kent Kane*, Philadelphia: Childs and Peterson, 1857; Margaret Fox, *The Love-Life of Elisha Kent Kane and Margaret Fox*, New York: Carleton, 1866; J. H. Hyslop, *Contact With the Other World*, New York: The Century Company, 1919; Rev. Hiram Mattison, *Spirit Rapping Unveiled*, New York: Mason Brothers, 1853; Robert Dale Owen, *Footfalls on the Boundary of Another World*, Philadelphia: J. B. Lippincott & Company, 1860; Blake McKelvey, *Rochester, the Water Power City*, Cambridge: Harvard University Press, 1945; Blake McKelvey, "The Rochester Area in American History," *Rochester History*, vol. XXI; Frank Meryl and Blake McKelvey, "Some Former Rochesterians of National Distinction," *Rochester History*, vol. XXI; Lloyd Morris, *Incredible New York*, New York: Random House, 1951.

Victoria Woodhull and Tennessee Claflin

Files of *Woodhull & Claflin's Weekly* and *The Humanitarian*; Official Record of Beecher-Tilton Trial, New York: McDivitt, Campbell & Company, 1875; Campaign Document of the Equal Rights Party, New York: Woodhull, Claflin & Company, 1872; Vanderbilt will case scrapbook, New York Public Library; *New York Independent* scrapbooks, New York Public Library; Theodore Tilton, "Victoria Woodhull," New York: *Golden Age*, 1871; Zula Maud Woodhull, "Affinities," *Westminster Review*, April, 1899; *The Churchman*, September 8, 1893; New York *Tribune*, January 11, February 21, and May 10, 1872, January 10, 1873, March 8, 1887, Beecher-Tilton case, January 12, 1875 to July 2, 1875; New York *World*, May 22 and November 20, 1871; New York *Herald*, January 20, 1870, February 13, 1870, April 2 and 12, 1870, May 27, 1870, December 21, 1870, June 3, 1871, November 20, 1871, January 11, 1872, February 20 and 21, 1872, April 11, 1872, May 9, 1872, June 6, 1872, January 10, 1873, July 3, 1924; Cincinnati *Enquirer*, July 21, 1876; Indianapolis *Daily Sentinel*, November 25, 1875; Boston *Herald*, November 5 and 11, 1892, February 24, 1894; June 3, 1910; Brooklyn *Argus*, September 19, 1874. Lyman Abbott, *Henry Ward Beecher*, Boston: Houghton Mifflin Company, 1903; Wayne Andrews, *The Vanderbilt Legend*, New York: Harcourt, Brace & Company, 1941; William C. Beecher, *A Biography of Henry Ward Beecher*, Rev. Samuel Scoville, assisted by Mrs. Henry Ward Beecher, New York: Charles L. Webster & Company, 1888: Tennessee Claflin, *Constitutional Equality*, New York: Woodhull, Claflin & Company, 1871; Lady Cook, *The Evils of Society and Their Remedies*, London: University Publishing Company, 1895; Heywood Broun and Margaret Leech, *Anthony Comstock*, New York: A. and C. Boni, 1927; G. S. Darewin, *Synopsis of the Lives of Victoria C. Woodhull and Tennessee Claflin*, London: J. H. Corthesy, 1891; M. F. Darwin, *One Moral Standard for All*, New York: Caulon Press, 1895; Mrs. E. F. Ellet, *Court Circles of the Republic*, Philadelphia: Philadelphia Publishing Company, 1872; Edmund B. Fairfield, *Wickedness in High Places*, Mansfield, Ohio: Myers & Bros., 1874; William Worthington Fowler, *Inside Life in Wall Street*, Hartford, Conn.: J. D. Denison, 1870; Ida Husted Harper, *The Life and Work of Susan B. Anthony*, Indianapolis: Bobbs-Merrill Company, 1899; Paxton Hibben, *Henry Ward Beecher*, New York: George H. Doran Company, 1927; Frederick Hudson, *Journalism in the United States from 1690–1872*, New York: Harper & Brothers, 1873; Madeline Legg,

Two Noble Women, London: Phelps Brothers, 1893; Denis Tilden Lynch, *Boss Tweed*, New York: Boni & Liveright, 1927; C. F. Marshall, *The True History of the Brooklyn Scandal*, Philadelphia: National Publishing Company, 1874; Lloyd Morris, *Incredible New York*, New York: Random House, 1951; Leon Oliver, *The Great Sensation*, Chicago: The Beverly Company, 1873; Emanie Sachs, *The Terrible Siren*, New York: Harper & Brothers, 1928; Don C. Seitz, *They Also Ran*, New York: Thomas Y. Crowell Company, 1928; and *The Dreadful Decade*, 1926; Robert Shaplen, *Free Love and Heavenly Sinners*, New York: Alfred A. Knopf, 1954; Arthur D. H. Smith, *Commodore Vanderbilt*, New York: R. M. McBride & Company, 1927; Matthew Hale Smith, *Sunshine and Shadow in New York*: Hartford, Conn.: J. B. Burr & Company, 1868, and *Twenty Years Among the Bulls and Bears of New York*, New York: American Book Company, 1870; Elizabeth Cady Stanton, Susan B. Anthony and Matilda Joslyn Gage (ed.), *The History of Woman Suffrage*, Fowler & Wells, 1881–1902; *Elizabeth Cady Stanton as Revealed in Her Letters, Diary and Reminiscences*, edited by Theodore Stanton and Harriot Stanton Blatch, New York: Harper & Brothers, 1922; Dixon Wecter, *The Saga of American Society*, New York: Charles Scribner's Sons, 1854; Lyman Beecher Stowe, *Saints, Sinners and Preachers*, Indianapolis: Bobbs-Merrill Company, 1934; Nathaniel P. Williams, *Famous Persons and Places*, New York: Charles Scribner's Sons, 1854; Victoria Claflin Woodhull: *And the Truth Shall Make You Free*, London: Blackfriars, 1894; *The Alchemy of Maternity*, Cheltenham: N. Sawyer & Company, 1889; *Breaking the Seals*, New York: Woodhull & Claflin, 1875; *A Fragmentary Record of Public Work done in America, 1871–1877*, London: G. Norman & Son, 1887.

Mrs. Jack Gardner

Mrs. Jack Gardner correspondence in the Isabella Stewart Gardner Museum, Boston, with Henry James, F. Marion Crawford, F. Hopkinson Smith, John Singer Sargent, James A. McNeill Whistler, and Henry Adams; Henry James to Mrs. Gardner July 5 and 22, 1879, January 29, 1881, December 7, 1881, January 23, 1882, June 5, 1882, March 18, 1888, February 2, 1899, December 27, 1899, June 24, 1890, January 29, 1891, June 7, 1891, September 3, 1892, May 1, 1893, August 4, 1893, April 3, 1898, December 27, 1899, September 3, 1910, October 24, 1911, April 20, 1914; F. Hopkinson Smith to Mrs. Gardner, December 22, 1898; James A. McNeill Whistler to Mrs. Gardner, January 1, 1889, February, 1901; John Singer Sargent to Mrs. Gardner,

January 1, 1889, November 1, 1889, March 9, 1894, August 27, 1894, March 2 and 5, 1898, September 14, 1902, June 16, 1903, June 28, 1904, May 12, 1909, October 28, 1917, May 31, 1918, December 28, 1918, April 17, 1920; F. Marion Crawford to Mrs. Gardner, November 25, 1893, December 10 and 20, 1893, January 24, 1894, June 28, 1894, July 28, 1894, March 23, 1895, July 20, 1895, January 25, 1896, August 23, 1896, March 1, 1897, February 21, 1898, February 7, 1901, June 12, 1907, August 11, 1907, December 31, 1907, January 21, 1909; Henry Adams to Mrs. Gardner, October 23, 1906; *Current Opinion*, September, 1924; *Literary Digest*, March 27, 1906; *Leslie's Weekly*, February 20, 1902; Nelson Lansdale, "Mrs. Gardner's Palace of Paintings," *Horizon*, July, 1959; General Catalogue compiled by Gilbert Wendel Longstreet under the supervision of Morris Carter, Boston: Printed for the Museum Trustees, 1935; Catalogue of the Exhibited Paintings and Drawings by Philip Hendy, Boston: Printed for the Museum Trustees, 1931, 2 vols.; Ella S. Siple, "Some Recently Identified Tapestries in the Gardner Museum," *Burlington Magazine*, November, 1930; George L. Stout, "Mrs. Gardner's Legacy on the Fenway," *Museum News*, May, 1960; New York *Times*, August 20, 1908, July 18 and 27, 1924, March 10, 1926, May 28, 1948; New York *Herald Tribune*, July 18 and 27, 1924, March 15, 1953; New York *World*, June 23, 1895, January 5, 1902, June 12, 1904, August 21, 1908; New York *Evening World*, July 19, 1924; New York *Journal and Advertiser*, December 17, 1899; New York *Sun*, February 24, 1903; Boston *Herald*, July 18, 1924; Boston *Post*, February 14, 1954; Charles Francis Adams, *An Autobiography*, Boston: Houghton Mifflin Company, 1916; Cleveland Amory, *The Proper Bostonians*, New York: E. P. Dutton & Company, 1947; Lucius Beebe, *Boston and the Boston Legend*, New York: D. Appleton-Century Company, 1935; S. N. Behrman, *Duveen*, New York: Random House, 1952; Bernard Berenson, *Sketch for a Self-Portrait*, New York: Pantheon, 1949; Bernard Berenson, *Painters of the Renaissance*, New York: G. P. Putnams Sons, 1894; Van Wyck Brooks, *New England: Indian Summer*, New York: E. P. Dutton & Co., 1940; Morris Carter, *Isabella Stewart Gardner and Fenway Court*, Cambridge: The Riverside Press, 1925; F. Marion Crawford, *A Lady of Rome*, New York: Macmillan, 1906; *Arethusa*, Macmillan, 1907; *Katherine Lauderdale*, Macmillan, 1893; *The Ralstons*, Macmillan, 1895; *To Leeward*, Boston: Houghton Mifflin Company, 1884; Leon J. Edel, *Henry James*, 3 vols., Philadelphia: J. P. Lippincott, 1953–1964; Florence Howe Hall, *The Correct Thing in Good Society*, Boston: Estes and Lauriat, 1888; Henry Lee Higginson, *Life and Letters of Henry Lee Higginson*; Boston, The Atlantic Monthly Press, 1921; Julia Ward Howe, *Reminiscences*

1819–1899, Boston: Houghton Mifflin Company; Percy Lubbock, *Portrait of Edith Wharton*, New York: D. Appleton-Century Company, 1947; Aline B. Saarinen, *The Proud Possessors*, New York: Random House, 1958; Ellery Sedgwick, *The Happy Profession*, Boston: Little, Brown & Company, 1946; Douglas and Elizabeth Rigby, *Lock, Stock and Barrel*, Philadelphia: J. B. Lippincott, 1944; Sylvia Sprigge, *Berenson*, Boston: Houghton Mifflin Company, 1960; Countess Eleanor Palffy, *The Lady and the Painter*, New York: Coward-McCann, 1951; Dixon Wecter, *The Saga of American Society*, New York: Charles Scribner's Sons, 1937.

Carry Nation

Carry Nation, *The Use and Need of the Life of Carry Nation*, Topeka: F. M. Stevens & Sons, 1908; Carry Nation, "My Mission," *National Magazine*, February, 1901; N. O. Nelson, "Mrs. Nation in Enterprise, Kansas"; "Onward March of Carry Nation," *Current Literature*, March, 1901; *Review of Reviews*, March, 1901; *The Hatchet*, July, 1906; *The Smasher's Mail*, February 21, 1901; "Intemperate Methods of Temperance Reformers," *The Outlook*, February 9, 1901; Herbert Asbury, *Carry Nation*, New York: Alfred A. Knopf, 1929; Carleton Beals, *Cyclone Carry*, Philadelphia: Chilton Company, 1962; Kansas City *Star*, 1899–1902; New York *Times*, 1902–1904; *History of Kansas*, vol. II, The American Historical Society, Inc., 1928; *American Monthly Review of Reviews*, 1902; London *Times*, 1908; *Peoria Journal*, 1901; *Topeka State Journal*, 1901–1902.

Nellie Bly

New York *World*, 1887–1895; New York *Herald*, September 25, 1887; New York *Journal*, January 31, 1920; New York *Times*, January 28, 1922, February 16, 1956; New York *World*, January 28, 1922; Pittsburgh *Dispatch*, November 22, 1885; Marjorie Rittenhouse, "They Called Her the Amazing Nellie Bly," *Good Housekeeping*, February, 1955; Elizabeth Cochrane (Nellie Bly) *Six Months in Mexico*, New York: J. W. Lovell Company, 1888; *Ten Days in a Mad-House*, New York: N. L. Munro, 1887; *The Mystery of Central Park*, New York: G. W. Dillingham, 1889; *Around the World in Seventy-two Days*, New York: The Pictorial Weeklies Company, 1890; Nina Brown Baker, *Nellie Bly*, New York: Henry Holt & Company, 1956; James W. Barrett, *The End of the World*, New York: Harper & Brothers,

1931; Willard Grosvenor Bleyer, *Main Currents in the History of American Journalism*, Boston: Houghton Mifflin Company, 1927; Emily Hahn, *Around the World with Nellie Bly*, Boston: Houghton Mifflin Company, 1959; Iris Noble, *Nellie Bly: First Woman Reporter*, New York: Julian Messner, 1956; Mignon Rittenhouse, *The Amazing Nellie Bly*, New York: E. P. Dutton & Company, 1956; Ishbel Ross, *Ladies of the Press*, New York: Harper & Brothers, 1936; Don C. Seitz, *Joseph Pulitzer*, New York: Simon and Schuster, 1924; *The Story of Nellie Bly*, New York: American Flange & Manufacturing Company, 1951.

Isadora Duncan

Isadora Duncan correspondence in Irma Duncan collection, New York Public Library; Isadora Duncan to Irma Duncan, June 10, 20, and 24, July 10 and 28, November 27, and December 16, 1924; Eleven scrapbooks, Dance Collection, New York Public Library; Edward Gordon Craig correspondence, Irma Duncan papers, Dance Collection, New York Public Library; London *Times*, April 21, 1913, September 14, 1927; New York *Times*, September 15, 1927; *Pall Mall Gazette*, October 23, 1915; Stark Young, "Isadora Duncan," *The New Republic*, November 28, 1928; Morris R. Werner, *To Whom It May Concern*, New York: Cape & Smith, 1931; Ernest Newman, "Dances of Isadora Duncan," *Living Age*, June, 1921; Harriet Monroe, "Golden Moments," *Poetry Magazine*, January, 1928; Nelia Pavlova, "Essenine and Isadora Duncan," *Revue Mondiale*, January, 1930; Arthur Ruhl, "Some Ladies Who Dance," *Collier's*, February, 1910; Mary Fanton Roberts, "Isadora—The Dancer," *Denishawn Magazine*, Summer, 1925; "Isadora Duncan," *La Danse*, March, 1921; Mabel Dodge Luhan, "Isadora Duncan," *Town and Country*, July, 1936; Max Eastman, "Isadora Duncan Is Dead," *The Nation*, September, 1927; "Isadora Dances the Marseillaise," *Current Opinion*, January, 1917; Robert Edmond Jones, "The Gloves of Isadora," *Theater Arts*; "Seeing Is Believing," *The Musical Digest*, November 13, 1923; Edward Steichen, "Isadora Duncan—A Photographic Study," *Vanity Fair*, August, 1923; Maria Theresa, "As I Saw Isadora Duncan," *The Dance Magazine*, November, 1928; Mme. Yokska, "Isadora Duncan," *Arts and Decoration*, August, 1927; Isadora Duncan, "I See America Dancing," New York *Herald Tribune*, October 2, 1927; "Isadora's Triumphs and Tragedies," *Literary Digest*, October 8, 1927; Hollister Noble, "Isadora Duncan: Liberator of the Dance," *Musical America*, September 24, 1927; Agnes de Mille, "The Revolution of Isadora," New York *Times*,

September 14, 1952; New York *World*, December 16, 1900; New York *Journal and Advertiser*, July 14, 1901; Boston *Herald*, May 22, 1904; Paris *Herald*, September 20, 1927; New York *Herald Tribune*, September 15 and 16, 1927, October 2, 1927; Boston *Transcript*, January 1, 1909; Pittsburgh *Gazette Times*, January 10, 1909; Countess Cassini, *Never a Dull Moment*, New York: Harper & Brothers, 1956; Mary Clarke, *Dancers of Mercury*, London: A. and C. Black, 1962; Mercedes de Acosta, *Here Lies the Heart*, New York: Reynal & Company, 1960; Floyd Dell, *Women as World Builders*, Chicago, Forbes & Company, 1913; Agnes de Mille, *The Book of the Dance*, New York: Golden Press, 1963; Mary Desti, *The Life of Isadora Duncan 1921–1927*, New York: Horace Liveright, 1929; Maurice Dumesnil, *An Amazing Journey*, New York: I. Washburn, 1932; Irma Duncan and Allan Ross Macdougall, *Isadora Duncan's Russian Days and Her Last Years in France*, New York: Covici Friede, 1929; Irma Duncan, *The Technique of Isadora Duncan*, New York: Kamin, 1937; Isadora Duncan, *The Dance*, The Forest Press, 1909; Isadora Duncan, *The Dance of the Future*, New York: The Bowles-Goldsmith Company, 1908; Isadora Duncan, *The Art of the Dance*, New York: Theater Arts, Inc., 1928; Isadora Duncan, *My Life*, New York: Boni and Liveright, 1927; Arnold Genthe, *Isadora Duncan: twenty-four studies*, New York: M. Kennerley, 1929; Lola Kinel, *This Is My Affair*, Boston: Little, Brown & Company, 1937; Prince Peter Lieven, *The Birth of Ballets-Russes*, Boston: Houghton Mifflin Company, 1936; Allan Ross Macdougall, *Isadora: A Revolutionary in Art and Love*, Edinburgh and New York; T. Nelson, 1960; Paul D. Magriel (ed.), *Isadora Duncan*, New York: Henry Holt & Company, 1947; Walter Terry, *Isadora Duncan*, New York: Dodd, Mead & Company, 1963; Sisley Huddleston, *Paris: Salons, Cafes, Studios*, Philadelphia: J. B. Lippincott Company, 1928; Princess Der Ling, *Lotos Petals*, New York: Dodd, Mead & Company, 1930; Mabel Dodge Luhan, *Movers and Shakers*, New York: Harcourt, Brace & Company, 1936; Carl Van Vechten, *Merry-Go-Round*, New York: Alfred Knopf Company, 1918; Sol Hurok, *Impresario*, New York: Random House, 1946; Hippolyta, "Isadora," *The New Yorker*, January 1, 1927; Joseph Kaye, "The Last Chapters of Isadora's Life," *The Dance Magazine*, April–July, 1929; Royal Cortissoz, "Reflections Apropos the Work of Isadora Duncan," *The New Music Review*, March, 1909; Mary Fanton Roberts, "The Dance of the Future as Created by and Illustrated by Isadora Duncan," *The Craftsman*, October, 1908; "Isadora Duncan's Art," *Literary Digest*, May 1, 1915.

Aimee Semple McPherson

New York *Times*, May 18, 1926 to January, 1927; Los Angeles *Times Mirror*, May 20, 1926 to January, 1927; New York *Times*, November 23, 1930, September 14, 1931, July 18, 1933, December 15, 1934, Febuary 18, 1935, November 27, 1936, May 11, 1937, September 14, 1942; New York *Herald Tribune*, February 21, 1927, September 6, 1933, October 15, 1933; New York *World*, September 5, 22, and 23, 1926; October 2, 1926; New York *Evening World*, February 19, 1927; New York *Journal*, November 13, 1926; New York *Evening Sun*, March 7, 1935, April 16, 1937; New York *Evening Post*, February 8, 1935, September 6 and 28, 1933; Brooklyn *Eagle*, September 6, 1933; Aimee Semple McPherson, *In the Service of the King*, New York: Boni & Liveright, 1927; Lately Thomas, *The Vanishing Evangelist*, New York: The Viking Press, 1959; Nancy Barr Mavity, *Sister Aimee*, Garden City, Long Island: Doubleday, Doran & Company, 1931; W. Teeling, *American Stew*, London: Herbert Jenkins Ltd., 1933.

Index

DATE DUE